Local History

and

Genealogical Abstracts

from

Jonesboro and Gas City Indiana Newspapers

1889–1920

Ralph D. Kirkpatrick

HERITAGE BOOKS
2011

HERITAGE BOOKS
AN IMPRINT OF HERITAGE BOOKS, INC.

Books, CDs, and more—Worldwide

For our listing of thousands of titles see our website at
www.HeritageBooks.com

Published 2011 by
HERITAGE BOOKS, INC.
Publishing Division
100 Railroad Ave. #104
Westminster, Maryland 21157

Copyright © 1996 Ralph D. Kirkpatrick

All rights reserved. No part of this book may be reproduced or transmitted in any form or by any means, electronic or mechanical, including photocopying, recording or by any information storage and retrieval system without written permission from the author, except for the inclusion of brief quotations in a review.

International Standard Book Numbers
Paperbound: 978-0-7884-0574-7
Clothbound: 978-0-7884-8811-5

FOREWORD

Jonesboro and Gas City are located in east-central Indiana in the old 'Trenton natural gas field' that was discovered, developed, and exhausted within approximately two decades, 1887-1910. Discovery and utilization of natural gas in and near these towns abruptly changed the local rural agricultural economy to an industrial society that urbanized convulsively.

Many local early settlers were Protestant Scots-Irish that came from Virginia, Ohio or the Carolinas. With the development of industry, particularly glassmaking, newcomers tended to come from northeastern states and they included several Roman Catholic families. The major overseas group that came in as immigrants were Protestants from Wales. They initially had their own Welsh-speaking church but later several of the Welsh families joined the local Baptist congregation.

The Mississinewa River divides Jonesboro from Gas City geographically, and in some instances, culturally and socially . The river was an important barrier to free movement and access in early days although it was always a source of ice to be stored for summer use and was a route of transportation prior to the development of a good road system. This beautiful stream is now used for recreation even though unwise farming practices and over-zealous agricultural drainage schemes cause it to be silt-laden and too low much of the year for canoeing or other boating activities.

The time period covered, 1889-1920, is rather long for so few abstracts because several years of the various newspapers are missing. I read and abstracted all known extant newspapers for this time period. Fortunately, various editors included reminisces from early settlers and early school teachers giving us a certain amount of early history dating back to before the Civil War.

I am indebted to the Twin City Journal-Reporter, the Gas City-Mill Township Public Library, and the Indiana State Archives for granting me free access to their original copies of various Jonesboro and Gas City newspapers.

Ralph D. Kirkpatrick, Ph.D.
Osage Farm
March 4, 1996

Abbreviations and conventions used:
att - attended
b - born in or date of birth
BC - Back Creek
BCMM - Back Creek Monthly Meeting of Friends
BCS - Back Creek Friends Common School
bldg - building
bur - buried at
ca - circa; about
Cem - Cemetery
ch - child of or children of
Ch. - Church
Coll - College
Co. - County
county name not followed by a state name is an Indiana county
CW - Civil War
d - died on
dec - deceased
dt - daughter of
EBPM - East Bethel Preparative Meeting of Friends
f - former or formerly
FFA - Fairmount Friends Academy
GC - Gas City
GAR - Grand Army of the Republic, Civil War veterans organization
grad - graduate or graduate of
HS - High School
Jnsbr - Jonesboro
KIA - killed in action
K of P - Knights of Pythias
m - married
mbr - member of
M.E. - Methodist Episcopal Church
mgr - manager
MH - Meetinghouse; building used by Friends for religious services
MM - Monthly Meeting; conducts business of a local group of Friends
M/M - Mr. and Mrs.
M.P. - Methodist Protestant Church
PM - Preparative Meeting; Friends group under care of a MM
Monthly Meeting or Preparative Meeting name not followed by a state
   name is in Indiana
prob - probably
(NAME) - maiden name of married woman or widow
'Name' - nickname
Name - name this person was known by or 'went by'
prop. - proprietor

RC - Roman Catholic or Roman Catholic Church
RR - railroad
s - son of or sons of
Sch - School
serv - served in or served as
SS - Sunday School
tchr - teacher
Twp - Township
vet - veteran or veteran of
WCTU - Women's Christian Temperance Union
wk - week
yr - year or years

ACHOR, W.H. - GC night policeman (G10/28/98)

ADAMS, Benjamin K. - att Western Coll of Embalming, Chicago (G7/16/97)

ADAMS, Mrs. Clarissa - b 30 Mar 1836; of Mill Twp (J8/11/16); wife of John; d 11 Mar 1917, bur Lancaster Cem (G3/16/17)

ADAMS, I.H. - s John Adams, both of Jnsbr (G10/5/17)

ADAMS, Jake - of Warren; s John Adams (J6/1/89)

ADAMS, John - b 5 Jul 1828; of Mill Twp (G7/27/17; J8/27/20)

ADAMS, John C. - Jnsbr Royal Movie Theatre prop. (J10/22/15)

ADAMSON, J.F.- moves his family to Gaston (G12/23/98)

ADAMSON, Mrs. J.F. - of GC; sister of Miss Katharine Lugar (G3/11/98)

ADAMSON, John - owned farm E on N. D St., Harrisburg in 1861; d in CW (J5/4/17)

ADAMSON, Joseph - s John Adamson; owned farm W of John Adamson's farm in 1861; his farmhouse stood at N. B St. & Third St., GC (J5/4/17)

ADAMSON, Mort - s M/M Virgil Adamson of North Grove area (G11/30/17; J12/27/18)

ADAMSON, Virgil - of North Grove area, s M/M John Adamson of Rigdon (G9/21/17)

ADDELBERGER, John - officer, Jnsbr K of P (G1/26/17)

ADDELBERGER, Mrs. John - dt Austin and Waity S. (ROLLAND) Freeman (J3/26/15)

ADDINGTON, Charles - Mgr, GC Brass Band (G10/1/97)

ADDISON, E.L. - s M/M William Addison of Knightstown (G5/20/98)

ADDISON, Mrs. E.L. - mbr GC Christian Ch. (G2/12/97); mbr '97 Club (G12/17/97)

ADKINS, Mrs. - of Van Buren, age 55, d at County Infirmary 8 Aug 1915 (J8/13/15)

ADLER, Anna - dt M/M J.W. Adler; 13 Dec 1897 given party for 11th birthday (G12/17/97)

ADLER, Herbert - and Ralph are s Mrs. J.W. Adler (G7/16/97)

ADRIANSON, Ralph - 8-yr old attempting to win pony and cart in GC merchants contest (J4/2/15)

AIRPLANE - flew over GC at altitude of ca 1,000 ft at 9:30 AM Tues (J5/16/19)

ALEXANDER, __ - of Alexander & Beital; 9 Mar 1897 opens saloon/restaurant on Alexander's Restaurant site (G3/12/97)

ALEXANDER, Dr. W.P. - mbr GC Christian Ch. (G2/12/97); birthday is 20 Feb 1897 (G2/26/97); mbr GC K of P (G7/23/97)

ALEXANDER, Walter - 20 Mar 1897 m Anna M. Lewis of GC (G3/26/97)

ALLEGREE, William - will manage T.H. Graham's GC Livery Stable (G8/20/97)

ALLEN, Eli - of North Grove area; bought a new El-Car (J8/3/17)

ALLEN, Ephraim O. - of Fairmount, preached at EBPM Sun (J5/26/16; G11/16/17); EBPM pastor (J10/29/20)

ALLEN, Irvin Palmer - of GC; s Mrs. Sam Holmes, step-s Sam Holmes; m Lydia R.; d 30 Sep 1915, bur GC Cem (J10/1/15; J10/8/15)

ALLEN, John - m Ethel Hawkins 19 Feb 1919 (J2/21/19)

ALLEN, Lucy - grad, Mill Twp Dist. No. 4 Sch who passed exam for County Diploma (G4/29/98; G5/13/98)

ALLEN, Orville - Mill Twp 8th grade grad 1916 (J5/12/16)

ALLEN, Verlou - Mill Twp 8th grade grad 1915 (J6/18/15); mbr North Grove PM SS (J9/7/17); mbr FFA basketball team (J2/7/19); of North Grove area; broke State Record for 220 yd. dash at FFA track meet with time of 22.8 seconds (J5/9/19)

ALLISON, Frank - employee of U.S. Glass Factory, GC; Mayor R. Brashear fined him $9.30 for assault (G1/1/97)

AMSDEN, W.M. - Attorney, office is on Main St., GC near the RR Depot (G4/28/93); played Santa Claus at GC Baptist Ch. Christmas Eve (G1/1/97); Attorney for GC (G8/5/98)

ANDES, Helen - 1920 Mill Twp 8th grade grad (J5/21/20)

ANDES, James E. - 1920 Mill Twp 8th grade grad (J5/21/20)

ANDES, Lily - 1919 Mill Twp 8th grade grad (J4/4/19)

ANDREWS, Gladys - local 3-yr old (J4/2/15)

ANDREWS, Mrs. Leslie - 25th birthday last Tues (J1/12/17)

ANSCHUTZ, Louis - b Germany 22 Jun 1855; m 23 Aug 1881 Mrs. Margaret Kettniss; d 2 Oct 1917; bur GC (G10/5/17)

ANSON, Mrs. Joe - of Huntington; sister of Mrs. W.E. Mason (J4/18/19)

ANTRIM, Mrs. C.J. - of Danville, IL is step-mother of Mrs. William Carroll of Jefferson area (J1/7/16)

APOSTOLIC FRIENDS/THE MODERN FRIENDS/JONESBORO HOLY ROLLERS - Pastor Charles D. Craig of Losantville was made to salute and kiss the flag and lead the congregation in singing patriotic songs because he preaches non-help to the Red Cross and non-violence; flags were nailed to walls of the church and on the steeple; Hiatt was recently rotten-egged in Losantville for the same cause (G7/26/18)

APPLE, Ray - young Fairmount man; killed Sept 1904 by street car at Deer Creek bridge (J10/3/19)

APPLEMAN, Rev. Glenn - m; new Jnsbr MM pastor (J9/26/19); raised in S. Marion; grad, Taylor Univ (J10/3/19)

ARHART, Jennie - age 39; d in County Infirmary 2 Feb 1917, bur Mt. Hope Cem (G2/9/17)

ARMSTRONG, Alie Christian - b Cass Co. 12 Dec 1878; s M/M Charles R. Armstrong; m Mrs. Hazel Baker Sep 1917; mbr Christian Ch.; d 6 May 1918, bur GC (G5/10/18)

ARMSTRONG, Arlie - officer, GC K of P (G7/14/11)

ARMSTRONG, Edward - GC Baptist pastor (G7/14/11)

ARMSTRONG, Harry Rex - b last Mon; s M/M Charles Armstrong of GC (J4/25/19)

ARMSTRONG, Walter Leroy - b 11 Nov 1915; s Charles and Mary Armstrong; mbr Christian Ch.; d 4 Sep 1916, bur Walnut Creek Cem (J9/8/16)

ARNETT, Charles Elwood - b 21 Jun 1880 near Fairmount; s Stephen and Ruth Ann Arnett; m 20 Jun 1913 Mattie Harvey; d 5 May 1917 in FL (G5/11/17; J5/11/17)

ARNETT, Cleo - will m Walter Pattison Apr 29 (J4/30/15); dt Ruth Ann Arnett (J5/7/15); taught at Dist. No. 4 Sch 1914-15 (J6/18/15)

ARNETT, Ernest - grad, Jnsbr HS 1911 (J4/29/21); f Earlham Coll student (J6/15/17); mbr Jnsbr MM (J7/27/17)

ARNETT, Robert - s Mrs. Arlie Arnett of North Grove area (J8/24/17)

ARNETT, Stephen - m Ruth Ann; d ca 1896 (J5/11/17)

ARNETT, Virgil - conductor on Marion, GC, and Jnsbr Electric Car Line for past 5 yr, has quit (G1/15/97)

ARNETT, Woodie - of Jnsbr; d in Orlando, FL (J8/17/17)

ASHCROFT, Richard - mbr Jnsbr Masons (G12/24/97)

ASHWELL, Mrs. Charles - mbr Jnsbr Presbyterian Ch. (G7/13/17)

ASPY, Rev. C.W. - Dunkirk Baptist pastor; is assisting Rev. D.L. Jamison in a revival at GC Baptist Ch. (G11/19/97)

ASPY, Rev. Lotus - of Fairmount; is holding revival at GC Baptist Ch. (G1/8/97)

ATKINSON, Frank - of GC; 8 Jan 1917 m Mary A. Deeren, dt Henry Leffler of GC; will live in GC (G1/12/17; J1/12/17)

ATKINSON, Guy - Ralph, Ray, Carl and Gail are s M/M Lewis Atkinson of Union Chapel area (J3/23/17)

ATKINSON, Lewis - brother of Mrs. Chester Parks of near Kidner Bridge; m (J3/30/17)

ATKINSON, Mrs. Lewis - of Union Chapel area is sister of Miss Marie Mitchell of Swayzee (G1/26/17)

ATWATER, Mrs. George - lives in W. Jnsbr (J10/6/16)

ATWOOD, Elijah - CW vet; d recently; mbr Jnsbr GAR Post; bur Jnsbr (G5/13/98)

AUSTIN, J.O. - mbr GC K of P (G7/23/97); recently sold Wilson Barber Shop to O.M. Patton (G8/6/97)

AXTON, Rev. Charles R. - Kokomo MM pastor for several yrs, is Jnsbr MM pastor beginning 1 Oct 1916 (J9/22/16; J10/6/16); wife dec; m 19 Apr 1917 Mrs. Rachel Pierce, widow of Edward N. Pierce (G4/20/17); will quit as Jnsbr MM pastor in Oct (J7/4/19); Supt. of White's Institute, Wabash Co. at $1,800 per year plus maintenance (J8/22/19)

AXTON, Victor L. - s Rev. Charles R. Axton; is in US Army in KY (J12/14/17)

BABB, David - age 90; of near Herbst; m; d 5 Nov 1919 (J11/7/19)

BABB, Katherine - mbr Jnsbr M.P. SS (J6/29/17)

BABB, Samuel - b Grant Co. ca 1834; of Herbst; m; d last wk, bur Thrailkill Cem (J12/12/19)

BACK CREEK - contractor Thomas Monahan completed work on cleaning stream bed from source in Madison Co. to Mississinewa River (J3/17/16); T.A. Snyder Preserve Co. of Fairmount polluted BC killing fish and damaging drinking water, according to suit filed by Town of Jnsbr (J10/31/19)

BACK CREEK MONTHLY MEETING OF FRIENDS - BCMM, including Jnsbr PM and North Grove PM, held 16 Sep 1915 at BC MH (J9/17/15); BC WCTU met at BC MH 8 Nov 1916 (J11/10/16); Carl Neal will preach Sun in the absence of pastor, Mattie Cammack-Gibson (J8/3/17)

BACK CREEK SCHOOL (Fairmount Twp Sch Dist. No.) - last day dinner 5 Apr (G4/12/18)

BACK CREEK WCTU - Mrs. Lin Wilson, mbr (J12/10/20)

BAILEY, Prof.__ - Instructor, GC Brass Band (G10/1/97)

BAILEY, J.F. - Fri sold his GC Sanitary Cut-Rate Grocery & Meat Market to George Frederick; will go into full-time evangelistic work (J10/22/15)

BAILEY, Mattie - mbr Jnsbr WCTU (J12/28/18)

BAINBRIDGE, Bessie - grad, GC HS 1919 (J4/11/19); b GC 21 Jun 1901 (J5/16/19)

BAINBRIDGE, Earl - mbr GC Christian Ch. (G11/23/17)

BAINBRIDGE, P.W. - of GC; father of Clara (G1/26/17)

BAIRD, Charles - of Jnsbr; m; s Mrs. Sarah Baird of Jnsbr (G11/5/20)

BAIRD, Mrs. Charles - dt Mrs. Elizabeth Cray (J2/11/16)

BAIRD, Hulda (BODKIN) - b Grant Co. 9 Mar 1855; m Thomas Baird 25 Feb 1873; mbr Jnsbr M.P. Ch.; d 26 Nov 1916, bur GC Cem (J11/30/16)

BAIRD, Fred - of Jnsbr; s M/M W.O. Baird of Gary; grandson Mrs. Sarah Baird of Jnsbr (G11/5/20)

BAIRD, Mrs. J.A. - of Jnsbr; mother of Mrs. J. Clifton Branden of Anderson (G2/9/17)

BAIRD, Mrs. Verd - of Jnsbr; mother of Mrs. Ernie Griffith of Casey, IL (J10/1/15)

BAIRD, W.O. - now of Gary; m; s Mrs. Sarah Baird of Jnsbr (G11/5/20)

BAIRD, Walter - 8th grade grad Jnsbr Sch 1918 (G5/10/18)

BAIRD, William - of Jnsbr; s M/M W.O. Baird of Gary (G11/5/20)

BAIRD, William R. - living in Jnsbr (G12/24/97)

BAKER, Joseph - one of men who rescued Wood Huff and Belle Whitson when they fell through ice into Mississinewa River (G1/1/97)

BAKER, Julia (LEONARD) - m William Baker; Oct 1904, d at her GC home (J10/10/19)

BAKER, Mrs. Laura - of GC; dt Mrs. Nancy Eakins of GC (G11/12/20)

BAKER, Rich - GC Tigers football team mbr (J10/6/16)

BAKER, Sarah Ann (SMITH) - b Page Co., VA 18 Oct 1848; dt James and Catherine Smith; m George W. Baker; mother of Mrs. Iva Petty; d 1 Feb 1918 (G2/8/18)

BALDWIN, Mrs. __ - mother of Mrs. Ben Rush of North Grove; d 14 Nov 1919, bur Marion cem (J11/21/19)

BALDWIN, A.M. - old Marion resident; d 24 Jul 1898 (G7/29/98)

BALDWIN, David - lived in Fairmount since 1873; Methodist; d recently (G2/11/98)

BALDWIN, Edgar M. - editor, Fairmount News; m Myra Rush at home of Cyrus Neal in Marion last wk, m by Rev. E.O. Ellis (J9/2/87); s Micah Baldwin (dec); brother of Nathan Baldwin and of Mrs. E.M. Hollingsworth (J8/22/19)

BALDWIN, Lafen - age 56; m; d in County Infirmary; bur Park Cem (G11/5/20)

BALDWIN, Lancaster D.- acquitted of bribery (G4/23/97)

BALDWIN, Louis/Lewis Jenkins 'Chink'/'Jenk' - officer, GC K of P (G7/14/11); 17 Apr 1919 his ice storage house in GC burned (J4/18/19); and wife celebrated 81st birthday 22 Oct 1919 of her father, John Donovan (J10/24/19)

BALDWIN, Nathan - age 68; s Micah Baldwin (dec); lived in Fairmount; d 17 Aug 1919 (J8/22/19)

BALES, Ernest - and three others took 30 frogs from the Mississinewa River Mon night (G7/30/97)

BALLARD, Roland E. - 1920 Mill Twp 8th grade grad (J5/21/20)

BALLINGER, Mrs. Albert - of College Hill area; d 5 Jul 1919, bur Jefferson Cem (J7/11/19)

BALLINGER, Carrie - of College Hill area, mbr Jefferson WCTU (G10/26/17)

BALLINGER, Clara Ella (McVICKER) - b near Upland 5 Feb 1892; m Alvin Cleo Ballinger 27 Oct 1908; d 4 Sep 1920, bur Jefferson Cem (J9/10/20)

BALLINGER, Mrs. Nettie - of Upland; mbr, Jefferson WCTU (J2/4/16)

BANDY, __ - of Bandy & Metcalf; owners of Park Meat Market on W side of First St. between N. D St. & N. E St., GC (G9/22/93)

BANDY, Mrs. Orlando - lives on Main St., GC; dt Mrs. Elizabeth Oder (G2/11/98)

BANKS, Rev. T.H. - Supt., County Infirmary (G3/12/97)

BANNISTER, __ - dt M/M James Bannister of S. C St., GC; b 13 Jul 1897 (G7/16/97)

BANNISTER, Lula - of Fairmount; wife of George Bannister; d 23 Jul 1918, bur Knox Chapel Cem (G7/26/18)

BANNON, Everett - 8th grade grad Jnsbr Sch 1919 (J4/18/19)

BARCLAY, Cora Ellen (KIMBLE) - b Adams Co., OH 19 Jul 1864; m Rev. James L. Barclay 3 Sep 1888; mbr M.E. Ch.; d 8 Jun 1920 in Jnsbr, bur Gaston Cem (J6/11/20)

BARCLAY, Rev. James L. - Jnsbr M.P. pastor (J8/24/17)

BARKALOW, James K. - 8 Apr 1889 sold his Jnsbr bakery/ grocery store to D.W. Hayworth (J6/8/89)

BARKDULL, Charles A. - of GC; age 26; m Edna M. Hollobaugh 4 Dec 1915, will live in GC (J12/10/15)

BARKDULL, Grant - lives on Fankboner farm N of Fairmount; has opened sugar camp of 107 trees with more trees yet to tap (J2/14/19)

BARKER, Everd - 8th grade grad Jnsbr Sch 1919 (J4/18/19)

BARKLEY, John - alto trombonist, GC Brass Band (G10/1/97)

BARLEY, William J. - of Marion; age 81; d 23 May 1917 (G5/25/17)

BARNARD, A.L. - age 79; of Jnsbr; had 11 children, 4 now living; d 6 May 1897 (G5/7/97)

BARNARD, Clinton - and Jacob are s A.L. Barnard (G5/7/97)

BARNHARDT, Mrs. William - operates boarding house in GC (G11/12/97)

BARNHART, Frank - mbr GC Fire Dept. (J3/4/04)

BARR, Rev. Daisy (DOUGLAS) - held revival at Fowlerton M.P. Ch. (J1/31/19); f of Fairmount; pastor, New Castle MM (J6/18/20)

BARRETT, Mrs. Martha E. - b Delaware Co. ca 1847; widow; d 19 May 1918, bur Alexandria cem (G5/24/18)

BARTMESS, E.S. - officer GC K of P (G7/23/97)

BARTMESS/BARTMUS, U.S.- b Wells Co. ca 1867; came to GC in 1896 (G3/18/98); officer GC K of P (G7/23/97)

BARTON, Ruth - 8th grade grad Jnsbr Sch 1918 (G5/10/18)

BARZE, B.F.- Citizen's Bank of Jnsbr Cashier, and First National Bank of GC Cashier/stockholder (G12/16/98)

BARZE, Virginia - dt M/M B.F. Barze of S. B St., GC; given party for 7th birthday 18 Dec 1897 (G12/24/97)

BASH, Rev. A.S. - m; GC Christian Ch. pastor (J4/6/17)

BASKETT, James - mbr Jnsbr M.P. Ch. SS (J6/29/17)

BASKETT, Janet - mbr Jnsbr M.P. Ch. SS (J6/29/17)

BASTIAN, Anna Jeanette (DUMOND) - b OH 22 Jul 1856; dt Lorenzo A. and Clemenzo Dumond; m James Bastian 4 Jul 1879; mother of Karl Bastian; mbr GC M.E. Ch.; d 24 Dec 1919, bur GC Cem (J1/2/20)

BASTIAN, Emmett - and Glen, s James Bastian (G7/14/11)

BASTIAN, Karl - mbr GC K of P (J4/25/19); s James and Anna J. (DUMOND) Bastian (J1/2/20)

BASTIAN, Miss Lois -mbr GC Lady Maccabees (J1/14/16)

BATEMAN, Mrs. Veda/Vida (STEPHENS) - missionary for WCTU in India, gave talk here Fri (J8/22/19); is visited by her mother, Sallie (WINSLOW) Stevens (J5/13/21)

BATES, Jacob - old Jnsbr resident; d Sep 1910 (J9/10/20)

BATES, John W. - old soldier, granted pension of $6.00 per mon. plus $1,700 back-pension (J6/24/87)

BAUMGARTNER, Ethel (MORRIS) - age 27; dt M/M Jasper Morris of near Kidner Bridge; m Jacob Baumgartner; d 12 Jul 1917, bur Jefferson Cem (G7/20/17)

BAY, Eva - North Bethel Sch tchr 1915-17 (J8/27/15; J9/1/16)

BAY, Lillie - neice of John Wilhoit (dec) of GC; his recently probated will left his estate to her (J10/13/16)

BEALL, Rev. M.E. - Jnsbr Presbyterian Ch. pastor (G2/12/97), and of GC Presbyterian Ch.; he came to these churches in 1895 but is now resigning (G3/26/97); becomes Editor, Ft. Wayne Gazette (G4/16/97)

BEALS, Elwood - of Linwood, KS; brother of Louisa Corder (J1/14/16)

BEALS, Thomas - of CA; brother of Louisa Corder (J1/14/16)

BEARD, D.H. - opens Jnsbr blacksmith shop (G8/19/98)

BEARD, Thomas - b 3 Apr 1837, lives in Mill Twp (G8/17/17; J8/27/20)

BEATTY, __ - only s of Jot Beatty; drowned long ago below Mississinewa River dam near present Rubber Works (J6/8/17)

BEAUMONT, Sam - fireman on first train to enter Grant Co. 16 Aug 1865 (J8/24/17)

BEAVER, Elijah - 11 Nov 1897 d at his N. Jnsbr home (G11/12/97)

BECK, Mrs. Katherine - of Marion; age 61; d 12 Mar 1917 (G3/16/17)

BECK, R.D. - mbr Jnsbr Masonic Lodge (G12/24/97)

BEEDY, Amanda Ellen - dt M/M John Beedy; m Russell Trout 24 Aug 1915; will live on farm E of GC (J8/27/15)

BEEDY, Matthew - of Upland; m Eva Clark 20 Nov 1916; will live in IL (J11/24/16)

BEEKMAN, Evelyn - age 7; dt M/M William Beekman of 3 mi. NW of Van Buren; accidentally shot and killed 12 Mar 1917 (G3/16/17)

BEERS, Mrs. Harry - dt Mrs. Margaret Marchal (J8/8/19)

BEGGS, Otto - of Kyle & Beggs; jeweler (G5/28/97)

BEHEM, Clara Helen - b 12 Nov 1897 near Washington Courthouse, OH; grad, GC HS 1915 (J5/21/15); Candy Sch tchr 1918-19 (G9/6/18)

BEITEL, Charles - opens new bowling alley in Opera House Block, GC (G4/1/98)

BEITEL, Orville - mbr GC Christian Ch. (G11/23/17)

BEITEL, Ursula - 1917 Mill Twp 8th grade grad (G5/11/17)

BELCHER, Rev. Joseph - Nov 1910, m; GC Baptist Ch. pastor for past 14 mons; given farewell dinner (G11/5/20)

BELL, Albert - has an ice house in GC (G6/4/97); sold his grocery at S. 3rd & D St., GC to D.A. Gilchrist (G8/12/98)

BELL, Mrs. D.M. - mbr Jnsbr WCTU (J4/16/15)

BELL, William F. - of SW of Fairmount; age 88; mbr Fairmount MM; d 26 Jul 1920 (J7/30/20)

BENBOW, Aaron - one of first residents of Harrisburg ca 1870; lived N of Main Street, E of RR (J6/8/17)

BENBOW, Hannah E. (JENKINS) - b 12 Sep 1840 3 mi. E of GC; dt Israel and Lydia Jenkins; m Thomas Benbow of Jnsbr 5 Sep 1858; mbr Jefferson Christian Ch.; d 7 Nov 1915, bur Jefferson Cem (J11/12/15; G11/12/20)

BENBOW, Ida S. - age ca 23; had a son born at Co. Infirmary last wk; this is her 4th illegitimate child (G2/11/97)

BENBOW, Jesse - had a log cabin home on site of Harrisburg ca 1870 (J4/13/17)

BENBOW, Robert Leaman 'Lee'- b 3 mi. E of GC 3 Jul 1868; s Thomas and Hannah E. (JENKINS) Benbow; m 1 Nov 1911 Kitty Ellars of GC; brother of I.S. Benbow of Fairmount; mbr Jefferson Christian Ch.; d 1 Apr 1919 (J4/4/19)

BENBOW, Susan - of GC; mother of Lee Swisher of Benton Harbor, MI (G11/23/17)

BENBOW, Thomas - b 11 Jun 1836; of Mill Twp (G8/17/17); lives E of GC; gets $8 per mon. vet pension (G12/23/98); of GC; 83rd birthday; father of Mrs. George Haines and Mrs. Chester Buffington (J6/13/19); 84th birthday (J6/18/20)

BENSON, Mrs. Charles - dt Mrs. Al Dye of GC; lives in Gary (G6/22/17)

BERRY, Martin - age 15; s M/M John Berry of GC; had foot crushed by RR car, foot was amputated (J1/2/20)

BEST, Mrs. Lewis - sister of Reuben King (G2/9/17); dt Mrs. Ben King of GC (G7/27/17)

BETHEL MONTHLY MEETING OF FRIENDS - pastor is Rev. Harvey Ratliff (J1/26/17)

BICKNELL PUBLISHING CO. - purchased GC Journal and the Jnsbr Journal recently (G12/3/97)

BICKNELL, Clarence - mbr GC Baptist Ch. (G5/14/97)

BICKNELL, Mrs. C.F. - wife of f owner of Jnsbr/GC newspapers; f lived in GC; d recently in NY (J12/27/18)

BIDDINGER, Frank - mbr GC Christian Ch. (J2/20/20)

BIDDLECUM, __ - of Biddlecum & Lottridge, has opened new carriage and blacksmith shop at S. A & Railroad Sts., GC (G5/28/97)

BIDDLECUM, Rev. Homer J. - f of GC; m; Friends pastor in KS; recently passed through on way to KS (J9/10/20)

BLAKELY, Mary Isabelle - dt Mrs. T.J. Blakely of Jnsbr (J4/18/19)

BLAKELY, Robert - s Mrs. T.J. Blakely of Jnsbr (J4/18/19)

BLAKELY, Mrs. T.J. - of Jnsbr; dt of Mrs. George Brighton (J4/18/19)

BLAND, Anna May - b Baltimore, MD 23 Sep 1898; started to sch 1904 in Fairmount; grad, GC HS 1917 (J5/18/17)

BLAND, Harry - GC All-Stars football team mbr (J10/6/16)

BLAND, William Block - b Yorkshire, England 10 Mar 1840; m 1859 Ellen Ryan; d at GC home 12 Feb 1919 (J2/14/19)

BLESS, William - of Kokomo; father of Mrs. Charles Rutherford and Mrs. Clarence Grosscup, both of GC (G11/5/20)

BLISS, James - GC All-Stars football team mbr (J10/6/16)

BLISS, Mrs. Rebecca - f of Jnsbr; d 15 Feb 1917; bur Jnsbr IOOF Cem (G2/23/17)

BLISS, Yevon - 10 yr-old dt of M/M Charles Bliss of GC; struck by auto in Fairmount while visiting her grandparents, M/M George Turner; she will recover (J10/6/16)

BLOCH, Edward - mbr/officer in GC K of P (G7/14/11)

BLOOM, Lawrence - mbr Jnsbr HS 1915-16 sophomore class (J10/8/15)

BOCHART, __ - s M/M Henry Bochart; b 24 May 1898 (G5/27/98)

BOCOCK, James - b Clinton Co., OH 15 Aug 1824; father of Mrs. John Smith; mbr Christian Ch.; d 7 Mar 1920, bur Atkinson Cem (J3/12/20)

BOGUE, Alvah - s M/M Elmer Bogue; 2 Apr 1916 m Jessie Marie Gift, dt M/M Jessie E. Gift of Jnsbr (J4/7/16)

BOGUE, Mrs. Mary E. - of GC; b 12 Sep 1837; husband d ca 1894; she recently d, bur Greentown (G10/4/18)

BOLAND, Mr.__ - a Quaker; instigated, at meeting at Fairmount Wesleyan Ch., the dynamiting of the Fairmount bldg leased as a saloon by Ira J. Smith (J7/1/87)

BOLES, Josiah - Candy Sch tchr 1855-57; owned the N 40-acres of the Davy Overman farm, sold it to David Entsminger and took his family to Wabash Co. (G6/1/17; J6/1/17)

BOLES, Maggie - Candy Sch tchr summer of 1855 (G6/1/17; J6/1/17)

BOLES, William - County Infirmary Supt. for past 3 yr; will be replaced March 1st (G2/9/17)

BOLLMAN, Elizabeth - b 10 May 1854 in Matrick, MA; dt Mrs. Bridget Keegan; m Abraham MacWilliam Bollman (dec) 22 Oct 1874 at Bunker Hill; mother of Mrs. Oscar Howard of GC; d 4 Sep 1915, bur at Marion (J9/10/15)

BOLLMAN, Fred - of GC; in US Army (J6/29/17); in France; brother of Miss Frances Bollman of Marion, and of Mrs. Oscar Howard of GC (G11/30/17)

BOND, __ - he and __ Ward had a sawmill in Harrisburg near river bridge ca 1869, then they moved the sawmill to Muncie Road near the Jack Crawford residence; the boiler exploded killing Ward, Bond was unhurt (J6/8/17)

BOND, E.L. - invites public to the annual Horticultural Picnic in his grove NW of Jnsbr on 15 Jun 1889 (J6/8/89)

BOND, John - is home in Jnsbr after his discharge from US Army (J4/18/19)

BOND, William - age 72; m; d 30 Jul 1917, bur GC Cem (G8/3/17)

BOND, Wilson H. - lives on farm SW of Jnsbr; m; had 25 bushels of wheat stolen (G9/22/93)

BONES, William - ca 1855 had farm immediately N of the Candy farm (J6/1/17)

BONGE, Elmer P. - is in army on way to France (G5/17/18)

BOOKOUT, __ - of Fairmount; drowned in Mississinewa River near Harrisburg long ago (J6/8/17)

BOOKOUT, Martha - see LECKLIDER

BOOKOUT, Rueben - of N. Jnsbr; m Nancy Terrell 4 mi. SE of Fairmount; 50th wedding anniv 14 Mar 1920 (J3/12/20)

BOTHWELL, I.L. - mbr Jnsbr Masons; is in army (G11/29/18)

BOURIE, __ - dt M/M Frank Bourie; b 30 May 1898 (G6/3/98)

BOURIE, Mae - Jnsbr M.E. SS officer (J1/12/17)

BOURIE, William - grad, Jnsbr HS 1919 (J4/18/19)

BOWERS, David - enlisted while teaching at Candy Sch during CW, d in war (G6/1/17; J6/1/17)

BOWERS, Frederick - last wk given party for 5th birthday at his home E of GC (J7/9/15)

BOWERS, Mrs. Hester L. - m Grant W. Hiatt 25 Oct 1920 in GC (J10/29/20)

BOWERS, William - of E of GC; while hauling firewood a log fell off his wagon onto him breaking his left leg in two places (J11/16/17)

BOWMAN, Elmer - of GC; s William H. Bowman; m; d of flu Wed (G11/29/18)

BOWMAN, Jess - s William H. Bowman (G11/29/18); of GC; filed to divorce wife, Elizabeth Bowman (J4/18/19)

BOWMAN, Mary M. (DILLON) - b 2 Mar 1846; m William Bowman 25 Dec 1865; d 21 Oct 1917, bur GC Cem (G10/26/17)

BOWMAN, Willard - of GC; s William H. Bowman (G11/29/18)

BOWMAN, William H. - is in Marion Soldier's Home (G11/29/18)

BOYCE, Thomas - s George Boyce; 14 May 1898 had party for 10th birthday (G5/20/98)

BOYD, L.C. - stockholder, Citizens' Bank of Jnsbr (G12/16/98)

BOYER, George - fined by GC Mayor Brashear last Fri for public intoxication (G1/1/97)

BRADFORD, C.C. - is Grant Co. Deputy Sheriff who stopped prize fight between Gayle Ruley and Frank Roberts, both of Jnsbr (G4/22/98); elected Grant Co. Sheriff (G11/18/98)

BRADFORD, Jesse T. - of Marion; age 80; d (J1/31/19)

BRADFORD, Mary R. -lives in Jnsbr (J7/18/19); b 8 Feb 1839 (J8/1/19)

BRADFORD, Moses - age 78; of Marion; d (G1/14/98)

BRADFORD, Noah - jailed for drunkenness (G11/19/97)

BRANDEN/BRANDON, Fern (BAIRD) - 2d dt M/M J.A. Baird of Jnsbr; m Aug 1914 J. Clifton/Clifford L. Branden of Anderson; lives in Anderson (G2/9/17)

BRANE, Miss Ferol - GC West Ward Sch tchr (J2/20/20)

BRANNEN, Harry C. - Jnsbr M.E. SS officer (J1/12/17); mbr/officer, Jnsbr K of P Lodge (G1/26/17)

BRASHEAR, Richard A. - of Brashear, Lay & Kyle; they have a GC store selling wallpaper (G9/22/93); GC Mayor (G1/1/97); mbr GC Baptist Ch. (G1/14/98); 8 Apr 1898 was 45th birthday (G4/15/98); lost Mayoral election to James H. Lay (G5/6/98)

BRASHEAR, Mrs. Richard A. - mbr/hostess of '97 Club last wk (G10/7/98)

BRELSFORD, A.W. - age 69; lived 2.5 mi SE of GC; m; d 6 Feb 1918, bur GC Cem (G2/8/18)

BRENNEN, William - GC Welshman employed at Morewood Tin Plate Works; tried to m Anna Jones, GC Welsh working at Morewood Tin Plate Works; her father stopped them since she is less than 18 yrs old (G12/10/97)

BREWER, Hazel - 1917 Mill Twp 8th grade grad (G5/11/17)

BREWER, Sherman - 1916 Mill Twp 8th grade grad (J5/12/16)

BREWER, Valie - 1916 Mill Twp sch 8th grade grad (J5/12/16)

BRIGGS, Bernard - of Jnsbr; s M/M Fred Briggs; m 1 May 1917 Mabel Crawford, dt M/M J.C. Crawford of GC (G5/4/17)

BRIGGS, Roland - s M/M Fred Briggs of Jnsbr (G2/9/17)

BRIGHTON, Irene - grad, Jnsbr HS 1919 (J4/18/19)

BRINDLE, Albert - mbr/officer, Jnsbr K of P (G1/26/17)

BRITT, Daniel S. - s Thomas Britt; of Marion (J2/20/20)

BRITT, Richard - s Thomas Britt; age 30; raised on farm near Jnsbr; mbr US Marines; d at sea of disease (J2/20/20)

BRITT, Thomas - b 2 Nov 1832; lives in Mill Twp (G7/27/17; J8/27/20)

BROAD, George O. - age 35; b Boston, MA; came to GC in 1894 (G3/18/98)

BROCK, Edna E. - grad, Jnsbr HS 1918 (G5/10/18)

BRODGON, Rebecca Jane (BATES) - b near Alexandria 20 Jan 1862; dt John and Sarah Bates; m 1880 Jasper Brogdon; mbr Second Salem Baptist Ch. of N of Marion; d 21 Feb 1919, bur GC Cem (J2/21/19)

BROGAN, Frank - s M/M John Brogan of GC; was killed in street car-train wreck in WV ca 1913 (J1/21/16)

BROGAN, Joseph - s M/M John Brogan of GC; m last Sat to Alma May Hicks of Hannibal, OH (J7/9/15)

BROOKS, Zeek - hauls straw for American Strawboard Co.; had been drinking, became belligerent with streetcar on River Bridge, lost argument (G10/8/97); of Jnsbr; arrested for public intoxication (G6/3/98)

BROSCHART, __ - dt M/M Henry Broschart; b 31 Dec 1896 (G1/8/97)

BROSKY, John Paul - b 22 Aug 1870 in Pittsburg, PA; m Lydia Bolinger 1903 in GC; lived in GC; d 16 Nov 1915, bur Riverside Cem (J11/19/15)

BROWN, __ - mother of John Brown of near Zeek Sch; d last Monday (J4/30/20)

BROWN, __ 'Doc' - bartender in Mississinewa Hotel, GC (G1/29/97)

BROWN, Charles H. - mbr GC Tribe of Ben Hur (G7/30/97)

BROWN, Dr. Charles N. - with s, Virgil, bought the 140-acre N.A. Wilson farm 1 mi. E of Fairmount for $31,500 or $225 per acre (J7/4/19)

BROWN, Mrs. Debbie - of Jnsbr; dt William Havens (G4/29/98)

BROWN, Joe - and George Meekins bought Charles Campbell's Jnsbr saloon (G11/26/97)

BROWN, John - f of near Swayzee; recently moved to his farm E of Jnsbr known as the Martin Whitson farm (J12/28/17); father of Mrs. Glenn Parsons (G2/8/18)

BROWN, Margaret - mother of Mrs. Cora Rutherford of GC (G11/23/17)

BROWN, Mrs. Maria - of Upland; age 83; d 3 May 1918, bur Jefferson Cem (G5/10/18)

BROWN, Tude - of S of Jnsbr on Wheeling Pike; wife is Julia Brown (G1/26/17)

BROWNING, Mattie Leona (CHAPMAN) - b near Jnsbr 14 Nov 1894; dt Guy and Emma Chapman; m Rev. Alva T. Browning 16 Jun 1916; mbr GC Christian Ch.; d 24 Jan 1919, bur GC Cem (J1/31/19)

BROWNLEE, James - b 15 Aug 1818; m __ Goldthwait; d 9 Aug 1897 (G8/13/97)

BRUBAKER, Helen - grad, GC HS 1917 (J5/18/17)

BRUCE, __ - of Bruce & Marks Manufacturing Co., GC; Co. formed ca 1893; Mr. Marks d 1894; L.K. Price of Marion will manage plant for Mr. Bruce (G1/1/97); W.F. Young is receiver for Bruce & Marks Manufacturing Co. (G10/29/97)

BRUMLEY, Fayanna - dt M/M Frank Brumley of Jnsbr; b recently (G2/19/97); Feb 1908 is given party for 11th birthday (J2/16/23); grad, Jnsbr HS 1916 (J1/5/17)

BRUMLEY, Frank - clothing robbed of $9.65 while swimming at dam last Thurs (G7/9/97)

BRUMLEY, George - has malaria fever (G6/24/95); is a barber (G3/5/97)

BRUMLEY, Grace - grad, Jnsbr HS 1916 (J1/5/17)

BRUMLEY, Guy - officer, Jnsbr K of P (G1/26/17)

BRUMLEY, Mrs. Henrietta - b 1 Jun 1833 (J8/13/15); b Guernsey Co., OH; m Samuel Brumley (dec ca 1897); lived in Jnsbr; d Mar 1916 (J3/10/16)

BRUMLEY, Holland Samuel - f of Jnsbr; age 17; s M/M S.H. 'Chink' Brumley; drowned in Michigan last wk, bur in GC IOOF Cem (G9/13/18)

BRUMLEY, Ruby - 8th grade grad, Jnsbr Sch 1918 (G5/10/18)

BRUMLEY, Samuel - of Jnsbr; d 21 Dec 1898 (G12/23/98)

BRUSHWEILER/BRUSHWILER, George - one of men who rescued Wood Huff and Belle Whitson when they fell through the ice into Mississinewa River (G1/1/97)

BRUSHWEILER, Mary (HANMORE) - dt Mrs. Mary Hanmore and sister of Mart Hanmore (G3/5/97)

BRYAN, Mrs. Herbert - age 18; dt Yuba Johns; granddt Mrs. Laura Johns (J2/4/16)

BRYAN, Russell LeRoy - age 4 wks; s Mrs. Herbert Bryan (J2/4/16)

BUCHANAN, John H. - age 73, Fairmount CW vet, killed in RR accident while working 1 Nov 1919 (J11/7/19)

BUCHANAN, Mrs. Olive - Mill Twp Dist. No. 2a Sch tchr 1920-21 (J8/27/20)

BUDD, Cleo - 8th grade grad, Jnsbr Sch 1918 (G5/10/18)

BUFFINGTON, Amy Sevilla (BENBOW) - dt M/M Thomas Benbow of GC; m 16 Oct 1912 Chester A. Buffington (J6/13/19)

BUFFINGTON, Chester A. - brother of Mrs. Leslie Lemon (G11/30/17)

BUFORD, Ed - sold his well drilling/repair rig to Richcreek & Burgess (G5/28/97); sold his livery stable at N. 3rd & A St., GC to Ike Roush (G7/29/98)

BURGESS, __ - of Richcreek & Burgess; purchased well drilling/repair rig from Ed Buford; in business (G5/28/97)

BURGESS, Albert - b OH 18 Sep 1850; widower; d 16 Jun 1919, bur GC Cem (J6/20/19)

BURGESS, H.H. - 11 Dec 1897 sold Fair Store to Evan Lewis (G12/17/97)

BURGESS, Harvey - brother-in-law of Miss Grace Harvey (G7/23/97)

BURGESS, Mary C. (CLARK) - b 23 Apr 1842 in Preble Co., OH; dt Edward and Eliza Clark; m 20 Jun 1859 Elijah Burgess (d 14 Mar 1896); d 19 Dec 1915, bur Jefferson Cem (J12/24/15)

BURGESS, Milo A. - m; lives on S. C St., GC (G5/27/98); cousin of William Rhoads of Rangoon, India (J1/16/20)

BURGHER, Mrs. George - of Peru; dt M/M Chris Hupp of Jnsbr; m (G11/30/17)

BURGOON, Daniel - b OH Jun 1841; farmer near Farrville; wife d ca 1916; d 25 Jul 1918, bur in OH (G8/2/18)

BURGOON, Mrs. Enoch - of GC; dt William Stelts (J9/10/15); mbr GC WCTU (J2/21/19)

BURGOON, Mrs. Sarah Elizabeth - b 9 Apr 1829; m Daniel Burgoon; lives in Mill Twp (J8/13/15)

BURK, B.F. - and Co. are Jnsbr druggists (J7/22/87)

BURKES, Robert - GC All-Stars football team mbr (J10/6/16)

BURNS, Anna - sister of Lenora Heal who is Mrs. Frank Heal of Marion (J7/9/15; J4/14/16); lives in Zeek Sch area (J10/22/15); age 50; m Peter Burns; d 3 Nov 1916 (J11/10/16)

BUTLER, Ben - s Ed Butler; is in Army in France with Co. of Engineers (J12/27/18)

BUTLER, Carrie (FITE) - of GC; mother of Harry Crawford of Gary (G12/7/17); b Brown Co., OH 17 Feb 1850; dt M/M Stephen Fite; m 1st ca 1881 James Crawford, a Harrisburg grocerman who d ca 1915; m 2nd 2 May 1917 George Edward Butler (G5/4/17)

BUTLER, Helen - age 4 wks; dt Mr. and Mrs. John Butler; d Sat, bur Mount Chapel near Rigdon (J4/23/15)

BUTLER, John - of Fairmount; d 25 May 1889 (J6/1/89)

BUTLER, Pansy - mbr Jnsbr MM SS (J7/27/17)

BUZBEE, Harvey - officer, Jnsbr Odd Fellows (J1/14/16)

CAIN, Annie - opened house of prostitution on S. E St., GC recently; police closed it (G4/15/98)

CAIN, Howard - of GC; in Gary enlisted in Co. F, 1st Ind. Inf.; will enter camp ca Aug 5th (G6/22/17)

CALLAHAN, Peter F. - GC bicycle worker (G1/1/97)

CAMPBELL, Charles V. - sold his Jnsbr saloon to Joe Brown and George Meekins (G11/26/97); d 29 Dec 1898 (G12/30/98)

CAMPBELL, Mrs. Ora - of Dayton, OH is dt Mrs. George Ryder of Zeek Sch neighborhood (J10/22/15)

CANDY, __ (WICKS) - wife of Uriah S. Candy (J6/1/89)

CANDY, Albert - taught in Candy Sch during his first term as a tchr (J6/1/17)

CANDY, Elra - brother of Uriah S. Candy (J6/1/17); mbr GC K of P Lodge (J4/25/19)

CANDY, Jacob - ca 1870 owned 80 acres in Harrisburg just E of the 80 acres owned by Dr. John A. Meek (J4/13/17)

CANDY, Uriah S.- one of first Harrisburg Sch tchrs ca 1875 (G4/13/17); came from Wayne Co. in Apr 1851 at age 3, family settled on W1/2 of SW1/4 of Sec 26, T24 N, R 8 E; 35 acres of farm had been cleared and fenced; farm had many squirrels, fish, walnuts, frogs, mosquitoes, paw paws, hickory nuts, and maple sugar trees; there was no ditching or window screens, in evening chip smoke was used to drive away mosquitoes; farm neighbors were: on N, William Bones; on E, Pierre Hossiers; on S, Piner Evans; on W, William Roush (G6/1/17; J6/1/17); owned 120 acres E of Thomas Kerns S of Main St. in area that became Harrisburg; his homesite is on S. C St. (J4/13/17); was issued 1st teaching license by Arthur W. Sanford who was examiner in Marion (J6/8/17); he was 3rd tchr to teach in Harrisburg Brick Sch in fall of 1876; he was assisted by Lida Jones and Pearly Champe (J6/1/17)

CANDY SCHOOL (Mill Twp District No. 1) - E of GC (G4/13/17); 1st frame sch bldg. erected in 1855 on SW corner of Candy farm; early tchrs were: Maggie Boles, summer of 1855; Mahala Moreland, summer of 1856; Josiah Boles, winters 1855-57; Thomas Knight, Amanda Ink, and Eli Wright before CW; David Bowers during CW (G6/1/17; J6/1/17); Candy Sch bldg. was often used for church services; early Candy Sch preachers were Rueben Kidner, New Light; Rev. Depo, New Light; Winston Jones, New Light; Rev. Rammels, Methodist; and Samuel Sawyer, Presbyterian (J6/8/17); U.S. Candy, Mary Smith, Albert Candy, Arminta

Eviston, and Elwood Ellis all taught their 1st terms as tchrs here (J6/1/17); Miss Jeanette Jones is 1919-20 tchr (J8/29/19)

CAPPER, Cynthia (HORNER) - b Preble Co., OH in 1830; m 21 Nov 1868 David Capper; Mar 1869 moved to Main & 1st St., Harrisburg; mbr GC Methodist Ch.; d 8 Jan 1898, bur IOOF Cem (G1/14/98)

CAPPER, David - m Cynthia 21 Nov 1868; moved to Main & 1st St., Harrisburg in Mar 1869 (G1/14/98); 1890 and earlier, ran a Harrisburg blacksmith shop (J3/30/17; J4/6/17)

CAREY, John T. - Mill Twp farmer whose sheep have been killed by dogs this spring (G5/7/97)

CAREY, Lizzie - was soon to m Charles Knight when he suddenly dec 28 Jul 1897 (G8/6/97)

CAREY, Mrs. Stanley - d 5 Jul 1919 (J7/11/19)

CARNEY, Miss Birdie - GC Baptist SS officer (G6/24/95)

CARNEY, J.W. - mbr GC Baptist Ch. (G1/14/98); lives on S. 1st St., GC; broke a leg while at work (G12/16/98)

CARROLL, Allie (LEWIS) - of Lake Galatia area (J2/2/17); sister of Mrs. Minnie Carroll (J8/24/17)

CARROLL, Albert - brother of James, John, Robert, and William (J5/21/15); bought a new auto (J7/9/15)

CARROLL, Bessie (IRVIN) - dt Mrs. W.N. Irvin of Fairmount; m Albert Carroll (J11/24/16)

CARROLL, Clyde Ernest - s Allie (LEWIS) Carroll (J2/2/17)

Carroll, F.M. - is GC glass worker (G1/1/97)

CARROLL, Hazel (YARBROUGH) - m Omer Carroll 19 Jan 1918 (G1/25/18); lives in Jnsbr; dt Mrs. Mary Yarbrough (J10/31/19)

CARROLL, John - brother of Bert, James, Robert (bur last Tues), and William; d May 14 at Hartford City (J5/21/15)

CARROLL, Minnie (LEWIS) - of Puckett; sister of Mrs. Allie Carroll (J8/24/17)

CARROLL, Omer - 25 Sep 1917, given party for 21st birthday (J9/28/17); m Hazel Yarbrough 19 Jan 1918 (G1/25/18)

CARROLL, Oren - s Allie (LEWIS) Carroll (J2/2/17); Mill Twp Sch 1920 8th grade grad (J5/21/20)

CARROLL, Palmer - student at FFA 1916-17 (J9/15/16)

CARROLL, Robert - age 42, d Sat at home near Lake Galatia, bur Riverside Cem (J5/14/15)

CARROLL, Mrs. William - of Jefferson Christian Ch. area; is step-dt of Mrs. C.J. Antrim of Danville, IL (J1/7/16)

CARTER, DeWitt - is Principal, Jnsbr Schs (G8/30/97)

CARTER, Edna Colene - b 9 Apr 1895; only child of DeWitt and Grace Carter; grad Jnsbr HS 1914; Jan 1915, att Glendale Coll (J10/6/16; J1/12/17)

CARTER, Frank - Mill Twp pupil; passed tchr license exam (G5/14/97); 8th grade grad Mill Twp Schs Commencement held in Deer Creek Friends MH last Thurs (G6/11/97)

CARTER, Frank/Fred - age 15; s George William Carter (dec); arrested for theft (J4/23/15); of Jnsbr; arrested for stealing horse and wagon (G11/23/17); sent to Plainfield Prison 30 Nov 1917 for horse theft, paroled 10 Nov 1919; arrested for stealing shoes (J7/9/20); age 20; confessed to theft of shoes, has been taken to Jeffersonville Reformatory; was m in Indianapolis 2 wks before arrest (J7/23/20)

CARTER, George E. - Mill Twp pupil, passed tchr license exam (G5/14/97); last Thurs 8th grade grad Mill Twp commencement held in Deer Creek Friends MH (G6/11/97)

CARTER, George William - father of Fred/Frank Carter, froze to death in a tree by Mississinewa River during flood of Apr 1904 trying to rescue a doomed family (J4/23/15); s M/M Wilson Carter; of N Jnsbr; m Anna (G3/4/98)

CARTER, Hallie - age 8; s M/M George W.'Will' Carter; Sat. drowned in Mississinewa River, bur IOOF Cem (G3/4/98)

CARTER, Lucy - sister of Sol Carter (J12/14/17); - see D. GIBSON

CARTER, Mary L. (BAIRD) - wife of Wilson Carter; lives in Jnsbr (J7/18/19); b 2 Mar 1839 (J8/1/19)

CARTER, Mrs. Newton - d 11 Mar 1917, bur Matthews Cem (G3/16/17; J3/16/17)

CARTER, Phoebe (WHITSON) - wife of Co. Commissioner Isaac Carter; d 23 Mar 1898 at her Liberty Twp home (G3/25/98)

CARTER, Rachel Edna - of Jnsbr; age 62; gets license to m Isaac J. Rominger of Jnsbr, age 74 (J10/6/16)

CARTER, Will, Jr.- lives in N. Jnsbr; while shooting a .38-cal. revolver at a dog killing his chickens, shot Will Simons in the back; Simons was on a load of hay driving through N. Jnsbr; he was merely blistered by the spent bullet; the dog escaped (G3/5/97)

CARTER, Wilson - records Mississinewa River levels; high water mark was 1841 at 6'7" higher than 6 Mar 1897 and in 1882 it was 3'1" higher than 6 Mar 1897 (G3/12/97); has contract to build new fence around IOOF Cem (G8/27/97); m; lives in Jnsbr (J7/18/19); b 19 Mar 1837 (J8/1/19); retired Jnsbr carpenter (J4/30/20)

CASKY, John - age 73; Fairmount Twp farmer; d 21 May 1920; bur Harmony Cem (J5/28/20)

CASSIDY, Anna - age 25; dt M/M Patrick Cassidy of GC; mbr Holy Family RC; d 10 May 1916, bur GC Cem (J5/19/16)

CAULEY, Nellie - m Mark Horn 3 Jun 1915 at St. Paul's RC Ch. in Marion (J7/2/15)

CHAMPE, Pearly - fall 1876 assisted Uriah S. Candy in teaching in Harrisburg Brick Sch (J6/1/17)

CHAPMAN, Mrs. J.G. - d 7 Dec 1897 at her N. Jnsbr home (G12/10/97)

CHAPPEL, Miss R. - GC Welsh person (G3/5/97)

CHASE, Margaret (JONES) - b ca 1889; dt M/M Charles Jones of Jnsbr; m 1st James Smith (dec ca 1915); mother of Warren and Ethel Smith; m 2nd 14 Jun 1917 H.M. Chase; d 3 Jan 1919, bur GC Cem (J1/10/19)

CHEEK, Marie - age 22; of GC (J10/1/15); see Leslie JOHNSON

CHILDS, Philip - infant s M/M Willard Childs; d 13 Sep 1915, bur Logansport (J9/17/15)

CLANIN/CLANNIN, Earl - of GC; s Jesse Clannin (age 58, farmer 3 mi. N of Swayzee, d last Fri) (J12/27/18)

CLAPPER, Asbury - s Henry Clapper of Jnsbr; abandoned his wife; arrested for adultery when found living at his father's house with an unrelated woman (G7/29/98); d last wk, bur Hartford City Cem (G8/26/98)

CLAPPER, Henry - b 6 Jan 1827, lives in Mill Twp (J8/13/15); d 17 Dec 1918, bur Hartford City (G12/20/18)

CLAPPER, Mrs. Henry - of N. Jnsbr; d 4 Sep 1916, bur Hartford City (J9/8/16)

CLAPPER, Herbert - of Jnsbr; is in army but is now home due to recent death of his father (G12/27/18)

CLAPPER, James - age 73; d County Infirmary 13 Apr 1917, bur Mt. Hope Cem (G4/20/17)

CLAPPER, Paris - b 5 Mar 1892; s Henry Clapper of N. Jnsbr; m Dec 1916; 1915 injured in motorcycle accident near David Winslow farm; d 5 Mar 1917, bur Hartford City (G3/9/17; J3/9/17)

CLAPPER, Paris - of Toledo, OH is s M/M C. Clapper of Jnsbr (J10/1/15)

CLARK, B.L. - mbr/officer, GC Odd Fellows (J7/9/15)

CLARK, C.H. - with W.M Taylor has purchased the Holbrook Bakery on Railroad Ave., GC (G2/5/97)

CLARK, Caroline - wife of Simon Clark; d 19 May 1898 at her home 3 mi. E of GC (G5/27/98)

CLARK, Charles - mbr/officer, Jnsbr K of P (G1/26/17)

CLARK, Dayton - is Jefferson Twp road Supt. (J10/22/15)

CLARK, Eva - of GC, moved to Fairmount (J10/22/15)

CLARK, M/M F.J. - have a Photograph Gallery on S. Main St., Jnsbr (J6/8/89)

CLARK, George B./G. - b 19 Mar 1837; lives in Mill Twp (J8/15/19); of Jnsbr; b PA; m Minerva (d ca 1907); serv in CW, mbr Jnsbr GAR; d 18 Jul 1920 (J7/23/20)

CLARK, James M./H. - of Fairmount; age 81; m; d 11 Mar 1917 (G3/16/17)

CLARK, Mrs. James - of 3 mi. SE of Jnsbr; d 23 Mar 1898 (G3/25/98)

CLARK, Orval/Orville Edward - 8th grade grad, Jnsbr Sch 1919 (J4/18/19)

CLARK, Rayfield - m 10 Apr 1917 Mary A. Wright, dt M/M Lewis Wright; will live in Jnsbr (J4/13/17)

CLARK, Mrs. Susannah D. - is att Washington, DC GAR Encampment (J10/1/15); pioneer resident of Jnsbr; is very ill; grandmother of Dar Dailey (G1/26/17); age 90; nurse in CW and in Spanish-American War; Clara Barton gave her a pin during CW (G8/30/18); b 11 Jan 1836 (J8/1/19); b in PA; m 1st Benjamin Day (dec); m 2nd 1861 Frederick Clark (d ca 1900); mbr M.E. Ch.; had CW pension, d 3 Jan 1920, bur GC Cem (J1/9/20)

CLARY, Mrs. Charles - of Indianapolis; dt Mrs. H.F. Parsons of GC (J1/7/16)

CLAY, M/M A.J. - of GC since ca 1911; m 24 Jan 1867 in Warsaw; he is now 74, she is 71; farmed E of GC ca 1897 to ca 1911 (G1/26/17)

CLAY, William O. - b Syracuse 15 Sep 1866/7; s M/M A.J. Clay; m; farmer 4 mi. E of GC; d 2 Mar 1919, bur GC Cem (G1/26/17; J3/7/19)

CLAYBORN, Robert - has contract to build new brick Zeek Sch for $782.00 (G6/17/98)

CLELAND, Mrs. Frank - of Jnsbr; sister of H. Hussey of Indianapolis (G4/9/97)

CLIFTON, R.M. - of GC; s James Clifton of Union City; m (G11/23/17); mbr GC Christian Ch. (J2/20/20)

CLINE, Mrs. A.E. - of N. E St., GC; dt Mrs. A. Langley of IL (G11/19/97)

CLINE, Adam H. - Commanding Officer, Jnsbr GAR (G1/8/97; J7/23/15); 24 Oct 1898, 15th wedding anniv (G10/28/98); of Jnsbr; is Co. Commissioner (J1/5/17); is seriously ill, having strokes (J4/18/19); mbr GAR (J4/2/20); b NY City 29 Sep 1845; s Jacob Frederick and Katherine (BASHTHER) Klein; m 1st Oct 1867 Mary E. Thornburg (d

Feb 1883) of Middletown; m 2nd Oct 1883 Lydia Pierce; stepfather of Gurtney Pierce; serv in 69th Ind. Inf. May 1862 to end of CW; wounded 3 times, captured 1 time; mbr M.E. Ch.; d 15 May 1920, bur Marion IOOF Cem (J5/21/20)

CLINE, Bessie (ENGLISH) - dt William H. English (J1/12/17)

CLINE, F.C. - President of a new social club (J3/4/04)

CLINE, Georgia - dt M/M Hubert Cline of Jnsbr; given party for 9th birthday last wk (G1/14/98)

CLINE, Hubert O.P.- Mill Twp Trustee with office in Jnsbr Bank Bldg. (G1/1/97); moves Trustee's Office to Main & 10th St., Jnsbr (G1/7/98); 30 Nov 1898, 30th birthday (G12/2/98); mbr Jnsbr Sons of Vets (G6/18/97; J3/4/04)

CLINE, Kathleen - dt M/M Hubert O.P. Cline; 5 Mar 1898 given party for 7th birthday (G3/11/98)

CLINE, Lydia - m 1st __ Pierce; m 2nd Adam H. Cline (J5/21/20); mbr GAR Women's Relief Corps # 143 (G1/8/97)

CLODFELTER, Noah J. - his proposed railway line has been taken over by Indiana Traction Co.; line will go from Elwood to Marion through Jnsbr and GC (G11/26/97); has now sold his Line to Marion Street Car Co. (G5/20/98)

CLOUSE, Susie - local 9-yr old (J4/2/15)

COAK, Richard - b ca 1915; of North Vernon; nephew of Clyde Swafford of Jnsbr; d, bur BC Friends Cem (G12/6/18)

COAT, Audrey - 8th grade grad, Jnsbr Sch 1918 (G5/10/18)

COATE, W.W. - of Coates & Lyons Co. of Marion; purchased Edge Tool Works from Bruce & Marks; Elmer Stump will be plant foreman as in the past (G5/27/98)

COATES, Bill - mbr Jnsbr M.P. Ch. SS (J6/29/17)

COBLE, William - of Richland Twp; age 60; wife d ca 1887; d recently (G3/23/17)

COGGESHALL, Edna Grace - Mill Twp pupil, passed exam for tchr license last wk (G5/14/97); 8th grade grad, Mill Twp sch 1897 (G6/11/97); dt Eli Coggeshall; d 13 Sep 1898 at Deer Creek of typhoid; her sister Ethel, d same day; 2 other family members also have typhoid (G9/16/98)

COGGESHALL, Ina - Mill Twp pupil, passed tchr license exam (G5/14/97); 8th grade grad, Mill Twp Sch 1897 (G6/11/97)

COLE, Agnes - 1920-21 Candy Sch tchr (J8/27/20)

COLE, Dudley - m 25 Nov 1916 Joyce Baker, dt M/M Joseph Baker; will live in GC (J11/30/16)

COLE, Miriam Watson - local 6-yr old (J4/2/15)

COLE, Rosanna - a Welsh person (G3/5/97); filed charges against GC saloon keeper Arthur Houyaux who assaulted her when she asked him to not sell whiskey to her husband (G3/4/98); of GC; age 56; m John Cole; d 26 Oct 1916, bur Riverside Cem (J11/3/16)

COLEMAN, Bennett Bryant - b 11 Dec 1827 (J8/13/15); of Jnsbr; came to Deer Creek 4 Apr 1847; m 1st 1849 Sarah 'Sally' Shugart (d 1861); Clerk, Deer Creek Anti-slavery MM then mbr Jnsbr Presbyterian Ch. (J12/15/16); 3rd Mill Twp gas well was 'Coleman Well' drilled near his home ca 1889 (J6/8/17); has 90th birthday party, his father also lived past 90 (G12/14/17); b Wayne Co., NC; m 2nd 1862 Anna Wilson (gored to death by bull 1882); m 3rd 1883 Mrs. Anna Martin; d 30 Oct 1918, bur GC IOOF Cem (G11/1/18)

COLEMAN, Daniel - lives in Marion; brother of Mrs. Frank Haynes; had 72nd birthday 26 Oct 1919 (J10/31/19)

COLEMAN, Howard - s M/M William Coleman of Jnsbr; Purdue Univ student 1917-18 (G12/28/17)

COLLEGE HILL SCHOOL (Jefferson Twp) - Edward Reasoner is drilling a water well for the sch (J10/13/16); Pearl Lynch is 1918-19 tchr (J2/21/19)

COLLINS, Cornelia - mbr Marion MM (G11/23/17)

COLLINS, John W. - age 34; s M/M William Collins; wife dec ca 1905; mbr Holy Family RC; d 25 Sep 1916, bur GC IOOF Cem (J9/29/16)

COLLINS, Nellie (HORNER) - lives S of Jnsbr; dt M/M Pete Horner (G3/22/18)

COLYER, __ - dt b 15 Jan 1917 to M/M Robert Colyer of Jnsbr (G6/22/17)

COLYER, Lawrence - 8th grade grad, Jnsbr Schs 1918 (G5/10/18)

CONELLEY, Cora - dt M/M Levi Conelley of E of GC; is Matthews Sch tchr; m Serg. James L. Pugh 14 June 1918 (J12/27/18)

CONELLEY, Mearl - Frog Coll Sch tchr 1916-20 (J9/1/16; G8/31/17; G9/6/18; J8/29/19); dt M/M Levi Conelley of E of GC (G9/7/17); Zeek Sch tchr for 1920-21 (J8/27/20), or Wise Sch tchr 1920-21 (G11/12/20)

CONELLEY, Ross Earl - brother of Mearl Conelley; att Ind Univ 1919 (J8/8/19); will grad Ind Univ June 1920 (J1/16/20)

CONELLEY, Vaughn - brother of Mearl Conelley; att Ind Univ (J8/8/19)

CONLEY, Edna - sister of Mrs. Chauncey Foust/Faust of Kokomo (J4/16/15)

CONLEY, Genevieve - local 9-yr old (J4/2/15)

CONLEY, Dr. L.H. - is GC Mayor; at time GC was established in 1892 he always wore a plug hat and made an interesting sight as he rode along Main St. through mud that came to his horse's knees (J3/30/17); assisted by Dr. McKinney, operated on W.M. Dunlap 14 Oct 1897 (G10/15/97); is GC Mayor (J10/6/16)

CONLEY, Mrs. L.H. - of GC; sister of Miss Edna Hixon of Middlebury (G2/12/97)

CONLEY, Robert - s Dr./M L.H. Conley of GC; 1920-21 Purdue Univ student (G11/12/20)

CONNER, __ - s M/M Frank Conner; b 26 Jul 1897 (G7/30/97)

COOK, Frank - local 8-yr old (J4/2/15); age 9; s M/M Newt Cook; d 1 Mar 1916, bur GC Cem (J3/3/16)

COOK, Jason - m Mrs. Anna Zent 13 May 1916; will live in GC (J5/26/16)

COOK, Karl - and Rufus, s Mrs. Mort Cook of GC (G7/13/17)

COOK, Loren - mbr GC Christian Ch. (G11/23/17)

COOK, __ - drowned in Mississinewa River while crossing on horseback many yrs ago (J6/8/17); Dr. A. Henley recalls, "Mrs. Cook and her 12-14 yr old son drowned at ford below river dam; they lived E of river; current was swift; Mrs. Cook was on horseback with son on behind her; near the middle of the river, the horse stumbled and threw both off in the swift current; the horse left them; water was waist deep and Mrs. Cook couldn't keep footing; son could have gotten out but stayed with his mother, he couldn't get her out, both drowned" (J8/17/17)

COOK, Mort - mbr GC K of P (J4/25/19)

COOK, Mrs. Mort - dt M/M John O'Neal of Knightstown; lives in GC (G7/13/17)

COOK, Newt - sold his barbershop to Alex Howard (J4/30/20)

COOMLER, Elmer - grad, Jnsbr HS 1897 (G5/7/97)

COOMLER, William R. - of Jnsbr; age ca 75; serv CW; broke hip falling down river bank at junction bridge (J9/1/16); mbr Jnsbr GAR Post No. 409 (J4/2/20)

COON, Margaret (LOVE) - age 82; m Michael Coon (dec); lived near Marion; d 13 Aug 1918 (G8/16/18)

COOPER, Rev. Harold - f Fairmount Congregationalist Ch. pastor; has been missionary in India several yrs, he and wife are coming home for health reasons (J7/23/20)

COOPER, Mrs. Harold - dt M/M Bennett Shugart of Fairmount (J7/23/20)

COOPER, Jessie - young dt M/M N.V. Cooper of GC (G6/22/17)

COOPER, Mrs. Russell - lives with husband in Connersville; dt M/M George Frederick of GC (G11/30/17)

COOVERT, John - b Cass Co. 7 Dec 1843; m; serv Co. E, 9th Ind. Inf. 4 yr, 4 mons during CW, wounded 2 or 3 times; d 21 Jun 1920 in N. Jnsbr, bur Riverside Cem (J6/25/20)

COOVERT, John S.- 1919 Mill Twp 8th grade grad (J4/4/19)

COPP, Frank - of GC; now in US Army (J6/29/17)

COPPOCK, Calvin - has wife (J6/8/89); age 73; of Jnsbr; CW vet; mbr GAR; d 11 Sep 1898, bur IOOF Cem (G9/16/98)

COPPOCK, Charles - of Jnsbr; m 25 Jan 1898 Mattie Warren of Warsaw; will live in Jnsbr (G1/28/98)

COPPOCK, Cyrus L. - is Vice-President of new Jnsbr social club (J3/4/04); operates a grocery (J3/4/04)

COPPOCK, Dorothy - mbr Jnsbr MM SS (J10/6/16; J8/27/20)

COPPOCK, Ebon - last wk purchased Lloyd Restaurant, GC; he will run it (G10/15/97)

COPPOCK, Edith (ELLIS) - dt Mrs. Jessie Haisley of Fairmount (J1/21/16); had surgery; is recuperating at home of mother (J10/6/16); mbr Jnsbr WCTU (J2/20/20)

COPPOCK, Harold - 8th grade grad, Jnsbr Sch 1919 (J4/18/19)

COPPOCK, James - brother of Mrs. Jerome Harter (J4/18/19)

COPPOCK, Joel - recently moved to Jnsbr from GC (J7/1/92); and wife celebrate 50th wedding anniv; live in Jnsbr (J6/23/16); b Mill Twp 23 Sep 1837; s John and Rachel (HOLLINGSWORTH) Coppock; m 17 Jul 1866 Nancy R. Fort, dt James D. and Ellen Fort; Pvt, Co K, 1st Ind. Cav. during CW; mbr Jnsbr MM; d, bur Riverside Cem (this Cem is on old John Coppock farm) (J11/10/16)

COPPOCK, N.J. - mbr Jnsbr Sons of Veterans (J3/4/04)

COPPOCK, Rachel (HOLLINGSWORTH) - m John Coppock, Friends Minister (J11/10/16)

COPPOCK, Winnifred - mbr Jnsbr MM SS (J7/27/17)

CORDER, Harry - s Robert Corder by his 2nd wife; contesting father's will leaving almost all to his 3rd wife (G12/16/98)

CORDER, Louisa (BEALS) - b TN 30 Oct 1839; dt Abner Beals; m Robert Corder (dec ca 1899); Jnsbr Presbyterian Ch. mbr; d 5 Jan 1916, bur Fairmount Cem (J1/7/16); left $500 to Jnsbr Presbyterian Ch. and lesser amounts to relatives including brothers Elwood Beals of Linwood, KS, Thomas Beals of CA, and sisters Caroline Krimm of Kansas City, KS and Mary A. Patterson of Kansas City, MO (J1/14/16)

CORDER, Robert - 4th gas well in Mill Twp was 'Corder Well' drilled on his land in Jnsbr ca 1890; well showed some oil (J6/8/17); is ill; his gas well in S. Jnsbr burst a pipe last wk (G12/10/97); Pres., Jnsbr Bank (G1/7/98); age 76; b in England;

came here 46 yrs ago; d 4 Aug 1898 (G8/5/98); his wife at time of his death was his 3rd; he left almost everything to her; his children by his 2nd wife are contesting the will (G12/16/98)

CORDER, Tom - f of Jnsbr; visits Jnsbr (J1/?/87)

CORN, Carrie (SIMONS) - dt M/M L.P. Simons of E of Fowlerton; m Rev. A.R. Corn; d (G7/12/18)

CORN, James - saloon keeper on W. Main St., GC (G1/22/97); b Tipton Co. 19 Aug 1849; m 1st Clara Headly (d ca 1884); m 2nd 3 Feb 1886 Rhoda Myers; d 4 Aug 1920, bur Sharpsville Cem (J9/10/20)

CORN, James A. - of Lake Sch area; s Mrs. Maggie Corn (J10/1/15)

CORN, Jason - 1916-17, 1921-22 att Zeek Sch (J3/30/17)

CORN, Joe - age 62; farmer on Muncie Rd. 8 mi. from Jnsbr had leg broken by horse falling on him (G2/11/98)

CORN, Laura Margaret - 1916-17 att Zeek Sch (J3/30/17)

CORN, Rhoda (MYERS) - of Jnsbr; dt Mrs. Albert Myers of Upland (J10/22/15); m 3 Feb 1886 James Corn (J9/10/20)

CORWIN, M/M Fred - their dt d 5 Jan 1918 (G1/11/18)

COURTNER, Rev. Arlie - has resigned as of next Aug as pastor of Jefferson Christian Ch. (G5/18/17)

COWGILL, Charles - of Jnsbr; ex-convict, suspect in the Zack Little murder in Fairmount 2 yrs ago; with Major Cowgill, was arrested for stealing feed from Charles Leach (G11/12/97)

COWGILL, Mrs. Josephine - of GC; age 76; d 13 Jan 1916, bur GC; husband survives (J1/14/16)

COX, A.J. - age 69; widower; leaves sons Walter and Reilly, and dt, Nellie Cox; d last Sun; bur Marion Cem (J1/28/16)

COX, D.W. - owns GC Pottery Works (G8/5/98)

COX, Earl - age 10; s M/M J.W. Cox of Jnsbr; 17 Aug 1898 broke his arm (G8/19/98); 22 Sep 1898 broke same arm again in different place (G9/23/98)

COX, Isaiah M. - of Marion; age 82; d 23 Mar 1917 (G3/30/17; J3/30/17)

COX, J.W. - s Aaron Cox of Indianapolis; m (G4/9/97); of Jnsbr; brother of Leslie Cox, Editor of North Manchester Leader (G1/28/98)

COX, Leslie - f of Jnsbr; f Editor of Sheridan Dispatch; has joined army (G7/8/98); mbr 159th Ind. Regmt.; is in Indianapolis ill with typhoid (G9/23/98)

COX, Ollie - 14 Jan 1898 was 16th birthday (G1/21/98)

COX, Quincy - s M/M Hiram M. Cox; 2nd Fairmount boy to be KIA in France this wk (G6/21/18)

COX, Reilly - Nellie, and Walter are ch A.J. Cox (dec) (J1/28/16)

COX, Webster -mbr Jnsbr Liberty Guards (G9/20/18)

COX, William - age 56; s M/M Oscar Cox; lived in Marion; killed by train in Jnsbr (J3/19/15)

COYNE, Alexander Hamilton - b Milford, OH 10 Mar 1857; s John and Jane Coyne; father owned sawmill at Hackleman; prior to 1871 he hauled hoop rolls to Ben Rothinghouse's cooper shop in Jnsbr (hoop rolls - small round hickory saplings split in half, the outside shaved and smoothed and the ends notched for joints); came to Harrisburg in 1871 at age of 15 and worked for farmer, William Smith, that yr plowing land that is now part of IOOF Cem; m 1st ca 1883 Jennie Harvey (d 4 Aug 1890); m 2nd 26 Sep 1891 Lucy E. Jackson; in 1871 he recalls wooden covered bridge (burned 5 Nov 1901) that linked Harrisburg with Jnsbr; he att brick sch on present site of West Ward Sch; Uriah Candy was first tchr there in 1876; Alex was mbr Christian Ch. (G4/6/17)

COYNE, John - ca 1871 had a sawmill in Madison Co. near Hackleman; father of Alex Coyne (J4/6/17)

CRABB, Fred - f of Jnsbr; age 33; s Jim Crabb of Jnsbr; m; d of flu last Sat, bur GC cem (G11/29/18)

CRAGUN, William - officer, Jnsbr K of P (G1/26/17)

CRAIG, C.A. - Zeek Sch area threshing ring finished 4 Sep 1915; threshing social held at C.A. Craig's Sep 8th (J9/10/15)

CRAIG, Charles C. - last wk bought license to m Adaline L. Beck (G12/24/97)

CRAIG, Dorothy - 8th grade grad, Mill Twp 1918 (G5/31/18)

CRAIG, Edna (BROCK) - Zeek Sch 1920-21 tchr (J8/27/20)

CRAIG, Francis - 8th grade grad, Mill Twp 1915 (J6/18/15); grad, Jnsbr HS 1919 (J4/18/19)

CRAIG, Orpha (GARRISON) - b Grant Co.; age 44; m Alex Craig; d 12 May 1916, bur Riverside Cem (J5/19/16)

CRAIG, William - father-in-law of Rev. Gilchrist (G10/15/97)

CRANDALL, Lydia - Mill Twp Dist. No. 3 Sch tchr 1914-16 (J6/18/15; J9/27/15)

CRANE, Otis - is Grant Co. Agricultural Agent (J4/16/15); of Lafayette; will speak Sun at Griffin Chapel (G10/5/17)

CRANFORD, Riley - of Zeek area has gone to High Point, NC to visit sister he has not seen in 50 yrs (J2/11/16)

CRAW, Miss Hattie - dt David Craw of Eaton; Jnsbr Asst. Postmistress (J10/22/15)

CRAWFORD, Grace - mbr GC Christian Ch. (J10/6/16)

CRAWFORD, Harry - s M/M James Crawford; 28 Jan 1898, 9th birthday (G1/28/98); of Gary; is s Mrs. Carrie Butler of GC (G12/7/17)

CRAWFORD, James C. - last Harrisburg Town Board Pres., winter 1891-92; had grocery store in Harrisburg prior to 1892 (J3/23/17), and prior to 1890; ca 1890 he became partner with George Harris to drill a gas well at W end of Main St., Harrisburg, hit gas and piped it to GC homes for heating (J3/30/17); sells Flour, Feed and Hay on A St. near Railroad Ave., GC (G9/22/93); is ill with piles & inflamed glands; had minor surgery (J10/13/16); of GC, b Hocking Co., OH 30 Oct 1846; s John and Susan Crawford; m 1st 13 Sep 1866 Sarah S. Wartman; m 2nd 17 Apr 1876 Mrs. Caroline Maine; serv Co K, 151st Ohio Inf. 2 May 1864 - 27 Aug 1864; d 18 Nov 1916, bur GC (J11/24/16)

CRAWFORD, William - 23 Oct 1897 m Clara Stech (G10/29/97)

CRAWSHAW, Frank H. - lived 3 mi. SE of Van Buren; age 59; never m; d 12 Oct 1916 (J10/20/16)

CRAY, Amos L. - is Justice of Peace and Insurance Agent with his office in B.F. Wiley's Furniture Store on corner of High St. & Water St., Jnsbr (J6/8/89); Asst. Cashier, Citizen's Bank of Jnsbr (G12/23/98); Jnsbr Odd Fellows Lodge officer (J1/14/16); b Henry Co. ca 1850; m 1st 1882 Marian Jennie Haley (d 1900); m 2nd Mary Hodupp; father of Fred Cray; d 17 Jul 1918, bur GC Cem (G7/19/18)

CRAY, Charles - grad, Jnsbr HS 1897 (G5/7/97); s M/M Amos Cray of Jnsbr; m; lives in Indianapolis (J7/9/15)

CRAY, Daniel W. - 9 Sep 1908 dropped dead in front of Rothinghouse Drug Store (J2/11/16)

CRAY, Elizabeth (SHEPARD) - of Jnsbr; b 6 Sep 1855 at Dillsboro; m Daniel W. Cray (dec) 22 Dec 1875; mbr Jnsbr M.P. Ch.; d 5 Feb 1916, bur Muncie (J2/11/16; J2/18/16)

CRAY, Frank - s Daniel W. and Elizabeth (SHEPARD) Cray (J2/11/16)

CRAY, Mrs. Fred - dt Mrs. Anna Hasting (J11/7/19)

CRAY, Hampton - of Jnsbr; Nov 1910, is Taylor Univ student (G11/12/20)

CREEK, Cort - of Fairmount; fell on ice, broke hip (J2/6/20)

CRETSINGER, Floyd - of College Hill area is s Holmes Cretsinger of Marion (G7/13/17)

CRILLEY, H.M. - of Fairmount; may have helped dynamite the Fairmount saloon of Ira J. Smith 25 Jun 1887 (J7/1/87)

CRIPE, Elizabeth - dt M/M Isaac Cripe of GC (J7/9/15)

CRIPE, Herbert - local 9-yr old (J4/2/15)

CRISPEN, Mrs. Floyd - b OH 1866; age 49; d at home in Jnsbr 10 Sep 1915, bur in Marion (J9/17/15)

CROSBY PAPER CO./NORTH MARION STRAWBOARD WORKS - hired E.L. Smith to drill gas well on Ras Hiatt farm N of Jnsbr on W side of river; gas needed for the paper company; good gas well came in on 2 Feb 1897 (G1/15/97; G2/5/97)

CROSBY, Emmet - of GC; now in US Army (J6/29/17)

CROSBY, Hannah Belle (BRANT) - b Shelby Co. 24 May 1869; dt Adam J. and Sarah A. Brant; m Thomas J. Crosby 14 Nov 1887; mbr Christian Ch.; d 20 Jul 1918, bur Mt. Pleasant Cem, Shelby Co. (G7/26/18)

CROW, George - mbr Jnsbr Masonic Lodge (G12/24/97)

CROWDER, C.F. - GC Weekly Journal publisher (G1/15/97); Crowder & Dunlap as the GC Publishing Co. is dissolved 14 Oct 1897; Will M. Dunlap retires, Crowder continues (G10/15/97)

CROWDER, Marguerite 'Maggie' - lives in GC; dt Mrs. S.M. Crowder of GC (G6/25/97; G6/17/98)

CROWDER, Mrs. S.M. - of S. 3rd St. & C St., GC; d 16 Jun 1898, bur Crawfordsville cem (G6/17/98)

CRUEA, Solomon - last Mon, m Lizzie Lewis of Jnsbr; will live in Jnsbr (G3/4/98)

CULP, Margaret Louise - b 9 Dec 1898 Greensburg, PA; grad, GC HS 1917 (J5/18/17); 1917-18 att Ind Univ (G11/23/17)

CULP, Samuel - of Smithton, PA; age 77; father of Mrs. Walter L. Leach; d 20 Mar 1918 (G3/22/18)

CUNNINGHAM, James - of Jnsbr; recently moved his drug store to Home Corner (G1/15/97)

CUNNINGHAM, Mrs. Jerome - of Jnsbr; sister of Miss Della and Miss Bertha Martz of Bluffton (J6/24/87)

CURRY, Hattie Jane - young dt M/M Will Curry of Lake Galatia area (G1/26/17)

CURRY, Jacob - employee of American Window Glass Works, GC; 8 Mar 1897 cut his hand badly at work (G3/12/97)

CURTIS, Sergt. A.A. - of GC; s Mrs. N.S. Curtis of GC; m; will be discharged from Army soon (J4/18/19)

CURTIS, Mrs. A.A. - dt James H. Snyder of Indianapolis (J4/18/19)

CURTIS, Ada - mbr GC Christian Ch. (J10/6/16)

DAILEY, Dar - grad, Jnsbr HS 1898 (G4/22/98); is in 160th Ind. Regmt.; has typhoid fever (G10/28/98); of St. Louis, MO; is visiting his very ill grandmother, Mrs. Susan Clark in Jnsbr (G1/26/17)

DAILEY, Don - is in 160th Ind. Regmt.; has typhoid fever (G10/28/98)

DAILEY, Mrs. Ed - dt Aaron Samms (J6/8/17)

DAILY, H.L. - age ca 60; m (wife dec); d 3 Jan 1916, bur IOOF Cem (J1/7/16)

DAILY, Jacob - Mill Twp octogenarian (J8/13/15)

DALE, Russell R. - of Fairmount; is on way to Canada for aviation training; is in Reserve Officers Corps (J7/27/17)

DANCER, Lulu (JOHNSTON) - of Marion is dt M/M A.J. Johnston of GC (G6/22/17); m Carl Dancer (G12/28/17)

DANIELS, Charles - s Mrs. W.O. Daniels of Jnsbr (G11/30/17)

DANIELS, Harry - b England 19 Jan 1872; s Mrs. Anna Daniels; m __ Kitselman; d 1 Sep 1916, bur GC Cem (J9/8/16)

DARTER, Frank - f of Jnsbr; s-in-law of Mrs. William McQuiston of Jnsbr; recently dec (G11/16/17)

DAUGHTERTY, Cyrus - driving with a young lady friend at dusk 14 Sep 1893 just S of BC Friends MH was held up by 2 men with revolvers, his watch and $4.50 were taken (G9/22/93)

DAVIDSON, J.H. - and wife are Mill Twp octogenarians (J8/1/19)

DAVIDSON, Jack - left GC ca 1889; s John Davidson, an old soldier living in Jnsbr; d recently in IL (G1/22/97)

DAVIDSON, John Milton - living in Jnsbr (G1/22/97); Mill Twp octogenarian (J8/27/20)

DAVIES, Mrs. D. - GC Welsh person (G3/5/97)

DAVIES, Owen - of Detroit, MI; f of GC; brother of Mrs. Richard Thomas of GC (G11/29/18)

DAVIES, Philip - GC Welsh person (G3/5/97)

DAVIES, Miss S. Jane - GC Welsh person (G3/5/97)

DAVIES, Mrs. W. - GC Welsh person (G3/5/97)

DAVIES, Mr. W.A. - celebrates St. David's Day with other GC Welsh (G3/5/97); mbr GC Baptist Ch. (G1/14/98)

DAVIES, Mrs. W.A. - mbr Welsh Union Congregational Ch., GC (G1/1/97); lives in GC; is Welsh (G3/5/97)

DAVIES/DAVIS, Dr. W.T. - grad of a Baltimore medical sch; hopes to set up practice in GC (G1/1/97); opened office in Mississinewa Blk. recently (G1/15/97)

DAVIES, William H. - in an Episcopal wedding, m 24 Jul 1897 Lizzie Jones at GC home of her parents (G7/30/97)

DAVIS, __ - s M/M Harry Davis; b 2 Dec 1897 (G12/3/97)

DAVIS, Mrs. David - is visiting f home in Wales (G5/27/98)

DAVIS, Edna - dt M/M Joseph Davis (J3/16/17)

DAVIS, Enoch - brother-in-law of Mrs.Walter L. Leach; recently d in Alabama (G1/11/18)

DAVIS, Miss Estella - Lake Sch tchr 1915-16 (J4/7/16)

DAVIS, Ethel (WILSON) - of Deer Creek; m __ Davis; sister of Homer and Ora Wilson (J8/24/17)

DAVIS, Evert - local 12-year old (J4/2/15)

DAVIS, Rev. H.A. - GC Christian Ch. pastor (G1/15/97); resigned as pastor here, will be a pastor in Marion (G2/26/97)

Davis, H.C. - mbr/officer, GC K of P Lodge (G7/14/11)

DAVIS, Dr. Joel R. - age 80; Marion physician; d (J4/23/20)

DAVIS, Rev. Joseph - of Bethel area; preached at Deer Creek MM last Sun (J8/10/17)

DAVIS, Nellie (SHUGART) - neice of Arthur Jay; Friends Minister, will preach at East Bethel PM Sun (J3/24/16); sister of Thurlow Shugart; dt M/M Bennett Shugart (G3/29/18); prob Deer Creek MM pastor (J4/16/20)

DAVIS, Paul Hubert - recently b, son of Clarence and Opal (LYNCH) Davis of College Hill area (G11/12/20)

DAVIS, Pierce/Percy - age 82; lived S of Upland in College Hill area; m; d 9 Aug 1917, bur Matthews Cem (J8/17/17)

DAVIS, Rufus - of Fairmount; age 45; m; d 11 Apr 1918 (G4/19/18)

DAVIS, Mrs. S.B. - of GC area; sister of Karry Lee, now in army (G7/20/17)

DAVIS, Mrs. Sylvester - of College Hill area; dt of Nate Curtis (G2/9/17)

DAVIS, Mrs. T.J. - Welsh; lives in GC (G3/5/97)

DAVIS, W.J. - Welsh; employed at Tin Plate Works, GC (G4/8/98)

DAY, Al - mbr GC Christian Ch. (J2/20/20)

DAY, Elizabeth - local 11-yr old (J4/2/15)

DAY, Maynard - mbr GC Christian Ch. (G11/23/17)

DAY, Mildred Louise - dt M/M Joseph Davis (J3/16/17)

DEAN, Calvin - age 69; of Fairmount; d 8 Dec 1918 (G12/13/18)

DEAN, Laura - of Jnsbr; m __ Dickey, then divorced ca 1894, took back name 'Dean' (G2/19/97)

DEER CREEK MONTHLY MEETING OF FRIENDS - Rev. Joseph Davis of Bethel preached Sun (J8/10/17); Rev. David Harris preached Sun (J8/17/17;J8/24/17; J8/31/17; J9/7/17; J10/12/17); Rev. Mattie Dempsey of Marion preached Sun (J10/19/17); Rev. Elmina Harris preached Sun; Rev. David Harris preached Sun 28 Oct 1917 (J11/9/17)

DEEREN, Amanda M. (MAY) - b Coshocton Co., OH 4 Jul 1854; m 26 Mar 1874 John W. Deeren; mbr Methodist Ch.; d 23 May 1918, bur GC Cem (G5/31/18)

DEEREN, James - age 92; is ill at home of s, Thomas Deeren (J10/29/15); b 5 Feb 1824; lives in Mill Twp (J8/13/15); Feb 1915 became age 91 (J2/6/20); b Guernsey Co., OH; lived in GC; m (wife d 19 Aug 1894); mbr M.E. Ch.; d 20 Aug 1916, bur Jefferson Cem (J8/25/16)

DEEREN, John Wilson - m; 22 Sep 1898 his home on S. A St., GC burns (G9/23/98); Oct 1909, and wife are parents of Mrs. Luke Wagoner of Chicago Heights (J10/10/19)

DEEREN, Mrs. Kemp - dt M/M Alvah Nesbitt of GC; with husband moved back to GC from Celabus, Cuba due to political unrest in Cuba (G6/22/17)

DEEREN, Thomas - of GC; s James Deeren (J10/29/15)

DEEREN, Thomas J. - b 26 Nov 1917; s M/M Kemp Deeren; family hopes to move back to Cuba soon (G12/7/17)

DEEREN, Vivian - local 11-yr old (J4/2/15)

DeLONG, Orville - 20th birthday 21 Nov 1916 (J11/24/16); s M/M John DeLong; in US Army; dropped dead 17 Dec 1918, bur GC Cem (G12/20/18)

DEMPSEY, Rev. Mattie (COATS) - of Marion preached at Deer Creek MM last Sun (J10/19/17)

DENNING, Miss Clara - of GC; and her sister Mary att christening of infant son of M/M C.C. Gordon (G1/1/97)

DENNIS, Allison - m Martha M. Rook; d 6 mon ago (J5/14/15)

DENNIS, Martha M. (ROOK) - sister of William Rook; age 67; d Fri, bur Riverside Cem (J5/14/15)

DEPO, Rev. __ - New Light/Christian preacher who sometimes preached in Candy Sch Building ca 1860 (J6/8/17)

DERRINGER, L.D. - baker for Knorre's Bakery, GC; m in KY last Wed Mamie Fields, GC Merchantile saleslady (J10/13/16)

DeSHON, Henry - b Fairmount 3 Jan 1888; s M/M James DeShon; m; killed 23 Dec 1916 by train, bur Marion IOOF Cem (J12/29/16)

DeWESE, Edith - a GC West Ward Sch tchr (J2/20/20); - see E. WILKINS

DICHARD/DISHART, John - prop., Brunswick Hotel, GC (G4/8/98); literally moved his Brunswick Hotel bldg. to Railroad Ave. & Main St., GC and re-opened it 13 Jun 1898 (G6/17/98)

DICKEY, Mrs. Harriett - f of Liberty Twp; mother of Mrs. Orestus Ballinger of SW of Fairmount; d 27 Sep 1920 (J10/1/20)

DILLA, Dan - is an Attorney; recently moved his office from Jnsbr to GC (G1/22/97)

DILLA, Floyd - s Mrs. Dan Dilla (G1/1/97)

DILLON, Mrs. Julia Ann - of Fairmount; age 86; recently d (G2/1/18)

DILTZ, Ina - 8th grade grad, Jnsbr Sch 1919 (J4/18/19)

DIMMICK, Iva Florence - b 19 Nov 1916; dt M/M Lester Dimmick (J11/24/16)

DIMMICK, Pearl - b 20 Sep 1889 near Somerset; m Marion Dimmick; lived near Lake Galatia; d ca 17 Sep 1915, bur Fairmount (J9/24/15)

DITMER, Elizabeth - age 47; m Jacob Ditmer; lived on Water St., Jnsbr; d last Mon (G6/4/97)

DITMER, Jake - was injured at work last wk (G10/15/97)

DITMER, Nina - grad, Jnsbr HS 1897 (G5/7/97)

DIXIE HIGHWAY - up to 1,000 autos will pass through Jnsbr on this highway Wed Nov 3rd driving entire length of the highway; autos from Jnsbr and GC may join the procession (J10/29/15)

DOHERTY, Arthur - of near Oak Ridge in Liberty Twp; sold his 120-acre farm for $36,000 or $300 per acre (J9/24/20)

DOLLMAN, James - age 65; killed 6 Mar 1916 in auto-street car accident, bur GC (J5/12/16)

DOLMAN, Frances - b 30 Apr 1914; dt M/M Frank Dolman; mbr Jnsbr MM; d 26 Nov 1916, bur GC (J11/30/16)

DONNELL, Rev. J.G. - new pastor of Jnsbr Presbyterian Ch. (J1/19/17)

DOYLE, Michael - age 70; farmer in Van Buren Twp; d last wk (J10/8/20)

DRAKE, Mrs. Anna - age 83; lived on farm NE of GC; m; d 22 Apr 1917, bur GC Cem (G4/27/17)

DRISCHEL, Edward B. - m E. Ethel Wise, dt M/M Sol Wise, in Louisville, KY last Thur (J6/18/15)

DROOK, Russell Dale - age 14; s M/M Earl Drook of Mier; accidentally killed by shotgun 24 Jul 1920 (J7/30/20)

DuBOIS, Amos - will teach in the Jefferson Twp sch recently closed due to illness of the tchr, Willis Peele (J1/?/87)

DuBOIS, Louisa - m Edgar J. DuBois; 31 Jan 1896 was injured when Marion City Railway car hit her buggy in GC at the River Bridge; she is now suing them (G8/13/97)

DUCKWALL, Cecil (GIFT) - f of Jnsbr; age 27; dt M/M Jesse Gift; m Guy Duckwall; d 1 Apr 1918, bur Marion (G4/5/18)

DUDLEY, Arthur - of Elwood is a converted f GC saloon man and gambler; will speak at GC Christian Ch. (J2/11/16)

DUDLEY, Rev. C.S. - pastor of Jnsbr MM (J5/7/15)

DUDLEY, Cecil - mgr, GC All-Stars football team (J10/29/15); GC All-Stars football team mbr (J10/6/16)

DULING, Mrs. Kate - of Matthews; sister of Mrs. George Ryder of Zeek Sch neighborhood (G11/16/17)

DULING, Mrs. Virgil B. - of Fowlerton; dt John and Mary Himelick (J4/4/19)

DULING, Mrs. William - of near Fowlerton; 75th birthday last wk; is 1/2 sister of Mrs. Newton Lucas (J7/4/19)

DUNCAN, George - one of first Harrisburg residents ca 1869; lived in a log cabin (J6/8/17)

DUNCAN, Lucille (LIGHTLE) - local 9-yr old (J4/2/15)

DUNKEL, Rev. J. Ambrose - of OH; Jnsbr Presbyterian Ch., pastor (G12/31/97); is also GC Presbyterian Ch. pastor (G1/14/98); will m 29 Jun 1898 Lula Baker of Tiffin, OH (G6/3/98)

DUNLAP, Andrew - m 7 Jul 1897 'Maggie' Cain in GC RC; both are of GC, live in Mississinewa Hotel, GC (G7/16/97)

DUNLAP, Will M. - m __ Monroe; bought 1/2 interest in GC Weekly Journal (G1/22/97); of Crowder & Dunlap operating as GC Publ. Co.; partnership is dissolved 14 Oct 1897, Dunlap retires; 14 Oct 1897 has surgery performed by Dr. Conley and Dr. McKinney (G10/15/97)

DURHAM, Rev. James H. - GC RC pastor (J12/10/20)

DWIGGINS, Mrs. J.W. - of GC; dt Enoch VanWye (G4/5/18)

DYE, Sarah - age 73; of near Fowlerton; m John S. Dye, they 1st settled on farm where tin plate factory was built when GC was founded, then moved to farm near Fowlerton; mother of James Albert Dye of GC, Edward Dye, W.D. Dye of Fowlerton, and L.P. Dye of Indianapolis; d 29 Jul 1917, bur GC Cem (G8/3/17; J8/3/17)

EAKINS, A. - mbr GC Tribe of Ben Hur (G7/30/97)

EAKINS, Joseph Mac - b Adams Co., OH 14 Feb 1845; m; d 12 Jan 1918, bur GC Cem (G1/18/18)

EAKINS, Willard - DePauw Univ student 1897-98 (G1/7/98)

EAST BETHEL FRIENDS PREPARATIVE MEETING (Fairmount MM of Friends) - Rev. Stroud, Taylor Univ., preached Sun (J3/19/15); John Morrish is SS Supt., Easter services Sun at 7:30 PM (J4/2/15); Ren Cline, of Fairmount, preached Sun (J5/7/15); Mrs. Ezra Newby preached Sun (J11/12/15); Rev. Metcalf of Jnsbr will preach AM Nov 28, Rev. Whybrew will preach PM (J11/26/15); revival starts Dec 28, Rev. Whybrew preaching (J12/24/15); revival being held (J1/7/16); SS oyster supper at home of Charles Jones 10 Feb

1916 (J2/11/16); SS has 60-75 weekly winter att, choir sang at dedication of Jnsbr MM MH, choir practice 7:30 Fri (J3/10/16); Easter services 7:30 Sun (J4/21/16); Rev. Oatley of Fairmount preached (J5/12/16); Ephraim Allen of Fairmount preached (J5/26/16); 86 in SS 11 Jun (J6/16/16); SS party for Vilas Leach (J6/30/16); choir sang at Jnsbr MM MH for funeral of Harvey Kirkpatrick 2 Jul (J7/7/16); Rally Day Sun 8 Oct 1916, all-day meeting with dinner (J10/6/16); Rally Day Sun (J12/15/16); revival will start Sun (G2/23/17; J2/23/17); Rev. Stroud of Upland is holding revival (G3/2/17; J3/2/17); all-day meet/ basket dinner Sun 6 May 1917; someone shot hole in side of MH (G5/4/17; J5/4/17); Sun is Children's Day program (G6/1/17; J6/1/17); Sun is all-day service, Rev. Chaffey to speak in AM, Rev. Monroe Vayhinger of Upland to speak in PM (G10/26/17); Rev. Allen of Fairmount preached Sun (G11/16/17); Rev. Pearson of Jnsbr will preach Sun (G12/7/17); Rev. Jones, of Fairmount, began revival Sun (G2/8/18); prayer meeting each Thurs at 7:30 (G4/12/18); Charles Pitt of Jnsbr preached Sun (G4/19/18); Sun all-day meeting, Rev. Jones will preach (G5/31/18); Ladies Aid Society meets (G9/27/18); SS each Sun, 9:45 AM (J12/26/19); ladies sold food at Clyde Wood's sale 20 Jan 1920, cleared $10 (J1/23/20); ladies sold food at Frank Relfe's sale 4 Sep 1920, took in over $50 (J9/10/20); all-day meeting/ basket dinner will be Sun Oct 24 (J10/22/20); Rev. Ephraim O. Allen of Fairmount is pastor (J10/29/20)

EASTES, J.N. - b Grant Co.; m; brother of William Eastes of GC; killed in work accident 12 Jul 1918 (G7/19/18)

EATON, Mary (GIBSON) - mbr Oak Ridge Friends WCTU (G10/22/97); of Radley; m; sister of Daniel and J.N. Gibson (J12/14/17)

EICHER, Carrie (HOPKINS) - of Jnsbr, age 23, dt M/M Albert Hopkins, m Charles Eicher, d 13 Mar 1916, bur Marion IOOF Cem (J3/17/16)

EICHORN, Mrs. Carrie - Mill Twp Dist. No. 2a Sch tchr 1915-16 (J8/27/15); North Grove Sch tchr 1917-18 (G8/31/17)

EILER, Esther - dt M/M Henry Eiler of Jnsbr, Sat m Arthur West of Fairmount, live in Fairmount (J6/11/15)

EILER, Ora E. - m 16 Jan 1918 Orpha Harris, dt M/M Newton Harris of Deer Creek area, she is grad-FFA (G1/18/18)

ELLERS, Barbara (JETT) - b Miami Co. 7 Oct 1844; m 1st 1861 Noah Bargerhuff; m 2nd 1877 William Ellers; mother of Mrs. R.L. Benbow of LaFontaine; mbr Jnsbr MM; d 4 May 1920, bur Riverside Cem (J5/7/20)

ELLIOTT, Richard - m Anna Peele 18 Jul 1915 (J7/23/15)

ELLIS, __ (SMITH) - b 13 Oct 1876 in Windfall, IN; dt M/M William Smith, m Fred Ellis, d 30 Jul 1916, bur Marion IOOF Cem (J8/4/16)

ELLIS, Clarence - age 16; drowned 1 Jul 1920 in Mississinewa River just downstream from Jct. Bridge (J7/2/20); b 10 Nov 1904 in Trafalgar; s Samuel and Nettie Ellis; bur Riverside Cem (J7/9/20)

ELLIS, Rev. Elwood O. - is Grant Co. Supt. of Sch (IJ7/1/1887); m Edgar Baldwin to Myra Rush at the Marion home of Cyrus Neal last wk (J9/2/1887)

ENGLISH, William H. - b 11 May 1847 in Defiance Co., OH; m 1st __, m 2nd Bessie, mbr Jnsbr M.E. Ch., lived in Jnsbr, d 3 Jan 1917, bur Riverside Cem (G1/12/17)

EUREKA - steamboat on Mississinewa River ca 1893, operated by Gene Marchal and 2 Marion men to take people 2 mi. upstream from near Jct. Bridge sight-seeing; sunk, wood salvaged to build a barn on S. C St. between 1st St. & Grant St. (J8/20/15)

EVANS, Amos - age 77, f of GC, widower, d 5 Apr 1918, bur GC Cem (G4/12/18)

EVISTON, Sarah A. (CRAW) - 79th birthday 21 Sep 1920 (J9/24/20); b Delaware Co. 21 Sep 1841; dt William C. and

Serena R. Craw; m 20 Apr 1862 George W. Eviston (d Jun 1879); mbr Jnsbr M.E. Ch.; d 14 Nov 1920, bur GC Cem (J11/19/20)

FABER, Mrs. W.R. - of Jnsbr; mbr Jnsbr M.E. Ch. (G11/30/17)

FAIRMOUNT FAIR - will be held Sept 12-16, 1887 (J9/2/87)

FAIRMOUNT NEWS - office is wrecked 25 Jun 1887 when a saloon next door is dynamited (J7/1/87); Edgar Baldwin is editor (J9/2/87)

FAIRMOUNT TOWNSHIP SCHOOLS - took over FFA prior to now (J5/16/19)

FAIRMOUNT WESLEYAN CHURCH - at a meeting 23 Jun 1887, it was decided to dynamite a saloon being set up in Fairmount (J7/1/87)

FANKBONER, George - Mill Twp Trustee when frame sch houses were first built in Sch Dist.#'s 2, 4, 5, and 6 (J6/1/17)

FANKBONER, S.R. - owner/operator, Jnsbr Flour & Meal Mill (J7/22/87); owns river dam, is removing it (G8/12/98)

FANNING, Mary (OLIVER) - b Clinton Co., OH 18 Jan 1847; dt M/M Winburn Oliver; sister of C.H. and of John Oliver; m 17 Aug 1867 George W. Fanning (d 25 Sep 1906); d 13 Jan 1918, bur Walnut Creek Cem (G1/18/18;J6/1/17)

FARMINGTON SCHOOL - Miss Echo Parks is 1916-17 tchr (J4/6/17); Miss Fae Fleming is 1920-21 tchr (J12/31/20)

FARROW, Rev. George L. - pastor of Jnsbr M.P. Ch. for past 4 yrs, leaves this pastorate (J8/24/17)

FAULKNER, Mount - Deacon, GC Christian (J1/7/16)

FAULKNER, Thelma - 1920 Mill Twp 8th grade grad (J5/21/20)

FEIGHNER, Irvin - mbr GC Fire Dept. (J3/4/04)

FELLOWS, Mrs. Fred - of Windfall; sister of Mrs. Nathan Hill (J10/6/16)

FELTES, Charles, Jr. - of GC, att St. Joseph's Coll (J9/3/15)

FELTON, Mansfield - of Marion; age 85; d 21 Nov 1917 (G11/23/17)

FERGUS, Warren - b Jefferson Twp 21 Sep 1837; m; serv Co. F, 23rd Iowa Inf. 3 yrs during CW; farmer near Matthews; d recently (G8/2/18)

FERGUSON, Eugene - of Jnsbr; b 15 Mar 1893; s M/M James Ferguson of Jnsbr; m; d of flu 4 Mar 1919 (J3/7/19)

FERGUSON, Jesse - tenant Van Buren Twp farm owned by Jesse Johnson, Upland banker; assaulted Johnson (G1/22/97)

FERREE, Martel/Martelle - mbr Jnsbr MM Young People's group (J8/27/20); - see M. PRINE

FERREE, Pauline - mbr Jnsbr MM Young People's group (J8/27/20)

FIELDS, Rev. A.S. - b 2 Dec 1830; lives in Mill Twp (J8/13/15); retired United Brethren Minister; d 7 Jul 1917, bur Saratoga, IN (G7/13/17)

FIELDS, W.S. - s Rev. A.S. Fields (G7/13/17)

FIKE, Mrs. Frank - b Kosciusko Co. 17 Jun 1852; d at home in Jnsbr 11 Jun 1915 (J6/18/15)

FISH, Mrs. Jane - born ca 1852; is mother of Mrs. Wallace Stewart; both live in GC (J10/6/16)

FISHER, Elsie - mbr GC Christian Ch. (J10/6/16)

FISHER, Joe - mbr GC HS baseball team (J4/16/15); att Marion Business Coll (J1/7/16); s M/M Charles Fisher of GC; works in Gary (G6/22/17)

FISHER, Thelma - mbr Jnsbr M.P. Ch. SS (J6/29/17)

FITE, Mrs. Alice - lives in Jnsbr (J1/5/17)

FITE, M/M Austin - of GC, parents of E.S. Fite of Arkansas City, AR and of A.R. Fite of Willis Springs, MO (J1/7/16)

FITE, Frank - GC Justice of Peace (J10/22/15); of GC; coal dealer; came to Harrisburg fall of 1890 (J3/30/17); officer in GC K of P (G7/14/11); and wife are mbrs of GC Baptist Ch. (J2/20/20)

FITE, Mary E. (HOPKINS) - b Covington, KY 22 May 1848; m Austin Fite in Dec 1865; d in GC 24 Apr 1918, bur Riverside Cem (G4/26/18)

FLANAGAN, Mrs. John - of Fairmount; dt Levi Winslow of S of Jnsbr (G10/26/17)

FLANAGAN, Martin - one of first residents of Harrisburg ca 1869 (J6/8/17)

FLEENOR, Henry Jackson - age 3; s M/M Nelson Fleenor; d 19 Aug 1915, bur Riverside Cem (J8/20/15)

FLEMING, Miss Fae - 1920-21 Farmington Sch tchr (J12/31/20)

FLEMING, James - given party for 23rd birthday last Tue by Christian Ch. youths (J4/2/15)

FLOWERS, William - age 71; of Jnsbr; m; d 30 Sep 1918, bur GC Cem (G10/4/18)

FOLK, W.H. - mbr GC Tribe of Ben Hur (G7/30/97)

FOLLET, Mrs. Lewis - dt W.A. Stephens of Logansport (G12/31/97)

FOLTZ, Oscar - mbr GC Christian Ch. (J10/6/16)

FOLTZ, Robert - mbr GC Christian Ch. (G11/23/17)

FORD, Nelson - age 88; brother of Elihu Ford of Marion; d E of GC last wk, bur Riverside Cem (J8/1/19)

FORD/FORDE, L. Harold - Jnsbr Presbyterian Ch. pastor (G9/22/93)

FORD, Vern - granddt of Leslie Lemons; d recently in MI (J4/6/17)

FOREHAND, Mrs. A.J. - of College Hill; dt Mr. Carson of Upland (G7/13/17)

FOREHAND, Ada - dt Mrs. Nancy Forehand of College Hill area (J4/30/20)

FOREHAND, James - b New Berne, NC ca 1809; s Lewis Forehand, came to GC area in 1827; m 1833 Anna Roberts (dt William Roberts who settled NE of GC on Walnut Creek) (J1/14/19)

FOREHAND, Mrs. Martha - of near Upland was given party for her 67th birthday last Sun (J2/4/16)

FOREHAND, Nancy (SKEEN) - dt Mrs. Mary Skeen of Jnsbr (G6/22/17); of College Hill area; sister of Daniel R. Skeen of Jnsbr (J2/6/20)

FOREHAND, Mrs. Rebecca - of College Hill, is mother of Josie Marine (J1/28/16)

FOREHAND, William - b near Kidner Bridge, Jefferson Twp 2 Nov 1836; s James and Anna (Roberts) Forehand; wife dec; d 8 Feb 1919, bur Converse Cem (J1/14/19)

FOREMAN, A.J. - of College Hill area; discharged by the army (G12/7/17)

FOREMAN, Harvey - appointed Deacon, GC Christian Ch. (J1/7/16); s John Foreman; m (G11/23/17)

FOREMAN, Iona (JAY) - dt Arthur W. and Flora Jay (G1/26/17)

FORSYTHE, A.N. - of GC; brother of Dayton and L.E. Forsythe (G10/21/98)

FORSYTHE, Dayton - mbr GC Christian Ch. (G2/12/97); age 29; brother of A.N. and L.E. Forsythe; d 13 Oct 1898 of malaria in Milroy (G10/21/98)

FORSYTHE, George B. - b 8 Aug 1864; brother of Lee E. Forsythe of Ottawa, KS; m; f of Jnsbr; d 18 Apr 1919 at Home Corner, Marion; bur Marion IOOF Cem (J4/25/19)

FORSYTHE, Lee E. - m; officer, GC Land Co. (G7/2/97); in US Army fighting in Phillipines; brother of Dayton and A.N. Forsythe (G10/21/98); officer, GC K of P (G7/14/11); of Ottawa, KS (J4/25/19)

FORT, Al - age 22; s John Fort; d at home S of GC 14 Nov 1897 (G11/19/97)

FORT, Charles - of Jnsbr; returned from penitentiary last wk; serv 6 yrs for killing Soldier's Home vet (G3/11/98)

FORT, E.C. - Jnsbr barber working in Min Murphy's barber shop (J7/1/87)

FORT, James D. - b 7 Feb 1815; of Jnsbr; oldest man in Grant Co. (J8/20/15); had 101st birthday (J2/11/16); b Greenup Co., KY; s Christopher Fort, Revolutionary War vet; m 1835 Nancy Ellen Witty; mbr Jnsbr MM; d 19 May 1916, bur Riverside Cem (J5/26/16)

FORT, Nancy Ellen (WITTY) - m 1835 James D. Fort; lived in Jnsbr; d 5 Jan 1897, bur Riverside Cem (J5/26/16; G1/8/97)

FORTNER, Elizabeth Jane (BURSON) - b 21 Dec 1841; m 1875 Reuben H. Fortner (dec); d 2 Nov 1919; bur Marion cem (J11/7/19)

FORTNER, John - employee of Sheldon's Glass Factory; m 16 May 1898 Eva Case of South F St., GC (G5/20/98)

FORTNER, Reuben H. - b 20 Jan 1854, m Elizabeth Burson 11 Feb 1873/1875, d 7 Aug 1916, bur Marion cem (J8/11/16)

FOSTER, Rev. DeWitt - is pastor of Marion Second Friends MM (J4/13/17)

FOSTER, Pvt. George H. - age 17; f of Fairmount; s John Foster; KIA in France (G6/21/18)

FOUST/FAUST, Jeanette (CONLEY) - of Kokomo; sister of Miss Edna Conley of GC (J4/16/15)

FOWLER, B. - of Jnsbr; is appointed Justice of Peace to replace William Shepard who resigned (G3/12/97)

FOWLER, Erastus 'Ras' - of Union City; s Jonathan W. and Jessie L. Fowler (G12/31/97); b Jnsbr ca 1861; m; lived in Union City; d 24 Nov 1920; bur Marion cem (J12/3/20)

FOWLER, Jessie L. - 80 yrs old on 27 Sep 1920 (J10/1/20)

FOWLER, John - of Jnsbr; d recently; father of Dave Fowler of Anderson (G4/9/97)

FOWLER, Jonathan 'Jot' W. - b 25 Mar 1836; of Mill Twp (J8/11/16); mbr GC IOOF Lodge (G1/1/97); will celebrate 59th wedding anniv, as well as his 83rd birthday on 20 Mar 1919; he is blind; lives in Jnsbr (J3/28/19); m Jessie L. Norton 25 Mar 1860; celebrated wedding anniv and birthday; mbr Jnsbr Presbyterian Ch. (J3/26/20)

FOWLER, Louis/Lewis - age ca 16; s M/M Daniel Fowler; seriously injured while swimming in Mississinewa River on Sun (G7/9/97); recently d from injury (G8/6/97)

FOWLER, Miss Ollia - 4 Jun 1889 grad, Hartford City (J6/8/89)

FOWLER, Pearl - of Jnsbr; lost in prize fight with Gale Ruley Sun AM at Schrader's Brick Works W of Jnsbr (G12/3/97)

FOWLER, Russell - grad, Jnsbr HS 1920 (J4/16/20)

FOWLER, Mrs. Viola - mbr Jnsbr WCTU (J2/20/20)

FOWLERTON - last Sun three bldgs burned, including the Childrey's Meat Market, Clover Leaf Creamery, Richard's Harness Shop, and Brown Bros. Barbershop (J1/21/16)

FOWLERTON METHODIST PROTESTANT CHURCH - Rev. Daisy Barr held revival here recently (J1/31/19)

FRAME, Mrs. Israelda - b 19 Aug 1829; of Mill Twp (J8/13/15)

FRANK, Lee C. - of Frank & Robbins Furniture Store in Opera House Blk., GC (G6/24/95); and wife left last Tue on a tandem bicycle for Troy, OH; distance is ca 100 mi., they hoped to be there that night (G5/21/97); 1902 is 1st new mbr in the GC Masonic Lodge (J4/4/24); Nov 1905, GC Treasurer for past 10 yrs (G11/5/20)

FRANTZ, Miss Lotus - of Fairmount; d 21 Jan 1920 of flu (J1/23/20)

FRAZEE/FRAZE, Emmett - 3 Mar 1897 is 34th birthday (G3/5/97); brother of J.M. Frazee of Rushville (G7/30/97)

FRAZEE, Mrs. Emmett - sister of Miss Lenora Carr of OH (G9/2/98)

FRAZEE, John - age 72; of Jnsbr; m; serv in CW; d 14 May 1916, bur GC Cem (J5/19/16)

FRAZEE, Mrs. John - age 74; of Jnsbr; m John Frazee; d 27 Jan 1919, bur beside husband in GC Cem (J1/31/19)

FRAZIER, Ananias - of Fairmount; spoke at Jnsbr Friends MH Sun night (J1/?/87)

FREDERICK, George - of Shatto & Frederick Grocery, Jnsbr; sold out to his partner, Charles Shatto (J10/8/15); f a GC glass blower; last Fri bought GC Sanitary Cut-Rate Grocery & Meat Market from J.F. Bailey (J10/22/15)

FREDERICK, Gladys - local 14-yr old (J4/2/15); recently had 17th birthday (G10/26/17); grad, GC HS 1918 (G5/10/18)

FREEMAN, Mrs. Bert - d of flu 28 Nov 1918 (G11/29/18)

FREEMAN, Daniel P. - of GC; in Army (J6/29/17); b in Richmond 26 Apr 1900; s M/M N.H. Freeman; twin of David P.; in Co. G, 28th Inf.; KIA in France 18 Jul 1918 (G8/9/18)

FREEMAN, David P. - of GC; in Army (J6/29/17); twin of Daniel P.; wounded in France Jul 1918 (G8/9/18)

FREEMAN, Floyd - of GC; in US Army (G2/9/17)

FREEMAN, Fred - age 33; s Lafayette Freeman; in US Army, d in KY 6 Jan 1918, bur in GC Cem (G1/11/18)

FREEMAN, Mrs. J.W. - sister of Albert Huffman of KS (G1/8/97)

FREEMAN, Lafayette 'Lafe' - widower; d in TX 6 Jan 1918, bur GC Cem (G1/11/18)

FREEMAN, Nina - 8th grade grad, Jnsbr Sch 1919 (J4/18/19)

FREEMAN, Richard H. - of GC; now in Army (J6/29/17)

FREEMAN, M/M W.M. - live in W. Jnsbr (G1/1/97)

FREEMAN, Waity S. (ROLLAND) - b Hancock Co. 11 Nov 1844; dt Chapman and Louisa Rolland; m Austin Freeman (dec); mother of Mrs. John Addelberger; d Jnsbr 21 Mar 1915, bur at Converse (J3/26/15)

FRIEDLINE, Elmer E. - mbr Jnsbr K of P (G10/7/98); of Jnsbr, is an attorney; Commander, Jnsbr Sons of Veterans (J3/4/04); replaces Elmer E. Heal as Mill Twp Trustee (J1/3/19)

FRIEDLINE, F.O. - Treas., new Jnsbr social club (J3/4/04)

FRIEDLINE, Jenness (HANNEN) - North Jnsbr Sch tchr 1920-21 (J8/27/20)

FRIEDLINE, Dr. Lloyd M. - s M/M E.E. Friedline of Jnsbr; is Indianapolis Veterinary Coll student (J4/16/15; J10/13/16)

FRIEDLINE, Mrs. Maude - of Jnsbr; dt Mrs. Mary Ann (BECHLER) Manley-Piddock (dec) (G11/5/20)

FRY, Agnes V. (STINE) - dt M/M John Stine; grad, GC HS 1897; m Rev. C.H. Fry; lives in Spokane, WA (G5/21/97)

FRY, Charley - brakeman on 1st train to enter Grant Co. (J8/24/17)

FRY, Harl - 1920 Mill Twp Sch 8th grade grad (J5/21/20)

FRY, Ivy - of GC; now in US Army (J6/29/17)

FRYER, Rev. Robert W. - came to Marion in 1882; age 70; serv Co. G, 52nd NY Regmt. during CW; ordained Baptist Minister; d 1 Jan 1918 (G1/4/18)

FURNISH, Wade - of GC; now in US Army (J6/29/17)

FURNISH, Mrs. Will - of Jnsbr; d last Tue (G10/1/97)

FUTRELL, M/M Abraham - of Jnsbr celebrated 50th wedding anniv last wk (G7/29/98)

FUTRELL, Guy - his funeral was at Jalapa last Tue (J4/2/15)

FUTRELL, Jack - opens saloon in Meek Blk., Jnsbr (J9/2/87); and Alt Hiatt run a Jnsbr bowling alley located next to the Jnsbr Bank (G9/9/98)

FUTRELL, Mabel - dt M/M William Futrell; m Edward J. Hiatt; will live in Attica (J4/9/15)

GADDIS, Bertha - age 10; of GC; d 21 Jun 1897 (G6/25/97)

GADDIS, M.L. - lives 2 mi. from Fairmount; his clover was stolen by A. Isaacs and others (G12/3/97)

GAPE, J.D. - mbr GC Baptist Ch. (G1/14/98); is leaving for old home in Wales (G5/20/98)

GARDNER, Hiram - has new 5-passenger Overland auto (G4/20/17; J4/20/17); tenant on Selby farm; moving to farm he owns near Lawrenceburg, TN (J8/22/19)

GARDNER, Jacob - of GC; is att Franklin Coll (G11/5/20)

GARDNER, James - of GC; now in US Army (J6/29/17)

GARDNER, John C. - s M/M James P. Gardner of GC; grad, GC HS 1914; now in US Navy; m 15 Dec 1917 Phyllis E. Donckers of Green Bay, WI (J12/21/17)

GARDNER, Mattie Brown - age 14; dt M/M Hiram Gardner; killed in auto wreck 20 Apr 1918 (G4/26/18)

GARNER, Joseph H. - of N. Jnsbr; b Covington 13 May 1862; m Maggie Viola Hickman ca 1877; d 4 Jun 1917, bur Riverside Cem (G6/8/17)

GARNER, Murval - took over teaching for wife (G12/13/18); 1919-20 North Grove Sch tchr (J8/29/19)

GARNER, Mrs. Murvel - North Grove Sch tchr 1918-19 (G9/6/18)

GARNER, Verna Mabel 'Lucy' (THOMPSON) - b Sweetser 10 Mar 1893; dt M/M T.H. Thompson; m Leroy Garner 11 Feb 1911; d 11 Mar 1918, bur Riverside Cem (G3/15/18)

GARNER, Voul - of GC; age 24; d of TB 6 Jan 1919, bur GC Cem; his brother, Faunce, d here of TB 28 Oct 1918, bur beside brother (J1/10/19)

GARNET, Robert - of Jnsbr; broke leg playing baseball in Weaver last Sun (G7/30/97)

GARRISON, Aline - dt M/M Ted Garrison of Lake Galatia area (G6/22/17)

GARRISON, Mrs. Ruben - of Jnsbr; m; d 27 Jun 1892; bur Bethel Cem (J7/1/92)

GARTHWAIT, __ - of Garthwait & Peel; sells real estate with office in Mississinewa Hotel Blk. (G6/24/95); of Garthwait & Sutton; dissolves partnership last wk; had been in GC real estate, insurance, and rentals (G6/4/97)

GARTHWAIT, Effie - dt W.P. Garthwait; is very ill (G7/9/97)

GARTHWAIT, Fred - clerk in Villar's Grocery (G7/23/97); brother of Charles Garthwait; m 7 Jul 1911 Violet M. Fisher (G7/14/11)

GARTHWAIT, Violet M. (FISHER) - dt Col. Samuel Fisher, wealthy retired farmer of Star City who commanded 46th Ind. during CW; m 7 Jul 1911 Fred Garthwait (G7/14/11)

GARTHWAIT, W.P. - succeeds W.A. Leach as mgr, Lovett's Opera House (G1/15/97); his 64 yr-old mother in Peoria, IL is sick (G12/17/97); of Garthwait & Son, managers of Lovett's Opera House, are having it repaired (G8/19/98); and George Harris buy Lovett's Opera House for $14,500 (G9/23/98)

GARY, Miss Edith Esther - age 20; d Mon at home of parents M/M R.G. Gary; bur Cumberland Cem, Matthews (J3/26/15)

GAS CITY - new name of Harrisburg 22 Mar 1892 (G3/23/17); 1889 a gas well was drilled in Jnsbr (J5/4/17), then partners James Crawford & George Harris drilled a gas well at the W end of Main St.; gas was piped to Harrisburg homes for heating; fall 1891 men leased land for gas and in spring 1892 bought land now in GC; GC Land Co. was incorporated 21 Mar 1892 and name of Harrisburg changed to GC; GC Post Office was established with Burr M. Harris, Postmaster; on 4 Apr 1892, there were 150 citizens in GC; soon lots sold for $200 to over $1,000 each and 8 factories were established in GC in 3 months in 1892; spring 1892, John Jackson was killed at Main St. RR crossing; spring 1892 most of GC was a wheat field, houses were built out in the wheat; Dr. L.H. Conley rode horseback through the deep mud of GC's Main St. wearing a plug hat; 1892, J.E. Ward and George Villars had a furniture store here (J3/30/17; J5/25/17); 11 Sep 1892, gas well drilled by James Crawford & Burr Harris at the lower end of Main St. blew out (J9/14/17); John and Sarah Dye settled on farm where tinplate factory was built at the time of GC's founding, Dyes then moved to a farm near Fowlerton (J8/3/17); 1892 Ed Pritchard established First National Bank of GC (G5/21/97); Dr. S.A. Goodin, Physician/Surgeon, has an office on Main St.; Dr. Knight and Dr. Vance have Jnsbr office on Main St. near Post Office and GC office in Thompson Blk.; John R. Hadley, Attorney, has office upstairs over People's Grocery; W.M. Amsden, Attorney, has an office on Main St. near the RR Depot (G4/28/93); Sep 1893, Brashear, Lay & Kyle have a wallpaper store; William F. Young, Twp Trustee, has his office over D.K. Ruley's grocery store; J.A. Miller has Livery Stable one-half block W of RR Depot; John A. Martin is a tailor on Main St. near First St.; William McDonald is contractor/builder sharing office with Dr. Goodin on Main St. near First St.; Bandy & Metcalf are prop. of Park Meat Market on W side of First St. between N. D & E Sts.; J.C. Crawford sells flour, feed & hay on A St. near Railroad Ave; J. Weinstein has clothing store; Herrold & Lusher sell clothing 3 doors W of Mississinewa Hotel (G9/22/93); Bruce & Marks Manufacturing Co. was formed ca 1893; Miss Lula Souttor has Dressmaker Shop on 2nd floor, Opera House Blk., Main St. (G1/1/97); Garthwait & Peel sell real estate in Mississinewa Hotel Blk.; Dr. G.W. McKinney & Dr. S.S.

Horne, Physicians/Surgeons, have offices in Jnsbr Bank Bldg and in GC Bank Bldg; Frank & Robbins have furniture store in Opera House Blk.; J.R. West has hardware store; Ward & Gordon own Furniture/Undertaking Establishment (G6/24/95); Lee Long's Flouring Mill will be located N of American Window Glass Plant (G1/8/97); John R. Hadley is City Attorney for GC; Ward & McCune's Hall is at 2nd & Main St. (G1/15/97); Central Union Telephone Co. will soon connect GC, Jnsbr, & Marion by phone; GC Journal established in 1892, Will M. Dunlap purchased one-half interest in it (G1/22/97); S.W. Nelson opens Meat Market on N. 1st St. between D & E St.; C.H. Clark and W.M. Taylor purchased Holbrook Bakery on Railroad Ave. (G2/5/97); Alf Jackson owns Livery Stable (G2/26/97); L.F. Stander moved his Fairmount cigar factory to N. B St. near 4th St., GC (G3/12/97); Alex Howard & A.D. Sprinkle combined their barber shops W of Centre Grocery; Frank Griffin is a city policeman (G4/9/97); first fire engine was purchased (G5/14/97); Biddlecum & Lottridge opened carriage & blacksmith shop at S. A & Railroad St.; O. Gordon's store at S. A & 1st St.; population is 6,000 (G5/28/97); Garthwait & Sutton dissolves real estate, insurance & rental partnership last wk (G6/4/97); 105 unlicensed dogs killed by police; Eli Smith is a policeman (G6/18/97); I.N. Hoagwood, Police Chief (G6/25/97); R.A. Brashear, Mayor (G7/2/97); L.D. Long & Co. Flouring Mill grinds its first batch of wheat (G7/9/97), mills 65 barrels of flour per day; powered by 35 hp Atlas engine (G7/16/97); Centre Grocery is sold to Capt. McCune by J.C. McCoy (G7/23/97); John Williams opens barber shop at 3rd & S. D St. (G7/30/97); Wilson Barber Shop and Oliver Shady Barber Shop are both on S. 3rd St.; A.O. Hartman Meat Market moved to S. 3rd St. (G8/6/97); 'Only' restaurant is on W. Main St.; A. Bell is iceman (G8/13/97); T.H. Graham owns a livery stable (G8/20/97), mgr, William Allegree; GC's 5-Mile Bicycle Road Race is held (G8/30/97); Jesse A. Jones is Truant Officer for GC, Jnsbr, & Marion (G8/30/97); Mrs. Wm. Barnhardt operates a boardinghouse (G11/12/97); F.J. Ley Meat Market is at S. G & 1st St. (G11/19/97); Waterworks and electric street lighting being installed by Seckner Contracting Co., Chicago (G12/3/97); Moody & Sons open new meat market in Commercial Hotel Bldg. on Main St. W of 1st St.

(G12/10/97); 13 Dec 1897 H.H. Burgess sold Fair Store to Evan Lewis (G12/17/97); Waterworks well was started last wk, will be 26' deep & 25' in diameter (G1/7/98); poles for electric lights are unloaded (G1/21/98); Waterworks well is complete with 6.5 million gal./day flow (G1/28/98); Arthur Houyaux is saloon keeper on S. 1st St. (G3/4/98); GC Cycle Co. makes Skipper Bicycles selling for $15 to $39 (G3/11/98); John Dichard is Brunswick Hotel prop.; Lon Maggart purchases GC Cycle Co. (G4/8/98); house of prostitution opened on S. E St., police closed it (G4/15/98); James H. Lay elected Mayor (G5/6/98); Western Strawboard Co. is in GC, as is Sheldon's Glass Factory (G5/20/98); Edge Tool Works is sold by Bruce & Marks to Coates & Lyons Co. of Marion (G5/27/98); Stegall & Magoto will operate a grocery store on Main St. (G6/10/98); GC Waterworks is complete and working; W.H. Lightle, Postmaster resigned; John Dishart moved his Brunswick Hotel to Railroad Ave. & Main St., it opened 13 Jun 1898; A.F. Griffin is Marshall (G6/17/98); 1 Jul 1898 Postmaster will be George S. Harris; GC has street lights (G6/24/98); E. Buford sold livery at N. 3rd & A St. to Ike Roush (G7/29/98); D.W. Cox owns GC Pottery; City Attorney is W.M. Amsden (G8/5/98); D.A. Gilchrist bought Albert Bell's grocery at S. 3rd & D St. (G8/12/98); GC and Jnsbr City Councils took option on river dam for $450 (G9/2/98); Harrie Pontious is landlord at Mississinewa Hotel; Jesse Jones is reappointed Truant Officer (G9/23/98); Charles Webster is Chief of newly organized GC Vol Fire Dept. (G9/30/98); W.H. Achor is night policeman (G10/28/98); B.F. Barze, Cashier of First National Bank of GC (G12/16/98); Vol Fire Dept. disbanded 1 Jan 1904; GC Fire Dept. organized this wk, Chief, Charles Webster, mbrs include William Kenny, Samuel Herald, Irvin Feighner, Frank Barnhart, and James Mann (J3/4/04); Aug 1904, Edward McCleary is City Marshall (J8/8/24); Nov 1905, L.C. Frank has been Treas. of GC for 10 yrs (G11/5/20); 1906 population was 4,647 (J8/26/21); population was 3,224 at 1910 census and 2,870 at 1920 census (J4/23/20); __ Sullivan, Mayor; Robert S. Green, Marshall and Ed McClary is night Marshall; Joe Heaton has ice cream parlor on S. 3rd St. (G7/14/11); Joe Kaufman, Asst. Fire Chief (J4/16/15); Ora Pratt and Harry 'Brigham' Young are city Constables; Thomas S. McKee is Water & Light Supt. (J7/23/15); George

Frederick bought Sanitary Cut-Rate Grocery & Meat Market from J.F. Bailey; Frank Fite, GC Coal Co. mgr (J10/22/15); L.H. Conley, Mayor; Burr Saunders, Fire Chief; Clyde Ward, in absence of Chief, is Acting Fire Chief; E.O. Nelson, Chief of Police (J10/6/16); A.D. Morgan operates a shoe repair shop on Third St.; W.J. Knorre, owner/operater of GC Bakery (J10/13/16; J3/27/17); GC sells its fire team, coal wagons, harness, feed and other horse supplies to Jacob Lygthle; barn man William Herring is out of a job since a new motor fire truck has been purchased (G2/9/17); GC now has motor fire truck (J6/15/17); GC's last hotel, the Avalon Hotel, has closed (G12/7/17); 17 Apr 1919, Chink Baldwin's ice storage house burned (J4/18/19); Frank Lerminiaux, Mayor (J4/25/19); John O. Reese is discharged as night policeman because of his problems with the Mayor (G11/26/20)

GAS CITY ALL-STARS FOOTBALL TEAM - Cecil Dudley, mgr; Pete Peery, Captain; team will play Jnsbr Wildcats Fri (J10/29/15); beat Jnsbr Wildcats 12 to 0 last Sat; 1916 All-Star team mbrs include Herman Thompson, Robert Burkes, Harry Bland, Jesse Hutchinson, Ray Stinson, Brian Williams, Francis McCormick, Lawrence Troxel, James Bliss, Jesse Lyons, and Cecil Dudly (J10/6/16)

GAS CITY BAPTIST CHURCH - 2nd church established in Harrisburg, soon after 1875 (J4/20/17); T.C. Smith is pastor; services at Lovett's Opera House (G9/22/93); W.M. Amsden played Santa Claus for Christmas Eve, 1896; church has new bell (G1/1/97); SS officers include James Grindle, John Sparks, Miss Birdie Carney, John Hughes, and organist Miss Stuart (G6/24/95); Rev. Lotus Aspy, Fairmount, has revival here (G1/8/97); D.L. Jamison, pastor (G1/15/97); 11:15 AM 9 May 1897 during morning services a cyclone blew off church cupola, no one was injured; mbr is Clarence Bicknell (G5/14/97); D.L. Jamison assisted by C.W. Aspy, Dunkirk Baptist Ch. pastor, is holding a revival (G11/19/97); mbrs include J.W. Carney, Robert Price, W.A. Davies, J.R. Hughes, R.A. Brashear, Mae Ward, Thomas Hewett, J.D. Gape, Noah Martin (G1/14/98); pastor D.L. Jamison resigns to return to sch (G5/20/98); 19 Jun 1898, Rev. Jamison's farewell sermon (G7/1/98); Aug 1903, E.B. English is pastor (J8/8/19); Rev.J.F.

Huckleberry resigns as pastor to take his family to the Pacific NW for the health of one of his children (G11/11/98); Nov 1910, Rev. Joseph Belcher is leaving after 14 mon. as pastor (G11/5/20); pastor is Edward Armstrong (G7/14/11); mbrs include Dai Morgan, Ollie Jones, Olwin Morgan, Cleo May (J7/23/15), Elizabeth Ann (Thomas) Trombgen (J10/8/15); Mrs. N.B. Leslie, pastor (J3/7/19); mbrs include Mrs. Clinton Ray, Mrs. Poe Trinkle (G11/5/20), Mrs. D.B. Simpkins, Mrs. Clarence Grosscup (G11/12/20)

GAS CITY BRASS BAND - has been formed; practice is in Ward & Gordon's Hall (G10/1/97); band has 26 pieces (G5/20/98); mbrs get uniforms (G6/10/98)

GAS CITY/JONESBORO JOINT CHAUTAUQUA - will be held in a tent Aug 28 - Sep 1,1915 (J4/16/15)

GAS CITY CHRISTIAN CHURCH - H.A. Davis is pastor (G1/15/97); mbrs include William Walters, Miss Jennie Moore, Miss Della Moore, Mrs. E.L. Addison, W.P. Alexander, Estella Smith, Dayton Forsythe (G2/12/97); Rev. R.S. Reynolds, pastor (G8/6/97), now resigns as of 1 May 1898 (G4/15/98); Aug 1903, S.D. Watts, pastor (J8/8/19); pastor is C.J. Sebastian (G7/14/11); mbr is Mrs. Abe Kendall (J10/8/15); new officers are W.C. McConnell, Elder; Harve Foreman and Mount Faulkner, Deacons; Abe Kendall, Trustee; S. Alice Jay, Roll Custodian (J1/7/16); Elders are W.E. Mason, A.D. Morgan, Geo. E. Myers, J.H. Vinson, D.W. Williams (J1/14/16); Arthur Dudley of Elwood is converted f GC saloon man and gambler will speak here (J2/11/16); Rev. J. Thomas W. Luckey, pastor, has resigned; Rev. Melvin Menges will be pastor Nov 1st; D.W. Williams, Board Pres. (J10/6/16); pastor Rev. Melvin Menges leaves (J3/9/17); Rev. A.S. Bash, pastor (J4/6/17); mbrs include Miss Gertrude Helm (G10/26/17), Mrs. Ora Lenfesty, Robert Foltz, Lester Mullen, Loren Cook, Earl Hatfield, Orville Beitel, Maynard Day, Earl Bainbridge (G11/23/17); Rev. R.A. Harmon of IL, pastor (J1/10/19); mbrs include J.E. Ward, R.M. Clifton, Wren Lewis, Frank Biddinger, W.P. Gray, Al Day (J2/20/20), and Harvey Oliver (J12/24/20); W.A. Jackson, pastor (G11/26/20)

GAS CITY CYCLE CO.- makes bicycles in GC (G2/11/98); makes Skipper Bicycles selling for $15 to $39 (G3/11/98); Lon Maggart purchases GC Cycle Co. (G4/8/98)

GAS CITY DAUGHTERS OF REBECCA LODGE NO. 506 - 28 May 1898 will give a supper (G5/20/98)

GAS CITY HIGH SCHOOL - 1897 grads are Percy Holbrook, Ina Hutchins, Grace Kearns, Stella Smith, May Ward, Agnes Stine, and Howell Thompson (G5/21/97); J.B. Wallis will be new Principal (G7/20/17)

GAS CITY HIGH SCHOOL BASEBALL TEAM - lost 5 to 2 to Fairmount HS in first game of season; Joe Fisher made one of GC's two runs (J4/16/15)

GAS CITY HIGH SCHOOL FOOTBALL TEAM - Sat lost 6 to 0 to Jnsbr HS (G1/1/97)

GAS CITY HOLY FAMILY ROMAN CATHOLIC CHURCH - pastor is Rev. James H. Durham (J12/10/20)

GAS CITY IOOF LODGE - mbrs include J.M. Fowler and J.T. Howard (G1/1/97); moves to new Morgan Blk. (G9/3/97)

GAS CITY K OF P, LODGE NO. 428 - officers are J.E. Ward, E.S. Bartmus, William Elwood, U.S. Bartmus, Harry Meekins, B.M. Harris, J.O. Austin, W.P. Alexander, Lee Seyfort, and Reese Lewis (G7/23/97); Dec 1905 is 10th anniv of GC Lodge (J12/24/20); officers include Elmer E. Heal, Frank Fite, Arlie Armstrong, Jesse Knopp, Robert Martin, George Lewis, W.O. Jones, H.C. Davis, J.E. Ward, L.A. Prickett, Lee Forsythe, L.J. Baldwin, Edward Bloch (G7/14/11), Elmer E. Heal (J10/6/16), Fred Jay, Tom Heal (J10/13/16), Isaac Harter (G10/5/17), Karl Bastian, Elra Candy, Mort Cook, Elmer Heal, Jesse Knopp (J4/25/19), Frank McManis, Harry McManis, and Robert Ray (J12/24/20)

GAS CITY LADY MACCABEES - Miss Lois Bastian, mbr (J1/14/16)

GAS CITY LAND CO.- local stockholders include A.F. Seiberling of Jnsbr and George S. Harris of GC (G3/12/97)

GAS CITY LIBRARY - was given the Indian stone collection picked up by George W. Smith (recently dec) on his farm during the past 40 yrs (J1/7/16)

GAS CITY MASONIC LODGE - Dec 1915, W.O. Swan is mbr (J12/24/20)

GAS CITY METHODIST EPISCOPAL CHURCH - pastor, Rev. Millard Pell (G1/15/97; G4/2/97; G5/27/98); was organized 1893; church bldg constructed 1895; Rev. Millard Pell, now of Knightstown, pastor 1894-98 (J9/17/20); Aug 1903 C.E. White, pastor (J8/8/19); pastor, Charles W. Shoemaker (G7/14/11); Rev. J.W. Walters, pastor for past two yrs; Rev. H.R. Godwin assigned here as pastor by church conference (J4/16/15); Rally Day was Sun (J10/6/16); pastor is A.C. Wischmeier (J3/7/19); Mrs. W.H. Perkins (dec) was mbr (J2/20/20)

GAS CITY METHODIST PROTESTANT CHURCH - first church in Harrisburg; began by holding meetings in the new brick sch building in 1875 (J4/20/17)

GAS CITY MILITARY CLUB - formed by Guy Mayberry as a Vol. Military Co.; Capt. Mayberry drilled the company this wk (G5/27/98); 25 mbrs are requested by the Regular Army for active service (G7/15/98)

GAS CITY '97 CLUB -meets today at home of Mrs. Will C. Jay (J1/14/16); meets in home of Miss Bessie Hoff (J2/21/19)

GAS CITY ODD FELLOWS LODGE - officers: R.C. Owen, W.E. Pollen, R.H. Morrow, Tillman Goble, H.L. Morrow, B.L. Clark, David Morgan, Walter Swisher, John Tulley, David Edwards, W.R. Stewart, and W.C. McConnell (J7/9/15)

GAS CITY PYTHIAN SISTERS LODGE - mbrs include Mrs. J.E. Leonard (J4/16/15), Mrs. Elmer Heal and Mrs. Elwood Jones (J10/6/16)

GAS CITY PRESBYTERIAN CHURCH - meets in Ward & McCune's Hall, 2nd & Main St. (G1/15/97); meets in GC Odd Fellow's Hall; Rev. M.E. Beall, pastor of Jnsbr and GC Presbyterian Chs., resigns (G3/26/97); Rev. J. Ambrose Dunkel, new pastor (G1/14/98); Aug 1903, W.D. Vater is pastor (J8/8/19)

GAS CITY PUBLISHING CO. - owned by Crowder & Dunlap; GC Weekly Journal, publisher is C.F. Crowder (G1/15/97); 14 Oct 1897 Crowder & Dunlap dissolved; Will M. Dunlap retires, Crowder continues (G10/15/97)

GAS CITY REBEKAH LODGE - celebrates 21st anniv in GC 26 Feb 1917; Mrs. John Stine is only Charter Mbr left (J3/2/17)

GAS CITY ST. GENEVIEVE'S ROMAN CATHOLIC CHURCH - pastor is Rev. F.C. Wiechman (G5/27/98)

GAS CITY ST. PAUL'S EPISCOPAL CHURCH - was organized Sunday with services in Opera House; C.G. West and Mr. Maliphant elected Wardens; W.M. Sills elected Sec.-Treas.; lots for church bldg. site bought on N. B St. (G9/22/93); new parsonage is being built (G7/23/97); Rector/pastor is F.B.B. Johnston (J3/7/19; J4/18/19)

GAS CITY TIGERS FOOTBALL TEAM - beat Upland team 45 to 0 last Sun; team mbrs include Eddie Gass, Frank Lerminiaux, Vern Miller, Rich Baker, and Henry Jones who had a shoulder dislocated during the game (J10/6/16)

GAS CITY TRIBE OF BEN HUR LODGE, COURT NO. 49 - officers are M/M C.A. Wiley, M/M J.E. Ward, M/M E.R. Jones, A. Eakins, and C.H. Brown (G7/30/97)

GAS CITY WELSH UNION CONGREGATIONAL CHURCH - meets Sundays in room above GC Bank; Rev. Mathew Hussey, pastor; mbrs include Mrs. W.A. Davies, Mrs. Rees Lewis, and Mrs. Sam Morgan (G1/1/97); old Welsh Church bldg. on 1st St. will be made into basketball gym (J10/1/15)

GAS CITY WEST WARD SCHOOL - tchrs are Miss Nelle Mullen (G11/23/17), Miss Ferol Brane and Miss Edith DeWese (J2/20/20)

GAS CITY WOMEN'S CHRISTIAN TEMPERANCE UNION - mbrs include Mrs. D.W. Williams, Mrs. A.K. Ludwig (J1/21/16; G11/30/17), Mrs. Lucy McKinney, Mrs. Leslie, Mrs. E.E. Hummel (J10/6/16), Mrs. Walter Lowe (G2/9/17), Mrs. D.B. Simpkins, Mrs. Enoch Burgoon, Mrs. John McCallum (J2/21/19)

GASS, Eddie - mbr GC Tigers football team (J10/6/16)

GATES, Dr. Leslie E. - closes his GC chiropractic office and moves to Indianapolis (J1/5/17)

GATES, Nora - of Shirley; widow; sister of Mrs. Lydia Hodupp; d, bur GC (J2/18/16)

GAYNOR, William - b 4 Jun 1855 Louden Co., VA; m Mary R. Bray 12 Nov 1879 in Arcola, IL; d 3 Jan 1916, bur Walnut Creek Cem (J1/7/16)

GEORGE, Mrs. Sarah - of 3 mi. E of GC; Apr 8 broke a leg (G4/15/98)

GERSTORFF, James William - of GC; recently m Mary Jones, f of GC; will live in GC (G5/18/17)

GIBSON, Bert - glass worker; last Thurs m Bessie Swisher; will live in Fairmount where he works (G1/1/97)

GIBSON, Daniel - brother of Mrs. Emily Collins of Swayzee (G2/9/17); of Jnsbr; b Randolph Co., NC 25 May 1851; came to near Hackleman in 1859; m 1st 1882 Lucy Carter, sister of Sol Carter; m 2nd ca 1899 Mrs. Mattie Cammack; was carpenter/ contractor, built many bldgs. in early GC; mbr Friends; d 11 Dec 1917, bur Marion Cem (G12/14/17; J12/14/17)

GIBSON, George - and wife of Muncie are parents of Mrs. John S. Young of Jnsbr (J10/22/15)

GIBSON, J.N. - of southern Grant Co.; brother of Mrs. Mary Eaton of Radley, of Mrs. Emily Collins of Swayzee, and of Daniel Gibson (J12/14/17)

GIBSON, Lucy (CARTER) - age 41; sister of Sol Carter; m 1882 Daniel Carter; lived on W. 6th St., Jnsbr; d 12 Mar 1898 (G3/18/98; G12/14/17)

GIBSON, Rev. Mattie Cammack (OSBORN) - mbr Jnsbr WCTU (J4/16/15); of Jnsbr; spoke at Huntington Co. WCTU meeting (J8/27/15); prob pastor of BCMM (J8/3/17); lectured for WCTU at Mier church (GC4/5/18); mother of Carlton Cammack of St. Louis, MO (J10/29/15; J11/21/19); f Howell Sch tchr (J8/20/20)

GIFT, Jesse E. - and wife are moving from Jnsbr to a farm 1 Mar 1897 (G2/26/97); moved from his farm to his home on Main St., Jnsbr (J3/4/04)

GIFT, Mrs. Phoebe E./A. - lives in Jnsbr (J7/18/19); b 10 Sep 1838 (J8/1/19)

GILCHRIST, Rev. __ - m __ Craig (G10/15/97)

GILCHRIST, D.A. - bought Albert Bell's grocery, South 3rd & D St., GC (G8/12/98)

GILCHRIST, W.F. - is Jnsbr Supt. of Schs (G8/20/97)

GILLESPIE, Oma - Mill Twp 8th grade grad 1917 (G5/11/17)

GILLESPIE, Park - Jnsbr Mason; is in army (G11/29/18)

GILLETTE, Lewis A. - b Canada 1854; m Susan E.; d 19 Dec 1916, bur Marion IOOF Cem (J12/22/16)

GILSON, Mrs. Mary - of Marion; sister of Mrs. W.E. Mason (J4/18/19)

GIRARD, Laura J. (LUGAR) - b Blackford Co. 18 Aug 1874; dt George and Martha Lugar; Sep 1893 m Hugh E. Girard; lived in GC; d 13 Jun 1917, bur GC cem (G6/22/17)

GIRT, Mabel (SCHULTZ) - f of GC; given divorce from Wm. Girt; resumed her maiden name (J1/7/16); - see SCHULTZ

GITHENS, Celena/Celina - 8th grade grad, Zeek Sch 1916 (J5/5/16); grad, Jnsbr HS 1920 (J4/16/20)

GITHENS, Edith - 8th grade grad, Zeek Sch 1916 (J5/5/16); grad, Jnsbr HS 1920 (J4/16/20); mbr Jnsbr MM Young People's group (J8/27/20)

GITHENS, Inez - d M/M John Githens; m James E. Shay of Kokomo 2 Aug 1920 (J8/6/20)

GITHENS, Theodore - 8th grade grad Jnsbr Sch 1918 (G5/10/18)

GLASGODINE, Miss Alin - GC Welsh person (G3/5/97)

GLASS, James - Jnsbr Odd Fellows officer (J1/14/16)

GOBEL, Linville 'Dutch' - last Mon m Acea G. Elston; both are of GC; will live in GC (G7/20/17)

GOBLE, Tillman - mbr/officer GC Odd Fellows (J7/9/15)

GODWIN, Esther - Deer Creek Sch tchr 1917-18 (G8/31/17)

GODWIN, Rev. I.R./H.R. - appointed as pastor for GC M.E. Ch. (J4/16/15); m; s Mrs. Mary Godwin (J10/22/15)

GOLDSMITH, Mrs. Fred - lives in Indianapolis (J7/9/15); lives in Lafayette; dt M/M Daniel Gibson of Jnsbr (J1/21/16); of Dayton, OH; dt Mrs. Mattie Cammack-Gibson (J8/3/17)

GOLDTHWAITE, George A. - of Marion; 1st Lieut., 24th Aero Squadron, pilot, awarded Distinguished Service Cross for heroism in action in France (J1/3/19)

GOLEY, John - b Ireland 25 Dec 1854; m Nancy Smith 11 Feb 1883; d 16 Oct 1917, bur Walnut Creek Cem (G10/19/17)

GOODIN, Dr. S.A. - Physician/Surgeon, has office on Main St. near First St., GC (G4/28/93; G9/22/93)

GOODYKOONTZ, Malinda - b OH 24 Feb 1836 (J8/11/16); of Jnsbr; 81st birthday (G2/16/17); m 1st 4 Aug 1856 Wesley Conguer (d 13 Nov 1861; their dt's are Mrs. Ed Howell and Mrs. James Leer); m 2nd 10 Dec 1882 Abraham Goodykoontz (d 13 Nov 1894); she has 1 living sister, Mrs. Maria Jones, of near Fairmount; d 27 Feb 1919, bur Park Cem (J2/28/19)

GOODYKOONTZ, Mrs. Nora - age 56; husband d ca 1916; lived in Liberty Twp; d, bur Fairmount cem (G10/4/18)

GORBY, W.A. - stockholder in First National Bank of GC (G12/16/98)

GORDON, __ - infant s M/M C.C. Gordon; was christened Sun (G1/1/97)

GORDON, Elizabeth 'Lizzie' N. (EATON) - m James Olin Gordon (G7/8/98); Dec 1913 is mbr '97 Club (J12/28/23); Jnsbr MM SS class tchr (J1/5/17); mbr Jnsbr MM (J4/25/19)

GORDON, Frederick - of GC; mbr Jnsbr MM SS (J7/27/17)

GORDON, James Olin - s Seth and Sarah (Jay) Gordon; m Elizabeth 'Lizzie' N. Eaton (G7/8/98); of Ward & Gordon; have Furniture Store/Undertaking Establishment at #148 Main St., GC (G6/24/95;G1/1/97); store is at S. A & 1st St., GC (G5/28/97); buys out Ward who retains undertaking business (G4/29/98); assaulted by Sam Holmes, teamster for a brewry; Holmes was angry at Gordon's "dry" sentiments (J7/23/15); charged with assault by Sam Holmes; charge is dropped (J10/1/15)

GORDON, Sarah (JAY) - dt Mrs. Lydia (HOLLINGSWORTH) Jay Harris (G3/11/98); m 11 Oct 1860 Seth Gordon; lived on farm E of GC (G7/8/98); schoolmate of Uriah S. Candy at Candy Sch prior to 1861; still living (J6/8/17)

GORDON, Seth - b Henry Co. 14 Aug 1831; s Richard and Susanna Gordon; came to Grant Co. ca 1853; m 11 Oct 1860 Sarah Jay; lived on farm E of GC; d 4 Jul 1898 (G7/8/98)

GOSSETT, John W. - f of Jnsbr; s M/M William Gossett of Fairmount; injured in service in France (G7/26/18)

GOSSETT, Mrs. Lena - North Jnsbr Sch tchr in 1914-16 (J6/18/15; J8/27/15)

GOSSETT, Thomas William - of Marion, f of Jnsbr, then of Fairmount; age 55; shot his wife, Nancy, then shot himself; both may die (J7/30/20); he and wife are recovering (J8/6/20); Nancy d 8 Aug 1920, bur Park Cem; husband held for murder (J8/13/20); formally charged with death of Nancy Ellen Gossett (J8/20/20); age 58; sentenced to life in Michigan City Prison for murder of wife (J9/24/20)

GOSSETT, Rev. William - age 77; m 20 Aug 1920 Mrs. Emma Johnson, age 66 (J8/27/20)

GOTSCHALL, Lawrence - 8th grade grad, Mill Twp 1916 (J5/12/16)

GOULD, Rosie - local 9-yr old (J4/2/15)

GRAHAM, Esther (WELBOURN) - granddt Rev./M J.H. Vinson; m Arthur Graham; lives in SD (J5/16/19)

GRAHAM, James - s of local liveryman; 2 Jun 1897 lost two fingers in work accident at Edge Tool Works (G6/4/97)

GRAHAM, James L. - d Sep 1905 (J9/10/20)

GRAHAM, Robert - s M/M Scott Graham of Farmington (J1/16/20)

GRAHAM, T.H. - owns a GC livery stable (G8/20/97)

GRAND ARMY OF THE REPUBLIC (GAR) MAGNOLIA POST No. 409/403 at Jnsbr - A.H. Cline is Commanding Officer (G1/8/97); has 16 surviving mbrs (J6/9/16)

GRAND ARMY OF THE REPUBLIC WOMEN'S RELIEF CORP No. 143 - Mrs. A.H. Cline is mbr (G1/8/97)

GRANT COUNTY - now has 945 miles of improved roads (J10/6/16)

GRANT CO. AGRICULTURAL AGENT - is Otis Crane (J4/16/15)

GRANT COUNTY FAIR - being held this wk in Marion, has poor attendance (J9/2/87)

GRANT COUNTY, FIRST RAILROAD - I.M. Miller of Marion recalls in early 1850's two RR's were projected to cross Grant Co., the Union & Logansport RR and the Cincinnati & Chicago RR; right-of-ways were cut out and much grading was done, but it fell through; interest began in 1864 to follow the old track to within a mile of the E Line of Grant Co., then run NW to Jnsbr, then cross to W of the river; because of this Harrisburg was on the map; work went on for about two yrs but the rails did not reach Grant Co. until the afternoon of 16 Aug 1865; about 5 PM that day, ties and rails were laid for about 80 rods into the fields of what is now the Millerton Farm so 3 cars of rails & 3 cars of ties were shoved ahead of the first iron horse entering the county; the engine was an old one having been used by the Indiana Central RR; it was bedecked with brass on all the angles and curves of its trimmings; for a whistle, a great brass horn at least 4 feet long was set over the boiler about midway; Newt Mitchell, engineer, delighted himself, as well as residents who came out of the swamps to see the curio, by frequent manipulations of the whistle; Sam Beaumont, fireman, and Charlie Fry, brakeman operated the first train of cars ever in Grant Co.; they brought the rails and ties from points east; having to bridge the river, rails were not laid into Marion until late Oct; some of the boys from around here who were employed on the construction said that the evening they reached the town of Marion, James Sweetser rolled out two kegs of beer and treated them all in honor of the event (J8/24/17)

GRANT COUNTY INFIRMARY - inspected last wk; Rev. T.H. Banks, Supt.; has 36 cattle, 76 hogs, 6 horses, ca 60 inmates; over 2,000 bu corn raised in 1896 (G3/12/97); William Boles, Supt. for past 3 yrs will be replaced by Elmer Handschey on March 1st (G2/9/17)

GRANT COUNTY SUPERINTENDANT OF SCHOOLS - is Charles Terrell of Jnsbr (J7/23/15)

GRANT COUNTY WOMEN'S CHRISTIAN TEMPERANCE UNION - Mary Eaton, mbr Oak Ridge Friends WCTU; Eunice Wilson, mbr BC Friends WCTU; Sue Ratliffe, mbr Deer Creek Friends WCTU; Anna Wilcuts, mbr South Marion Friends WCTU (G10/22/97); county convention at Jnsbr Friends MH; 300 White Ribbon babies present; baby of M/M Wint Ruley won the baby contest (J10/6/16); county has 1,760 mbrs, a gain of 149 mbrs over last yr; Mrs. Della Kirkpatrick of BC Friends is Vice-Pres. (J10/10/19)

GRAVES, William - s George Graves (J4/18/19); of Zeek area, bought new Ford roadster (J10/8/20)

GRAY, Abbey T. - of GC; age 47; m twice; he d 9 Feb 1917, bur Jefferson Cem (G2/16/17; J2/16/17)

GRAY, Ada - "great actress" to be at Lovett's Opera House Sat and Mon eve in "East Lynn" (G1/1/97)

GRAY, Ada Z. - mbr Jnsbr MM SS (J7/27/17); 1919 Mill Twp 8th grade grad (J4/4/19)

GRAY, C.C. - mbr Jnsbr Sons of Veterans (J3/4/04)

GRAY, Forrest - s M/M Frank Gray of Jnsbr; has broken his arm (G11/16/17)

GRAY, Katherine (CROSBY) - b Shelby Co. 15 Sep 1870; dt Darius and Katherine Crosby; m 1st 1898 James L. Graham (d

1905); m 2nd 29 Dec 1910 W.P. Gray; step-mother of Ezra and Scott Graham; mbr Christian Ch.; d 11 Mar 1920; bur GC Cem (J3/19/20)

GRAY, William P.- of GC; brother of Abbey T. Gray (J2/16/17)

GREEN, Robert S. - GC Marshall (G7/14/11)

GREEN, Rev. W.H. - Pastor, Jnsbr M.P. 1887-89 (J6/1/89)

GREEN, Mrs. W.H. - mbr Jnsbr M.P. Ch. (J10/22/15)

GREEN, William - age 111 yrs; War of 1812 vet, was with Harrison at Tippecanoe; d 11 Nov 1898 at home of dt, Mrs. Charles Swafford in Jnsbr (G11/11/98; G11/18/98)

GREEN TWP DIST. No. 6 SCHOOL - 1st sch, a log structure built in 1855, was recently moved to the Fleenor Grove to preserve it (J7/30/20)

GREENWOOD, Elmer, Jr. - s M/M Elmer Greenwood; d 2 May 1915, bur Riverside Cem (J5/7/15)

GREENWOOD, Harry Webster - m 18 Jan 1917 Louise Godwin; will live in GC (G1/19/17)

GREENWOOD, Lillian - grad, GC HS 1919 (J4/11/19); b in Tarentum, PA 2 May 1901 (J5/16/19)

GREENWOOD, Louise (GODWIN) - dt Rev/M I.R. Godwin (G1/19/17)

GRIFFIN CHAPEL M.P. CHURCH - is first church E of river on Soldier's Home Pike (J4/20/17); was organized 10 Mar 1864 (J5/4/17); Sunday, Otis Crane will speak (G10/5/17)

GRIFFIN SCHOOL, CENTER TWP DIST. No. 5 - Hazel Dexter Hayes att ca 1903-11 (J5/18/17); located N of GC; will have box social tonight (G12/7/17)

GRIFFIN, A./O. Frank - GC policeman (G4/9/97); GC paid him $11.50 for burying part of the 105 unlicensed dogs killed by police (G6/18/97); 18 Sep 1898 dogs killed 25 of his domestic rabbits in his yard (G9/23/98); buys 2 bloodhounds for use in police work (G10/21/98)

GRIFFIN, Mrs. A.F. - dt W.A. Daniels (d 26 Jul 1898) of Kenton, OH (G7/29/98)

GRIFFIN, Mrs. Martha - age 90; Wed d at County Infirmary; bur Jefferson Cem (J2/20/20)

GRIFFIN/GRIFFITH, William - b 25 Aug 1834; lives in Mill Twp (G7/27/17; J8/27/20)

GRIFFITH, Alvah - s Mrs. Jane Griffith of GC; is in Europe with US Army (G7/13/17)

GRIFFITH, Ernest - and wife and family recently moved back to Jnsbr from Yale, IL (J10/6/16)

GRIFFITH, Mrs. Ernest - of Casey, IL is dt Mrs. Verd Baird of Jnsbr (J10/1/15)

GRIFFITH, May Adeline - b GC 17 Aug 1899; 1917 GC HS grad (J5/18/17)

GRIFFITH, Mrs. Orlo - dt Mrs. Mant Leer of North Grove area (G11/30/17)

GRINDLE, James - GC Baptist Ch. SS officer (G6/24/95); is very ill (G1/14/98)

GROSSCUP, Clarence W. - s Charles W. (dec) and Dora G. Grosscup; lives in Fairmount (G6/22/17)

GROSSCUP, Mrs. Clarence - of GC; dt William Bless of Kokomo (G11/5/20); mbr GC Baptist Ch. (G11/12/20)

GROSSCUP, Mrs. Dan - of Mt. Vernon, OH; sister of Mrs. W.E. Mason (J4/18/19)

GROSSCUP, Phillip Harrison - b Tiffin, OH 7 Aug 1892; s Charles W. (dec) and Dora G. Grosscup; 5 Feb 1916 m Merial Reynolds of Muskegon, MI; lived GC until ca 1915 then moved to MI; d 18 Jun 1917; bur GC Cem (G6/22/17)

GROVES, Mary Trulock - b Dearborn Co. 13 Apr 1852; lived in Fairmount and Jnsbr; d recently (J3/26/15)

GRUNDEN, C. Frost - s Thomas Grunden of near Kennard; with wife visits family at Kennard (G12/2/98; G12/30/98)

GULICK, Emma - Mill Twp pupil; passed exam for teaching license (G5/14/97); 8th grade grad in commencement 10 Jun 1897 held in Deer Creek Friends MH (G6/11/97)

GUTHRIE, Clarence - age 4; s W.H. Guthrie; 9 Apr 1898 saved from drowning by a tramp (G4/15/98)

GUTHRIE, W.H. - sells his GC store to George H. Wallace of Rochester (G2/11/98)

GUYER, Easton A. - b Miami Co. 27 Jul 1842; m Catherine J. Mackey 21 Apr 1864; mbr Christian Ch.; d 25 Apr 1918, bur GC Cem (G5/3/18)

HADLEY, John R. - Attorney; office over People's Grocery, GC (G4/28/93); City Attorney for GC (G1/15/97); has disappeared, foul play ? (G4/9/97); fired as GC Attorney; reported sick in Chicago hotel (G4/16/97); sent letter to his sister from Indianapolis (G5/7/97); is back in GC; says he was visiting parents in Friendswood (G5/21/97); is attorney for Clodfelter Line (G11/19/97)

HAILEY, Ann (OLIVER) - dt Wemburn Oliver; lives 3 mi. SW of GC (J6/1/17)

HAINES, Mrs. George - dt Thomas Benbow of GC (J6/13/19)

HAISLEY, Chester - m; moves from Jnsbr to Marion; works for Penn RR (G11/16/17); age 29; of SE of Fairmount; s M/M Clint Haisley; d 3 Sep 1920; bur Park Cem (J9/10/20)

HAISLEY, Harvey - age 67; lived in Liberty Twp; mbr Friends; d 20 Sep 1920 (J9/24/20)

HAISLEY, Mrs. Jesse - of Fairmount; is mother of Mrs. Cyrus Coppock (J10/6/16)

HALEY, Miss Flossie - f of Jnsbr; d recently (J1/7/16)

HALL, Jane (LOOP) - b 9 Jun 1839 in Roanoke Co., VA; m Louis Hall (d May 1912) 30 Mar 1854 Salem, VA; mbr Jnsbr M.E. Ch.; d 19 Nov 1915, bur Riverside Cem (J11/26/15)

HALL, Orville E.- of Marion; m 19 May 1917 Melba Ethel Jay, dt Earl Jay (G5/25/17)

HALL, Zela - mbr Jnsbr MM SS (J7/27/17)

HALSTEAD, Bessie - lives on Main St., GC; 24 Sep 1898 had party for her 7th birthday (G9/30/98)

HALTON, Mary - local 10-yr old (J4/2/15)

HAMILTON, Frank - m 3 Jan 1898 Minnie Mahoney; will live in GC (G1/7/98)

HAMMOND, D.S. - Jnsbr Adventist Ch. Elder (J7/9/15)

HAMMOND, Mrs. Katie - age 82; of Fairmount; d at County Infirmary last Mon; bur Park Cem (J8/8/19)

HAMMOND, Sarah - age 71; widow; mbr Jnsbr M.P. Ch.; d 24 Dec 1917, bur GC Cem (G12/28/17)

HANAHAN, John - farmer; m __ Riley, dt William Riley native of Ireland (G7/9/97)

HANDLEY, Mrs. Sarah - of Upland; is dt M/M Lewis Morgan of GC (G11/12/20)

HANDSHEY/HANDSCHEY, Elmer - will become Supt. of County Infirmary March 1st (G2/9/17)

HANE, A.T. - f of Fairmount, moved to GC (J4/18/19)

HANMORE, John M. - lives E of GC; recently his buggy was destroyed when hit by a runaway team of horses pulling a wagon (G6/11/97)

HANMORE, Mart - s Mrs. Mary Hanmore (G3/5/97)

HANMORE, Mrs. Mary - age 84; d Jnsbr 28 Feb 1897, bur Jnsbr IOOF Cem (G3/5/97)

HANMORE, Sarah A. - schoolmate of Uriah S. Candy at Candy Sch prior to 1861; still living (J6/8/17)

HANNAN/HANNON, Frank B. - Jnsbr tailor; his business has failed (G11/12/97)

HANNAN, Joseph - grad, Jnsbr HS 1920 (J4/16/20); s M/M Frank Hannan of Jnsbr; 1920-21 Purdue Univ student (G11/26/20)

HARDY, Cora Mae - b Daviess Co. 10 Aug 1886; dt John R. and Martha J. Hardy (Martha d Jul 1914); mbr GC Baptist; d 26 Dec 1919, bur Walnut Creek Cem (J1/2/20)

HARMON, Mrs. Jacob - age 37; of GC; m; d 10 May 1898 (G5/13/98)

HARP, Alexander - b 26 Aug 1846 Van Wert Co., OH; 1869 m Dorothy Granger (d GC 28 Aug 1910); was a Baptist; d Kendallville 21 May 1915, bur Riverside Cem (J5/28/15)

HARP, Florence E. - dt A. Harp, S. F St., GC (G11/19/97); - see G.F. MARCHAL

HARP, Nellie (COLEMAN) - m William Harp (G11/5/20); of GC; dt Mrs. P.C. Coleman of Warren, OH (J12/27/18)

HARP, William - Nov 1910 m Nellie Coleman (G11/5/20); of GC; brother of Mrs. Florence Marchal of GC and of Walter Harp of Laurens, SC (J7/9/15)

HARRIGAN, Joseph E. - Mill Twp 1920 8th grade grad (J5/21/20)

HARRINGTON, J.H. - may have helped dynamite the Fairmount saloon of Ira J. Smith 25 Jun 1887 (J7/1/87)

HARRINGTON, Seth William - b 15 Jun 1868; m Ella; d Thur in GC at age 46 yr, 11 mon, 25 da (J6/18/15)

HARRIS, Burr M. - spring 1892, first Postmaster of GC (J3/30/17); gas well drilled with James Crawford at the lower end of Main St., GC, blew out 11 Sep 1892 (J9/14/17); m Anna M. Davis last Tue (G4/14/93); mbr GC K of P (G7/23/97)

HARRIS, Clara (POTTHOFF) - dt Henry Potthoff of Young America; m Phil J. Harris (s M/M D.W. Harris, d 18 months ago); art tchr in GC sch before m; d 1 Apr 1919 (J4/4/19)

HARRIS, Rev. David - of Deer Creek MM area; preached Sun at North Grove PM (J3/16/17), Sun at Deer Creek MM (J8/17/17; J11/9/17); Mill Twp octogenarian (G8/16/18); performed m of grand-s Telfer Walthall and Helen Gammel 28 Dec 1918 (J1/3/19)

HARRIS, Dora - 5 Jul 1898 was granted divorce from Charles Harris (G7/8/98)

HARRIS, Dorothy - grad, Jnsbr Sch 8th grade 1914 (J5/9/24); grad, Jnsbr HS 1918 (G5/10/18)

HARRIS, Elizabeth (MALIPHANT) - b South Wales, Aust. 29 Aug 1839; m in Aust. 1864 __ Harris (d 1875 in Australia); mother of W.G. Harris of Jnsbr; d 2 Jun 1919, bur GC Cem (J5/23/19)

HARRIS, Rev. Elmina B. - preached at Deer Creek MM Sun (J11/9/17)

HARRIS, Francis - grad, GC HS 1912 (J10/7/21); dt Prof./ M F.L. Harris of GC; 1915-16 Ind Univ student (J1/7/16)

HARRIS, Fred - of Deer Creek; bought new Dodge auto recently (J11/9/17)

HARRIS, George S. - ca 1890 with partner James Crawford drilled 1st gas well at W end of Main St., Harrisburg; gas from the well was piped to Harrisburg homes for heating (J3/30/17); this well blew out 11 Sep 1892 (J9/14/17); of GC; GC Land Co. stockholder (G3/12/97); will be new GC Postmaster 1 Jul 1898 (G6/24/98); stockholder in First National Bank of GC (G12/16/98)

HARRIS, Hannah - age 67; m Obadiah Harris (dec); d 7 Apr 1915, bur GC (J4/9/15)

HARRIS, Janet - grad, Jnsbr HS 1920 (J4/16/20)

HARRIS, Lowell R.- Mill Twp 8th grade grad 1917 (G5/11/17)

HARRIS, Luvenia (JONES) - b OH 27 Apr 1840; dt Daniel and Millie Jones; m ca 1864 Elam Harris (d ca 1905); lived in Jnsbr since 1854; mbr Friends; d 14 Nov 1919, bur Marion cem (J11/21/19)

HARRIS, Lydia (HOLLINGSWORTH) - m 1st __ Jay; m 2nd __ Harris; sister of Moses and Parker Hollingsworth; mother of Sarah (JAY) Gordon (G3/11/98)

HARRIS, Mary M. - 1919 Mill Twp 8th grade grad (J4/4/19)

HARRIS, Mina - dt M/M Newton Harris of Deer Creek (G6/22/17)

HARRIS, Nancy (OSBORN) - b Wayne Co. 12 May 1825; of Mill Twp (J8/13/15); m Noah Harris 23 Aug 1845 at Deer Creek Anti-slavery Friends MH; mother of Lizzie S. Ruley, Mayme Harris, Sarah J. Hill; mbr Jnsbr MM; d 2 Feb 1916, bur GC IOOF Cem (J2/4/16)

HARRIS, Noah - age 90; m Nancy; d 7 Aug 1913 (J2/4/16); in late-1850's his was the only house in what became Harrisburg (J5/4/17); founder of Harrisburg ca 1868 (J4/13/17); has a plant nursery in Jnsbr (G2/12/97)

HARRIS, Obadiah - of Jnsbr; last wk fell, broke leg (G5/14/97)

HARRIS, Phil J. - age 30; s D.W. Harris; m; lived NW of Jnsbr; d 30 Sep 1917 (G10/5/17)

HARRIS, William - and Ernest Harris have purchased the Jnsbr Garage (J8/1/19)

HARRISBURG - became GC 22 Mar 1892 (G3/23/17); U.S. Candy recalls in mid-1850's, there was forest S of Main St. from 3rd St. to foot of hill where cem is; forest was on N side of Main St. to foot of hill (J6/8/17); in mid-1850's the original highway W from 1st St. was ca 8 rods S of Main St.; 1st river bridge was wooden trestle where Streetcar Bridge is now, it rotted down, for 2 yrs in late 1850's people forded river below the dam; a wooden covered bridge was erected in 1861 where Streetcar Bridge is now, George Webster was the contractor (J6/8/17); in late 1850's only the house of Noah Harris was in what became Harrisburg; then there was no bridge over the river, people forded river below the mill dam then forded Back Creek to go to Jnsbr or they used canoes to cross river; there was no cem E of river; the first cem E of river belonged to the Jnsbr Odd Fellows and is now known as Riverside Cem (J5/4/17); May 1861 as CW began, no RR came through Grant Co.; John Adamson (d in CW) owned farm E on N. D St., his son Joseph Adamson owned farm W of John's farm, Joseph's farmhouse stood at N. B & Third St.; Dr. Samuel Horne, Sr. owned farm on S. B St. (J4/27/17); Penn RR came through Harrisburg in 1867/1868; station name was "Jnsbr" until 1892 when GC was organized; beginning 1884, Penn RR passenger trains stopped in Harrisburg; Harrisburg was laid out as a town by Noah Harris shortly after RR came through; at this time, Dr. John A. Meek owned 80 acres E of First St., Jacob Candy had 80 acres E of Meek, Thomas Kerns had 80-acre farm S of Main St. from RR to Third or Fourth St., Uriah S. Candy had 120 acres E of Kerns; U.S. Candy home site was on S. C St., Thomas Kern's farmhouse home is on S. B St. near First St., Jesse Benbow lived in a log cabin in what is now GC (J4/13/17); Candy recalls 1st train arrived summer of 1869; 1st Harrisburg residents were: 1st, Joseph Morrow family, 2nd was Elam Hiatt family (later moved to IA), then Noah Harris, then George Duncan moved into a log cabin, Shingleton Wise family, also Martin Flanagan, then Aaron Benbow moved N of Main St. E of RR; Bond & Ward had a sawmill near the river bridge where later Jack Rook had a tow & hemp factory after the sawmill was moved to Muncie Rd. near Jack Crawford residence (J6/8/17); had ca 200 people in 1871, wooden covered bridge (burned 5 Nov 1901) across Mississinewa River near where streetcar bridge is now; Wm. Smith owned a farm near river, one of his fields is now new part of Jnsbr IOOF/ Riverside Cem; Harry Wiley of Jnsbr had a planing mill on riverbank just N of where street-car bridge is; Jack Rook had a factory which made tow from flax straw for making rope; Hartson Oliver had a barrel shop (G4/6/17; J4/6/17); Pennsylvania RR completed through Harrisburg in 1867/1868, Noah Harris then laid out town, children went across river to Jnsbr Sch or went to Candy Sch until 1876 when 1st brick sch was built in Harrisburg, Uriah Candy was 1st brick sch tchr and Billy Owen was 2nd tchr (G4/13/17); 1st Harrisburg Sch was built by E. W. Pemberton, Trustee (J6/1/17); no churches were in Harrisburg in 1874, people went to church in Jnsbr or at Griffin's Chapel; 1st Harrisburg church was the M.P. which held services in the new brick sch, then came the Baptist Ch. (J4/20/17); U.S. Candy recalls, 1st church in Harrisburg was held in sch by Moses Smith, a Missionary Baptist preacher; Smith's congregation later built a church on the S side of Main St. E of the RR (J6/8/17); 1st brick sch built 1874, Billy Owens was 1st tchr, Uriah Candy was 2nd tchr (GC4/27/17); according to U.S. Candy, 1st brick Harriburg sch was built in 1874, with Wm. Owens teaching 1st term, George A. Osborn teaching 2nd and U.S. Candy teaching beginning the fall of 1876 assisted by Lida Jones and Pearley Champe; after Candy the next tchr was Robert H. Patterson (J6/1/17); beginning 1884, passenger trains stopped in Harrisburg at the Jnsbr Station; Jnsbr Station became GC Station in 1892 (J4/13/17); 1889, gas was struck in Jnsbr (J4/27/17); fall of 1890 there were but two stores in town, owned by James Crawford and by William Oliver; David Capper ran blacksmith shop; only industry in town was a sawmill owned/operated by John Hartzel; after Jnsbr struck gas, James Crawford and George Harris drilled a gas well at W end of Main St.; gas was piped from this well to Harrisburg homes for heating; in fall 1891, men leased land for gas and in spring 1892 bought land now in GC; the GC Land Co. was formed; Harrisburg became GC (J3/30/17); 2nd gas well drilled in Mill Twp was drilled March and April 1889 on N side of W end of the Harrisburg brick street (J6/8/17); James Crawford and A.D. Morgan had grocery stores here before 1892; James Crawford, recently dec, was last Harrisburg Town Board Pres. in 1892 (J3/23/17); spring of 1892, most of Harrisburg was a wheat field, houses were built in the wheat as the town of GC came into being (J3/30/17)

HARRISON, Mary E. - of GC; age 48; dt Mrs. Sarah Griffin of Marion; d last Mon, bur GC cem (G11/12/20)

HART, __ - dt M/M John Hart; b 30 Jul 1898 (G8/5/98)

HART, Patrick - d County Infirmary 14 Apr 1917 (G4/20/17)

HARTER, Isaac - mbr GC K of P Lodge (G10/5/17)

HARTER, Jerome N. - mbr Jnsbr K of P (G10/7/98; J6/1/23); of Jnsbr; m Mrs. Lydia Hodupp 23 Apr 1916 (J4/28/16)

HARTER, Lydia Ann (COPPOCK) - sister of James Coppock (J4/18/19)

HARTER, Mrs. Vera - sister of Miss Hazel Myers (J4/16/15)

HARTER, W.H. - of Marion; age 60; father of Matthews Sch tchr; m; killed on RR in Mar 1918 (G3/15/18)

HARTMAN, A.O. - moved his meat market to South 3rd St., GC (G8/6/97)

HARTMAN, Amelia - age 72; b Germany; m Otto Hartman (retired GC butcher); d 4 Jun 1916, bur IOOF Cem (J6/9/16)

HARTZEL, John - 1890 ran Harrisburg sawmill, the only industry in town (J3/30/17)

HARVEY, A.P. - sells Waterbury watches in his St. John Sewing Machine Office in Jnsbr (J6/8/1889); sells his "New Machine" sewing machine sales/repair business to retire to Curtisville (J3/4/04)

HARVEY, Miss Grace - sister-in-law of Harvey Burgess; while riding bicycle, ran into horse driven by William Taylor; horse and buggy passed over bicycle bruising Grace (G7/23/97)

HARVEY, Gulie - 1898-99 North Grove Sch tchr (G8/19/98)

HARVEY, J.S. - mbr Jnsbr Masonic Lodge (G12/24/97)

HASTING, Anna - age 76; of Fairmount; widow of John Hasting; mother of Mrs. Fred Cray; mbr Fairmount MM; d 2 Nov 1919 (J11/7/19)

HASTY, Orville - s M/M Tom Hasty; m 29 Apr 1916 Lula Moon, dt M/M Robert Moon of near Hackleman; will farm near Hackleman (J5/5/16)

HATFIELD, Earl - mbr GC Christian Ch. (G11/23/17)

HAVENS, Gabrilla (CLARK) - age 97, sister of James Clark (G3/16/17); of Fairmount, celebrates 99th birthday 25 Feb 1919 (J2/28/19); mother of Mrs. William H. Mann of Fairmount (J7/2/20)

HAVENS, William - celebrated his 89th birthday 22 Apr 1898 at Jnsbr home of his dt, Mrs. Debby Brown (G4/29/98); of Jnsbr; b 23 Apr 1810; d Sep 1910 (J9/3/20)

HAWKINS, Miss Ethel - of Kokomo; neice of Mrs. Otto Henley (J12/27/18)

HAYES, Hazel Dexter - b Center Twp 18 Jan 1897; att Griffin Sch 8 yrs; grad, GC HS 1917 (J5/18/17)

HAYNES, Charles - s M/M Dan Haynes of Lake Galatia area (G6/22/17)

HAYNES, Dan - of E of Jnsbr; bought new Maxwell auto (G6/15/17)

HAYNES, Ernest - lives in Marion (G12/7/17)

HAYNES, Frank M. - at his 73rd birthday party at his home Sun 21 Aug 1915, group picture was taken (J8/27/15); 150 friends and relatives were present 22 Aug 1920 for his 78th birthday (J8/27/20)

HAYWORTH, D.W. - 8 Apr 1889 bought Jnsbr bakery/grocery store from James K. Barkalow (J6/8/89)

HAYWORTH, Mrs. Nora (COPPOCK) - of Laura, OH; is visiting her parents in Jnsbr (J7/1/87)

HEAL, Athalia - b near Fowlerton; m John C. Heal (d ca 1905); d Feb 1916, bur Otisco, Clark Co. (J2/25/16)

HEAL, Bernice - att Ind Univ; visits parents in GC (J4/2/15)

HEAL, Chester - of Gary; visits parents in GC (J4/2/15); grad, GC HS 1910; 1910-11 att Marion Normal (J9/24/20); in 1st Ind. Inf. on Mexican border due to Pancho Villa raids (J8/4/16); in Gary enlisted in Co. F, 1st Ind. Inf., will enter camp ca Aug 5th (G6/22/17); is Lieut. at Camp Pike, AR (G6/14/18)

HEAL, Delight - att Purdue Univ; visits parents in GC (J4/2/15); Candy Sch tchr 1915-18 (J8/27/15; J9/1/16; G8/31/17)

HEAL, Elmer E. - Zeek Sch tchr 1898-99 (G8/19/98); mbr GC K of P (G7/14/11); Mill Twp Trustee (J6/18/15); brother of James Heal of Cleveland, OH (J10/1/15); GC K of P officer (J10/6/16; J4/25/19); replaced as Mill Twp Trustee by Elmer E. Friedline (J1/3/19)

HEAL, Mrs. Elmer E. - mbr GC Pythian Sisters (J10/6/16)

HEAL, Flossie M.- of GC; Dec 1909 m Jesse C. Knopp of Frankton (J12/19/19)

HEAL, James - s Mary Heal (G2/5/97); of Cleveland, OH; brother of Elmer E. Heal of GC (J10/1/15)

HEAL, Mrs. Le<u>nora</u> - of Marion is sister of Mrs. Anna Burns of Zeek Sch neighborhood (J7/9/15; J10/22/15)

HEAL, Nellie (MULLEN) - dt Jehu Mullen; grad, GC HS; m 20 Nov 1917 Thomas Heal (G12/7/17); lives in GC (J12/27/18); 1918-19 GC West Ward Sch tchr (J1/3/19)

HEAL, Paul E. - b Marion 19 Mar 1899; grad, GC HS 1916 (J5/19/16); of GC; 1917-18 att Ind Univ (G11/30/17)

HEAL, Philip W. - s M/M Thomas Heal of GC; works in Gary; is a 125-lb amateur in wrestling finals (J1/28/16)

HEAL, Thomas, Sr. - mbr GC K of P Lodge (J10/13/16)

HEAL, Thomas, Jr. - in Gary enlisted in Co. F, 1st Ind. Inf.; will enter camp ca Aug 5th (G6/22/17); of GC; now in US Army (J6/29/17); s M/M Thomas Heal; nephew of Elmer E. Heal; grad GC HS; m 20 Nov 1917 Nelle Mullen, dt Jehu Mullen (recently d); he is in US Army (G12/7/17); is in TX, commissioned 2nd Lieut. (G10/18/18); is discharged, is on way home from TX (G12/27/18; J12/27/18)

HEALE, Caroline (LEWIS) - of GC; mother of William Heale of Gary (J12/27/18)

HEALE, Isaac - of St. Mary's, OH; is s Mrs. Caroline Heale of GC (G1/26/17)

HEALE, William James - of Gary (G2/9/17; J12/27/18)

HEATH, Clara - Mill Twp Sch 1920 8th grade grad (J5/21/20)

HEATH, Mervin - local 6-yr old (J4/2/15)

HEATON, Amanda M. (HAMILTON) - b Henry Co. 2 Aug 1857; dt John and Elizabeth Hamilton; m 8 Mar 1876 Joseph Heaton; d 23 Oct 1920, bur Tipton Co. (J10/29/20)

HEATON, Joseph - has ice cream parlor on S. 3rd St., GC (G7/14/11)

HEAVILIN, M/M John W. - of E of Fairmount; celebrated 30th wedding anniv last Sun (J1/5/17)

HELM, Gertrude - of GC; mbr GC Christian Ch. (G10/26/17); - see A. THOMAS

HELM, Nancy - b OH 1839; f of Jnsbr; m 1st 1858 Walter D. Jay (d ca 1871); m 2nd F.M. Helm (d 1895); Arthur E. Jay is s; helped organize Emily E. Flinn Home in Marion; f mbr Friends, mbr Marion M.E. Ch.; d 27 Aug 1920 (J9/3/20)

HENDERSON, Mrs. Alice - mbr Jnsbr WCTU (J2/20/20)

HENDERSON, James - of GC; is in US Army (J6/29/17)

HENDERSON, Mrs. R.T. - dt A.L. Barnard of Jnsbr (G5/7/97)

HENLEY, Dr. A. - may have helped dynamite the Fairmount saloon of Ira J. Smith 25 Jun 1887 (J7/1/87); is retired and living in Melbourne, FL (J8/17/17)

HENLEY, Delbert - age 24; of Fairmount; raped his 12-yr old cousin, Minnie Thrift, dt M/M Alex Thrift of Fairmount; she is pregnant (G12/31/97); released from custody because of insufficient evidence of rape (G9/16/98)

HENLEY, Elizabeth - att Zeek Sch 1915-16 (J5/5/16)

HENLEY, M/M Otto - celebrated 15th wedding anniv 25 Dec 1919 (J1/2/20)

HENLEY, Mrs. Otto - is aunt of Miss Ethel Hawkins of Kokomo (J12/27/18)

HENRY, Elizabeth - 1919 Mill Twp 8th grade grad (J4/4/19)

HENRY, G.A. - beginning Sep 1897, will be Dean, Law Dept., Marion Normal Coll (G7/9/97)

HENRY, John - f barber in Spence's Barber Shop, Jnsbr; skipped town last wk owing money (G1/15/97)

HENRY, William - f of GC; age 32; m (wife is dt of Mrs. Lena Broschart); d 23 Apr 1916, bur GC Cem (J4/28/16)

HENSCHEN, Mabel - grad, GC HS 1918 (G5/10/18)

HERALD, Samuel - mbr GC Fire Dept. (J3/4/04)

HERNLEY, Frank M.- is m to Sadie Hodupp; moved to Portland last Tue (J6/8/89); of Jnsbr; s Mrs. Needham of New Castle (G5/14/97)

HERNLEY, Sadie (HODUPP) - dt Mrs. Matilda Hodupp of Jnsbr; m Frank M. Hernley (J6/8/89; G7/9/97)

HERRING, John - age 53; never m; d 18 Nov 1915, bur Riverside Cem (J11/26/15)

HERRING, William - barn man for GC; is out of a job because GC sold its fire horses (G2/9/17)

HERROLD, C.A. - of Herrold & Lusher; sell clothing/dry goods in GC store three doors W of Mississinewa Hotel (G9/22/93; G8/24/95)

HERROLD, George - s M/M C.A. Herrald of GC; 1920-21 Purdue Univ student (G11/26/20)

HERRON, Roxie - grad, Jnsbr HS 1897 (G5/7/97)

HEWETT, Thomas - mbr GC Baptist Ch. (G1/14/98)

HEWETT, Mrs. Thomas - lived on S. D St., GC; d 27 Apr 1898 (G4/29/98)

HEWITT, Raymond - Mill Twp 8th grade grad 1916 (J5/12/16); age 16; s M/M Thomas Hewitt; lived 4 mi. SE GC; mbr Jnsbr MM; d 25 Aug 1916, bur Riverside Cem (J9/1/16)

HIATT, Alt - and Jack Futrell run the Jnsbr Bowling Alley located next to the Jnsbr Bank (G9/9/98)

HIATT, Anna - m Erastus Hiatt; killed by train near her home 1 mi. N of Jnsbr 17 Sep 1910 (J5/5/16; J9/17/20)

HIATT, Rev. C.E. - s Calvin Wasson Hiatt; pastor of Marion MM (J4/13/17)

HIATT, Calvin Wasson - b N. Jnsbr 30 Sep 1833; m; was a building contractor; mbr South Marion MM; d 8 Apr 1917 (G4/13/17; J4/13/17)

HIATT, Charles D. - Jnsbr MM pastor (G4/30/97; G5/27/98); and Miss Maud Miller had the recent revival at Jnsbr MM (G10/29/97); of Losantville, pastor of "Holy Rollers", recently rotten-egged at Jnsbr Pentacostal Friends Ch. because of his objection to the war (G7/26/18)

HIATT, Edward J. - m Mabel Futrell, dt M/M William Futrell; will live in Attica (J4/9/15)

HIATT, Elam - and family lived in Harrisburg ca 1869; later moved to Iowa (J6/8/17)

HIATT, Grant W. - m Mrs. Hester L. Bowers 25 Oct 1920 in GC (J10/29/20)

HIATT, Harley H. - b Mill Twp E of GC 27 Apr 1899; s A.F. and Amanda Hiatt of Marion; m 5 Dec 1918 Martha Louisa Shaner of Emporia, KS; mbr GC Baptist Ch.; d 12 Jul 1920, bur Marion cem (J7/16/20)

HIATT, Harold - of Jnsbr; 1909-10, att Purdue Univ (J12/24/20)

HIATT, Levi - of Amboy; brother of Calvin Wasson Hiatt of N. Jnsbr (J4/13/17)

HIATT, M/M Lon - live SE of GC (G9/3/97)

HIATT, Ras - farm is N of Jnsbr, W of river; E.L. Smith is hired to drill gas well here for Crosby Paper Co./North Marion Strawboard Works; good gas well came in 2 Feb 1897 (G1/15/97; G2/5/97); s Dan Hiatt of Jnsbr; m (G7/29/98)

HIATT, Robert - age 2.5 yr; s M/M Ras Hiatt; d 24 Jul 1898 (G7/29/98)

HIATT, Sarah (NELSON) - b Grant Co. 17 Dec 1861; dt Jackson and Lacey Ann Nelson; m 1st 17 Dec 1881 Jesse Oliver (d 8 Sep 1893); m 2nd 7 Aug 1896 William S. Hiatt (d 5 Feb 1919); mbr Christian Ch.; d 15 Nov 1920, bur Jefferson Cem (J11/5/20)

HIATT, William - age 23; s Mrs. Matilda Hiatt of W of Jnsbr; in US Army; d in MO, bur GC Cem (G1/18/18)

HIATT, William S. - b near Zanesville, OH 1 Apr 1856; m 1st 16 Dec 1876 Jennie Deeren; m 2nd 7 Aug 1896 Mrs. Sarah Oliver; mbr Christian Ch.; d 5 Feb 1919 at his home in GC, bur Jefferson Cem (J2/14/19)

HIGHLEY, A.C. - is Jnsbr Schools Supt. (J3/4/04)

HIGHLEY, Arthur K. - m 26 Sep 1916 Mabel Nelson, dt M/M S.W. Nelson (J9/29/16)

HIGHLEY, Asa - and wife are mbrs Jnsbr MM (J1/5/17)

HIGHLEY, Mrs. Ace - of W. Jnsbr is sister of Robert Metcalf (J9/3/15)

HILL, Arl - is having house built in Jnsbr (G4/22/98)

HILL, Charles H.- plans to go to Klondyke gold fields with Arl Hill next spring (G8/30/97); is in State of Washington on his way to the Klondike (G12/3/97); was headed for Klondike but took job as Chief Pantryman on steamer headed for Manila (G5/27/98)

HILL, Chris - is Jnsbr butcher (G4/1/98)

HILL, Dan - att Valparaiso Coll 1888-89 (J6/1/89)

HILL, Emmaline (PHILLIPS) - sister of Mrs. Fred Fellows of Windfall (J10/6/16); mbr Jnsbr WCTU (G6/22/17); mbr Jnsbr MM SS (J7/27/17); 60th wedding anniv 26 Aug 1918 (G8/23/18); age 76 (G8/30/18)

HILL, Ernest C. - m 27 Jan 1919 Olive Haynes, dt John Williams of Upland (J1/31/19)

HILL, Jack - of Jnsbr; won Jnsbr Bicycle Race of 24 Jul 1897 in 15 min, 51 sec (G7/30/97); was 3rd in GC 5-Mile Bicycle Road Race (G8/30/97)

Hill, Nathan - mbr Jnsbr MM SS (J7/27/17); 60th wedding anniv 26 Aug 1918 (G8/23/18); age 79; f lived on farm S of Jnsbr (G8/30/18)

HILL, Miss Nellie - of Jnsbr; student in Greencastle (G1/8/97)

HILL, Paul - 1915-16 Howe Sch tchr near Puckett (J10/1/15)

HILLIGOSS, Mrs. Harriett - GC Sch tchr 1894-96 (G6/24/95)

HILLMAN, Coll - m; of GC; s Mrs. Margaret E. Hillman (J10/22/15)

HILLMAN, Margaret - GC Christian Ch. mbr (J10/6/16)

HILLMAN, Margaret E. - came to GC ca 1875; age 63; widow; d 15 Oct 1915, bur Walnut Creek Cem (J10/22/15)

HIMELICK, __ (NELSON) - of Jnsbr; mbr Jnsbr M.P. Ch. (G11/12/20)

HIMELICK, Bertha - dt M/M George Himelick; m Ira Knight of Upland 12 Aug 1915; will live in Upland (J8/20/15)

HIMELICK, Clarence - m; of Jefferson Church area was given dinner for 30th birthday last Sun (G11/26/20)

HIMELICK, Mrs. Dora - mbr Jnsbr M.P. SS (J6/29/17)

HIMELICK, Edward - s M/M Earl Himelick of Jnsbr; given party last Sat for 6th birthday (J10/13/16)

HIMELICK, M/M Ernest - live in Jefferson area (J1/28/16)

HIMELICK, George - farmer near Jefferson Ch.; has 22 milk cows; is installing a 2-unit Hindman Milking Machine (J10/22/15)

HIMELICK, Lloyd - s M/M Ernest Himelick (J1/28/16)

HIMELICK, Mrs. Lottie - mbr Jefferson WCTU (J1/28/16)

HIMELICK, Lucille - mbr Jnsbr M.P. SS (J6/29/17)

HIMELICK, Mary - b ca 1845; m John Himelick; mother of Mrs. Virgil B. Duling of Fowlerton; d last wk (J4/4/19)

HIMELICK, Mrs. Mary - funeral Sun in Summitville (J5/14/15)

HIMELICK, Robert - mbr Jnsbr M.P. SS (J6/29/17)

HIMELICK, Waldo - farmer SE of GC; m 1 Jan 1920 Fern Roe, dt Mrs. Anderson Roe (J1/2/20)

HINKLE, Rev. Milo - Jnsbr MM pastor (G7/14/11)

HINTON, Clarence - of Marion; m 15 Oct 1916 Elsie Daniels, dt Mrs. Harry Daniels of GC (J10/20/16)

HOAGWOOD, Holl C. - with 3 others, took 30 frogs from the river last Mon night (G7/30/97); plays tuba in GC Brass Band

(G10/1/97); m 23 Oct 1897 Mamie Hicks in a triple wedding (G10/29/97)

HOAGWOOD, I.M.- will establish drug store on Main St., Jnsbr; James McPherson will run it (G2/12/97)

HOAGWOOD, I.N.- is GC Chief of Police (G6/25/97)

HOAGWOOD, John - 26 May 1897 injured at work at Window Glass Plant, GC (G5/28/97); with 3 others, took 30 frogs from the river last Mon night (G7/30/97)

HOBBS, __ - s M/M W.H. Hobbs; b 14 Jul 1897 (G7/16/97)

HOBBS, Rev. Charles - s Mrs. Jane Hobbs of Fairmount; m; d 23 Oct 1919 (J10/31/19)

HOBBS, Sarah C. - 21 Apr 1898 had 4th birthday (G4/22/98)

HOCKETT, Georgia - dt M/M Clint W. Hockett of North Grove area (J3/16/17; G5/18/17)

HODUPP HOTEL AND RESTAURANT, Jnsbr - has been purchased by H.B. Holmes of Kosciusko Co. (G1/8/97)

HODUPP, Mrs. __ - widow; Jnsbr hotel mgr. (JI8/10/89)

HODUPP, Charles - and Lorin Pemberton bagged 40 quail 14 Nov 1898 within 3 mi. of GC (G11/18/98)

HODUPP, Hubert - 1913-14 att Earlham Coll (J1/11/24); s Mrs. Jerome Harter; wounded in France (G7/19/18); is home from service (J7/11/19); att Purdue Univ (J5/7/20)

HODUPP, Mrs. Matilda - of Jnsbr; is very ill at home of her dt, Mrs. F.M. Hernley (G7/9/97); 18 Nov 1897 funeral in Jnsbr (G11/19/97)

HOFF, Miss Bessie - mbr '97 Club (J2/21/19)

HOFFRON, John - is a tailor in Jnsbr (J6/1/89)

HOLBROOK, Percival F. - grad, GC HS 1897 (G5/21/97)

HOLDER, Velma - 1920 Mill Twp 8th grade grad (J5/21/20)

HOLLINGSWORTH, Daniel - of Summitville; moved to Jnsbr last Tue (J6/8/89)

HOLLINGSWORTH, Mrs. E.M. - dt Micah Baldwin (dec); sister of Nathan Baldwin (J8/22/19)

HOLLINGSWORTH, Moses - b Union Co. 24 Nov 1824; s Richard and Sarah Hollingsworth; came to Grant Co. ca 1839; m 23 Jun 1844 Sarah Ann Russell; 1858 moved to IA; brother of Parker Hollingsworth of KS; mbr Friends; d 12 Feb 1898, bur in OR (G3/11/98)

HOLLIS, Willis - age 54; d at County Infirmary last Mon; bur in Mt. Hope Cem (J1/21/16)

HOLLOBAUGH, Edna M. - of Marion; age 19; m Charles A. Barkdull 4 Dec 1915; will live in GC (J12/10/15)

HOLLOWAY, Eri - of Liberty Twp; backed his auto over head of his 2 yr old son, causing serious injury (J5/23/19)

HOLLOWAY, Leslie Doris (WOOD) - m Cleo Holloway last Sat (J2/20/20)

HOLMAN, Wanda Lucille - b GC 15 Dec 1915; dt M/M Charles Holman; d 26 Aug 1916, bur Marion IOOF Cem (J9/1/16)

HOLMES, __ - s M/M John Holmes; b 31 Dec 1896 (G1/8/97)

HOLMES, Burr - s M/M D.W. Holmes of Jnsbr; m; is Corp. in army (G12/28/17)

HOLMES, Charles - of GC; in Army (G5/18/17; J6/29/17)

HOLMES, Mrs. Jennie - 17 Nov 1897, her funeral was at Jnsbr Friends MH (G11/19/97)

HOLMES, Sam - brewery teamster; assaulted Olin Gordon on a GC Street; James Persinger, Walter Phillips, a cripple, and Henry Sims, an elderly man, tried to come to the defense of Gordon; Holmes' companion, Jesse Street, then struck each of Gordon's friends; Gordon is a "dry" and Holmes and Street are "wets" (J7/23/15)

HOLMES, Mrs. Sam - m 1st __ Allen; m 2nd Sam Holmes (J10/8/15)

HOLMES, M/M W.D. - of Jnsbr; parents of Mrs. Ben Petty of Dayton (J10/29/15)

HOLTZMAN, Mrs. Henry - mother of Theron Harry Martin (dec) (G11/29/18)

HOOPER, Harry - of Fairmount; murdered Fairmount Town Marshal Jim Payne several yrs ago, is up for parole (J4/4/19)

HOOVEN, Margaret - of GC; m Arthur Hooven; d 11 Jan 1917; may have been poisoned (G1/19/17; J1/19/17)

HOOVEN, William - age 17; s Mrs. William Hooven of GC; was refused enlistment in the army in Marion; went to OH, enlisted under the false name, John W. Huff (G10/5/17)

HOOVER, Jonathan - of Blountsville recently d; brother of Mrs. Susan Peele of Jnsbr (G7/20/17)

HORN, Mark H. - nephew of Mrs. Caroline Horne (G2/4/98); m 30 Jun 1915 Nellie Cauley at St. Paul's RC Ch. in Marion (J7/2/15)

HORNE, Dr. Brose S. - a speaker for the "wets" (i.e., persons wanting the legalization of alcoholic drink sales); last Mon PM he was attacked and beaten by L.A. Prickett, a leader of the "drys" (J7/23/15); s Dr. Samuel Horne, Jr.; grandson of Dr. Samuel Horne, Sr. (J5/4/17); 4 Jul 1917 was seriously injured in an auto accident in which Edith Howard was bruised (J7/6/17)

HORNE, Mrs. Caroline E. - age 73; d 20 Dec 1897 at her home at 2nd St. & Water St., Jnsbr (G12/24/97)

HORNE, Charles E . - s Mrs. Caroline E. Horne (G12/24/97)

HORNE, Loretta (ZEEK) - b Boston, IN 29 Sep 1854; came to Jnsbr in 1859; m Dr. S.S. Horne; mother of Mrs. Belle Lucas; d 28 Nov 1919, bur Riverside Cem (J12/5/19)

HORNE, Mark - grad, Jnsbr HS 1920 (J5/7/20)

HORNE, Dr. Samuel S.,Jr. - s Dr. Samuel Horne, Sr. (J5/4/17); has Barkalow Bldg. office on High St., Jnsbr (G4/28/93); & Dr. G.W. McKinney, Physicians/Surgeons, have offices in Jnsbr Bank and in GC Bank Bldg. (G6/24/95); with Dr. McKinney, successfully operated on William Swisher's lip cancer (G1/1/97); lives in S. Jnsbr with his wife (G4/2/97); with Dr. McKinney, successfully operated on Mrs. Elisha Jay 3 Oct 1898 (G10/7/98)

HORNE, Dr. Samuel, Sr. - owned farm on S. B St., GC prior to existence of GC (J5/4/17)

HORNER, __ - dt M/M Leroy Horner; m Eldo Patterson (G11/30/17)

HORNER, Ashton 'Pete' - bought a new Studebaker auto (G6/14/18)

HORNER, John - m Vera Melba Lewis, dt M/M H.B. Lewis, Thur at her home in Amboy, will live in Jnsbr where he is a tchr (J5/14/15)

HORNER, Leroy - 10 Mar 1897 his body was brought from Sweetser and buried in IOOF Cem (G3/12/97)

HORNER, Leroy - bought a Chevrolet auto (G6/14/18)

HORNER, Mrs. Leroy - 52nd birthday party Thur (J4/16/15); given party for 57th birthday 9 Apr 1920 (J4/16/20)

HORNER, Mrs. Leslie - dt M/M Jess Tetrick of near Leisure (G12/28/17)

HORNER, Mary (McFARREN) - b 6 Jun 1839; m David Horner (d ca 1908); lived in Upland; d 13 Aug 1919, bur Shiloh Cem (J8/15/19)

HORNER, Rebecca - of Jnsbr; age 80; m; d 28 Oct 1915, bur IOOF Cem (J11/5/15)

HORNER, Ulysses - of near Jnsbr; he says he's President of the World; is taken to the Richmond Asylum (G11/11/98)

HORNER, Virginia Arleen - b 5 Jun 1918; dt M/M Leslie Horner (G5/14/18)

HORNER, William - with Mary Band, bought a marriage license last wk (G4/9/97)

HOSSIERS, Pierre - ca 1855 had the farm immediately E of the Candy farm (J6/1/17)

HOUSTON, Clarence - of GC; in US Army (J6/29/17)

HOUYAUX, Arthur - saloon keeper on S. 1st St., GC; fined for assault on Mrs. Rosa Cole who had asked him not to sell whiskey to her husband (G3/4/98)

HOUYAUX, Ellen (WRIGHT) - b KY 28 Dec 1868; dt M/M William Wright; m 1st __ Austen; m 2nd Arthur Houyaux; lived in GC; d 15 Sep 1919 (J9/19/19)

HOUYAUX, Mrs. Thersee - b Belgium; age 57 yr, 3 mon., 11 da; m Arthur Houyaux; d Fri at home in GC, bur Maumee, OH (J4/30/15)

HOWARD, Alex - and A.D. Sprinkle have combined their barbershops W of Centre Grocery, GC (G4/9/97); m; sold his barbershop to Newt Cook, went to FL for winter, and is now back in GC having re-purchased his f barbershop (J4/30/20)

HOWARD, Edith - 4 Jul 1917 was bruised in auto accident in which Dr. Brose Horne was seriously injured (J7/6/17)

HOWARD, Emmet - of Elwood; s John Howard (G4/23/97)

HOWARD, J.T. - mbr GC IOOF Lodge (G1/1/97)

HOWARD, Margaret (BOLLMAN) - dt Abraham Mac-William (dec) and Elizabeth (d 4 Sep 1915) Bollman (J9/10/15); lives in GC (G11/30/17)

HOWE SCHOOL - near Puckett; Paul Hill is 1915-16 tchr (J10/1/15)

HOWE, Lawrence - of Berne; son-in-law of Jnsbr attorney Henderson Oliver (G8/27/97)

HOWE, Mildred - mbr Jnsbr MM SS (J7/27/17)

HOWE, Ray - of Jnsbr; placed 2nd in GC 5-Mile Bicycle Road Race (G8/30/97)

HOWELL, E.H. - m; father of George Howell; grandfather of Howard Howell (J12/27/18)

HOWELL, Ed - of North Grove area; brother of John Howell (J1/5/17)

HOWELL, Mrs. Ed - dt Wesley and Malinda Conguer (J2/28/19)

HOWELL, Mrs. Ellen - lives in North Grove area (J3/16/17)

HOWELL, Ethel - Mill Twp 8th grade grad 1916 (J5/12/16); mbr North Grove PM SS (J9/7/17); FFA student (G1/11/18)

HOWELL, Fred - farmer living 2.5 mi. W of Jnsbr; injured last Sat when his buggy upset in Jnsbr after being hit by a 2nd buggy (J7/23/15)

HOWELL, George - s M/M E.H. Howell; m; father of Howard Howell (J12/27/18)

HOWELL, Gordon - Mill Twp 8th grade grad 1916 (J5/12/16); mbr North Grove PM SS (J9/7/17); FFA student (G1/11/18)

HOWELL, Grace (NEAL) - 4 Oct 1917 is birthday (G10/5/17)

HOWELL, Hazel - dt Isaac N. Howell; age 20; of Jnsbr; has license to m Allison D. Jenkins of Marion, age 30 (G2/9/17)

HOWELL, Homer - 24 Jul 1897 placed 2nd in Jnsbr Bicycle Race (G7/30/97)

HOWELL, Howard - s M/M George Howell (J3/16/17)

HOWELL, James O. - s John Howell; slightly wounded while serv with US Army overseas (J5/16/19)

HOWELL, John - brother of Ed Howell of North Grove area (J1/5/17)

HOWELL, Marion - 1916-17 att Zeek Sch (J3/30/17)

HOWELL, Zenna - dt Mrs. Ellen Howell of North Grove area (J3/16/17); Deer Creek Sch tchr 1918-19 (G9/6/18); of North Grove area; started sch at Muncie Normal Institute 5 May 1919 (J5/9/19)

HUBERT, Daniel - b 3 Jun 1850 near Sweetser; s John and Caroline; m Sarah Leming 1 Dec 1872; mbr Jnsbr M.P.; lived in Jnsbr; d 22 Aug 1915, bur GC (J8/27/15)

HUBERT, John - m Caroline; given land near Sweetser for serv in Mexican War (J8/27/15)

HUCKLEBERRY, Rev. J.F. - age ca 31; m; new pastor, GC Baptist Ch. (G7/29/98); will resign as pastor and go to Pacific NW for health of one of his children (G11/11/98)

HUFF, John W. - of GC; in Army (J6/29/17); false name assumed by William Hooven when enlisting in the army in OH (G10/5/17)

HUFF, Wood - employee of U.S. Glass Factory, GC; fell through ice into Mississinewa River with Belle Whitson while they were skating; they were rescued (G1/1/97)

HUGHES, Cleftie - s M/M Samuel Hughes; m (J8/8/19)

HUGHES, Elvira (HODSON) - of Jnsbr; age ca 63; m J.M. Hughes (d ca 1918); d last wk; bur GC Cem beside husband (J8/13/20)

HUGHES, James N. - of Jnsbr; b Greene Co. 12 Jul 1845; m 2nd Anna Jenkins; serv 3 yrs Co. H, 6th Ind. Cav. during CW; mbr Friends; mbr Jnsbr GAR Post; d 12 Dec 1917, bur GC Cem (G12/21/17)

HUGHES, John R. - GC Baptist SS officer (G6/24/95; G1/14/98)

HUGHES, LaVonne - dt M/M Samuel Hughes (J10/10/19)

HULTS, Ina - age 9; dt M/M Elmer Hults near Upland; d 13 Jan 1918, bur Jefferson Cem (G1/18/18)

HUMMEL, Mrs. E.E. - GC WCTU mbr (J10/6/16)

HUMMEL, Georgia - dt M/M G.W. Hummel of GC; given party for her 12th birthday 5 Oct 1915 (J10/8/15)

HUMPHREY, Ernest - of GC; in US Army (J6/29/17)

HUNT, Elmer J. - age 61; m Melissa A.; retired farmer living in Marion; killed on RR last Sun; bur Marion IOOF Cem (J1/16/20)

HUNT, Jacob G. - b OH 21 Jan 1835; s Nathan and Rachel Hunt; m Sarah F. James in Oct 1861; mbr Friends; d in GC 14 Oct 1918, bur in OH (G10/18/18)

HUNT, Kenneth - 8th grade grad, Mill Twp 1918 (G5/31/18)

HUNT, Milford L. - of E of GC; s Elmer J. and Melissa A. Hunt (J1/16/20)

HUNT, Morton P. - m 25 Aug 1897 Louna Henderson of Jnsbr (G8/30/97)

HUNT, Nathan W. - of Rigdon; age 78; d 17 Apr 1920 (J4/23/20)

HUNT, Mrs. Sarah M./F. - b 1 Dec 1838; of Mill Twp (J8/15/19; J8/27/20)

HUNT, Walter Earl - Nov 1905, is elected Mayor of GC (G11/12/20)

HUNTER, __ - s M/M Andy Hunter; b 2 Jun 1898 (G6/3/98)

HUNTER, Andy - is Justice of Peace (G5/20/98)

HUNTER, Rev. J.W. - Jnsbr Presbyterian pastor (G7/14/11)

HUSSEY, Rev. Mathew - pastor, Welsh Union Congregational Ch., GC (G1/1/97); att St. David's Day celebration (G3/5/97); resigns pastorate, returns to Wales (G4/9/97)

HUSTON, Mrs. James - of GC; mother of Mrs. J.L. Worley of GC (G10/5/17)

HUTCHINS, Hazel - grad, GC HS 1918 (G5/10/18)

HUTCHINS, Ina - grad, GC HS 1897 (G5/21/97); - see Ina McCORMICK

HUTCHINS, Kenneth - m; father of Willis Hutchins; recently d (G11/12/20)

HUTCHINSON, Jesse - GC All-Stars 1916 football team mbr (J10/6/16)

HUTCHINSON, Sarah - b 4 Oct 1837; m; of Mill Twp (G8/16/18; J8/27/20)

HUTCHINSON, William - of GC; age 78; m; d 8 Mar 1918, bur GC Cem (G3/15/18)

ICE, Mrs. Catharine - recently d in Fowlerton; bur Fairmount cem (G11/23/17)

ICE, Gulia - mbr Jnsbr MM Young People's group (J8/27/20)

ICE, Henry Weldon - age 19; of Fowlerton; bought license to m Winifreda Bobbette Waterman, age 21 of Jnsbr (J10/1/15)

ICE, Martha J. (NELSON) - b NC; m 1869 Benjamin J. Ice (d 1903); mother of Mrs. Omer Roush, grandmother of Bert Ice; mbr Jnsbr Presbyterian Ch.; lived in Harrisburg, then in Jnsbr; d 13 Jun 1919, bur GC Cem (J6/20/19)

ICE, Sarah J. - m James Ice of Jnsbr; d 3 Jun 1898 (G6/10/98)

ICE, Mrs. Sidney S. - age 88; mother of B.J. Ice; d 9 May 1898 in GC; bur Matthews Cem (G5/13/98)

IHRIG, M/M John - of Converse are parents of Mrs. Chris Hupp of Jnsbr (J10/22/15)

INDIANA TRACTION CO.- takes over holdings of Noah J. Clodfelter Line; will go from Elwood to Marion through Jnsbr and GC (G11/26/97); owns toll road between Jnsbr and Fairmount, toll will be abolished (G12/24/97); track is practically complete between Fairmount and Jnsbr, average width of right-of-way is 21.5 feet (G1/14/98)

IIAMS, Billy - works in Pierce's Grocery, Jnsbr (J4/30/20)

IIAMS, George M.- 8th grade grad Jnsbr Sch 1919 (J4/18/19)

IIAMS, William J. - s M/M Ora Iiams of Jnsbr; wounded 9 Oct 1918 while in Army in France (G11/29/18; J12/27/18)

ILIFF, Rev. M.F. - Jnsbr M.P. pastor (G5/21/97)

INK, Amanda - Candy Sch tchr for 2 terms prior to CW (G6/1/17; J6/1/17)

INK FORD of MISSISSINEWA RIVER - near home of Robert Wilson (G6/7/18)

INK SAWMILL - ca 1855 was S of County Infirmary (J6/8/17)

ISAACS, Alfred - saloon keeper on S. 3rd St., GC (G2/5/97); nearly d in Marion jail when an artery in his head ruptured, in jail for selling liquor on Sun; m widow several yrs ago (G2/19/97); was released from jail after laying out fines for 6 mon. (G8/30/97); arrested for stealing clover seed (G10/22/97); on trial for theft of clover seed (G11/26/97); sent to Michigan City Prison for 1-4 yrs for theft from M.L. Gaddis, 2 mi. from Fairmount (G12/3/97); is home on parole from prison (G12/16/98)

ISENHART, Evelyn - att Zeek Sch 1915-16 (J5/5/16); 8th grade grad 1918 (G5/31/18)

ISENHOFF, Andrew - b 5 Feb 1822; of Mill Twp (J8/13/15); d at County Infirmary 23 Jan 1918, bur IOOF Cem (G1/25/18)

JACKS, Emil - injured when motorcycle struck Ed Tyner's auto (J5/7/20)

JACKS, Hallet Barber - b 16 Dec 1844; s Jeremiah and Hester; m Sarah Parks (dt Silas and Sarah Parks) 29 Oct 1870; serv 3 yr, 6 mon. in 34th Ind. Inf. during CW; d 16 May 1915 at Vet Admin. Hospital, Marion; bur Riverside Cem (J5/21/15)

JACKS, Harry - local 11-yr old (J4/2/15)

JACKS, Mrs. Hattie - age 74; d 6 Dec 1897 at home of son, Hallet Jacks on S. B St., GC (G12/10/97)

JACKSON, Alf - owns GC Livery Stable (G2/26/97)

JACKSON, Mrs. Byron S. - sister of Miss Ella Gifford of Kokomo (G4/9/97); dt Dr. Gifford of Kokomo (G12/16/98)

JACKSON, John - killed at GC Main St. crossing of RR; widow still lives in GC (J3/30/17; J6/8/17)

JACKSON, Mrs. Lydia - of GC is sister of George W. Harvey (dec) (G11/12/20)

JACKSON, Mary - grad, Jnsbr HS 1910 (J5/7/20)

JACKSON, Nellie - age 9; dt M/M Byron Jackson; last Mon injured by fall from hayloft (G6/11/97)

JACKSON, Rev. W.A. - GC Christian pastor (G11/26/20)

JACOBS, Hazel (MYERS) - is Marion Coll student (G11/5/20)

JACOBS, Rosella (WINTERS) - age 25; f of Jnsbr; dt M/M Matt Winters; m Otis Jacobs ca 1916; sister of Verlin Winters of Marion; d 21 Jul 1920, bur Marion cem (J7/30/20)

JAMISON, Rev. D.L. - pastor, GC Baptist Ch. (G1/15/97); assisted by Rev. C.W. Aspy, holds revival in his church (G11/19/97); resigns pastorate in order to return to sch (G5/20/98); 19 Jun 1898 was his farewell sermon (G7/1/98)

JAMISON, Mrs. D.L. - sister of Miss Mabel Browse (G6/11/97); mbr '97 Club (G1/14/98)

JAY, __ - dt M/M Earl Jay; b 29 Mar 1898 (G4/1/98)

JAY, Anna (SCOTT) - 3 Oct 1898 underwent successful surgery performed by Dr. McKinney and Dr. Horne (G10/7/98)

JAY, Arthur W.- and wife were injured when horse pulling their buggy ran away (G3/25/98); uncle of Nellie Davis, will att East Bethel PM Sun (J3/24/16); b Grant Co. 3 Feb 1856; m Flora Clark; was sch tchr in earlier days; later was a farmer; mbr Bethel MM; d 17 Jan 1917 at his home, "The Pines", 2 mi

W of Jnsbr on 6th St. Road; bur Marion IOOF Cem (G1/19/17; J1/19/17; G1/26/17)

JAY, Belle - dt M/M Will C. Jay; enters nursing sch Mon (J10/29/15); is student nurse at Indianapolis City Hospital (J1/14/16)

JAY, Carl S. - 8th grade student, Deer Creek Sch; passed exam for County Diploma (G4/29/98; G5/13/98); s Arthur W. and Flora Jay (G1/26/17)

JAY, David - f mbr Deer Creek Anti-slavery MM, mbr Center PM; grandfather of Rolinda 'Rolly' Whitson (J11/30/16)

JAY, Dr. E.L. - s M/M Lawrence Jay; lives in Clarksville, TX; visited parents last Sun (J1/5/17)

JAY, Earl - with brother, Leroy, purchased RR car of potatoes in NJ last wk (J10/6/16)

JAY, Mrs. Earl - of GC; dt Mrs. Sarah J. Nottingham (G9/23/98)

JAY, Erastus - grad, Jnsbr HS 1910 (J5/7/20)

JAY, Fred - GC K of P mbr (J10/13/16)

JAY, Fred M. - of Gary; s M/M Will C. Jay (G7/14/11)

JAY, Jamie - age 6; s M/M W.C. Jay of S. B St., GC; d 13 Apr 1898 (G4/15/98)

JAY, Jesse - during a wind storm the roof of his home, 1 mi. N of Jnsbr, was blown into river where it floated away; his wife and dt, who were in the house, were not injured (G4/28/98); b Miami Co., OH 17 Feb 1840; s Denny and Mary Jay; m Susan Winslow 16 Feb 1865; mbr Jnsbr MM; of N of Jnsbr; d 1 Mar 1918, bur GC Cem (G3/8/18)

JAY, Jesse - of GC; brother of Lambert Jay of Wichita, KS (J1/14/16)

JAY, Jessie - dt Mrs. Louie Jay of Jnsbr (G11/16/17)

JAY, Lawrence - m; father of Dr. E.L. Jay of Clarksville, TX (J1/5/17); moved to Akron, OH; s Jesse Jay of Jnsbr (G12/7/17)

JAY, Leota L. (NOTTINGHAM) - b 23 Jul 1861 Jefferson Twp; dt M/M James Nottingham; m Earl Jay 21 Aug 1880; mbr Methodist Ch.; d 14 May 1916, bur GC Cem (J5/19/16)

JAY, Mahala (GORDON) - dt Richard and Susannah Gordon; of Marion; sister of Seth Gordon (G7/8/98)

JAY, Melba Ethel - b 29 Mar 1898 in GC; dt M/M Earl Jay; grad GC HS 1915 (J5/21/15); - see O.E. HALL

JAY, Riley - of Fairmount; age 63; m; brother of Mrs. Gulia Shugart and Arthur W. Jay; mbr Fairmount MM; d 8 Oct 1915 (J10/15/15)

JAY, Roll - m Alpha Harris 3 Aug 1889, both of Jnsbr (J8/10/89)

JAY, Sarah Alice - Roll Custodian, GC Christian Ch. (J1/7/16); b Jnsbr 13 Sep 1862; dt Elisha Benson and Anna (SCOTT) Jay; att Oberlin Coll, Univ of Chicago, and Valparaiso Normal; sch tchr in Mill, Monroe, and Franklin Twps.; then 5 yrs as White's Institute tchr, then 30 yrs in GC making a total of 44 yrs as tchr; f mbr Friends, mbr GC Christian Ch. (G10/7/98)

JAY, Watt D. - mbr/officer, Jnsbr K of P (G1/26/17)

JAY, William A. - b GC 25 Dec 1897; s M/M Will C. Jay; grad, GC HS 1915 (J5/21/15); in Gary enlisted in Co. F, 1st Ind. Inf.; will enter camp ca Aug 5th (G6/22/17); of GC; now in US Army (J6/29/17)

JAY, William C. - att Valparaiso Coll 1888-89 (J6/1/89); Sect., GC Land Co. (G2/26/97); s Elisha Benson and Anna (SCOTT) Jay (G10/7/98)

JAY, Mrs. William C. - dt Mrs. Jennie Dillworth of Indianapolis (G12/31/97); hostess in her home for '97 Club meeting today (J1/14/16); lives in GC (G7/13/17)

JEFFERSON CHRISTIAN CHURCH - Rev. Arlie Courtner has resigned as pastor effective next Aug (G5/18/17)

JEFFERSON CHRISTIAN CHURCH CEMETERY - Tas Shoemaker is Sexton (J12/24/20)

JEFFERSON TWP - 1919-20 Sch tchrs: Dist.# 1 - Pete Ballinger; Dist.# 7 - Jay Pugh; Dist.# 8 - Theodore Bragg; New Mulberry Sch - Opal Wilson (J8/15/19)

JEFFERSON WCTU, in Jefferson Christian Ch. area - mbrs include Mrs. B.H. Stephens (J1/7/16), Mrs. Lottie Himelick (J1/28/16), Mrs. Nettie Ballinger of Upland (J2/4/16), Carrie Ballinger of College Hill area (G10/26/17), Mrs. Bertha Snyder (J2/11/16; G11/23/17), Mrs. John Tippey (G12/7/17), and Elva Marley (G11/12/20)

JENKINS, Allison D. - age 30; of Marion; purchased license to m Hazel H. Howell recently (G2/9/17)

JENKINS, G. - GC Welsh person (G3/6/97)

JENKINS, Mrs. J. - GC Welsh person (G3/5/97)

JENKINS, Mrs. Lewis - of Warren, OH; is dt M/M David Jones of GC (J10/29/15)

JENKINS, Mabel - youngest child of M/M Thomas Jenkins (dec); adopted recently by M/M William D. Myers (G1/15/97)

JENKINS, M/M Thomas - of GC; both d last summer leaving six children (G1/15/97)

JENNINGS, Hal - s M/M George Jennings of Jnsbr; 1920-21 Purdue Univ student (J12/31/20)

JENSEN, Jeppe - pastor of Union Chapel (G11/29/18)

JETT, Eileen - dt M/M John Jett of Deer Creek area (J7/27/17; J4/18/19)

JETT, Garn - of Deer Creek, recently bought auto (G5/18/17)

JETT, Irene - and Margaret are dts M/M Garn Jett of Deer Creek (J8/3/17); mbr North Grove Friends SS (J9/7/17)

JETT, Vance - s M/M John Jett of Deer Creek (J7/27/17; J4/18/19); 1919 Mill Twp 8th grade grad (J4/4/19)

JOHNS, __ - s M/M Will Johns; b 16 Jun 1897 (G6/18/97)

JOHNS, Anna Jane (BRAKE) - b 24 Jun 1847 in Wabash Co.; dt James and Elizabeth Brake; m Yuba Johns 31 Mar 1896; d 25 Mar 1916 at home in GC, bur GC (J3/31/16)

JOHNS, Henry Pierce - b 18 Jan 1847 in OH; s Nathan and Nancy (PIERCE); m Laura B. Cornell 16 Nov 1870; had practiced medicine; d 3 Dec 1915, bur Bunker Hill (J12/10/15)

JOHN(S), Mrs. J.W. - GC Welsh person (G3/5/97)

JOHNS, Mrs. Laura - age 65; mother of Yuba Johns; grandmother of Mrs. Herbert Bryan; g-grandmother of Russell LeRoy Bryan (J2/4/16)

JOHNS, Lavina Margaret (JENKINS) - b Swansee, Wales 15 Jan 1857; widow of W.T. Johns; mbr St. Paul's Episcopal, GC; d 22 Aug 1917, bur GC Cem (G8/24/17; J8/24/17))

JOHNS, William Thomas - b Wales 20 Jan 1850; s William and Ruth (Thomas); m Lavinia Jenkins 27 Dec 1873 in Wales; d 26 Nov 1915 at home in GC, bur Riverside Cem (J12/3/15)

JOHNS, Yuba - age 43; s Mrs. Laura Johns; m (J2/4/16)

JOHNSON, Elizabeth - mbr Jnsbr WCTU (J12/27/18)

JOHNSON, Harry - grad, GC HS 1919 (J4/11/19); b Fairmount 20 Jun 1900 (J5/16/19)

JOHNSON, Janet (MYERS) - m Solomon Johnson 4 Jan 1894 (G4/12/18)

JOHNSON, Jesse - Upland banker; assaulted by Jesse Ferguson, his Van Buren Twp farm tenant; he is over 70 yrs old (G1/22/97); his will contested; he had 3 children: Jesse Johnson, Bertha Schaum, Lula Holiday Johnson (J4/2/15); was farmer E of GC; had owned 1,700 acres of farm land in IN, IL, and MO (J10/8/15)

JOHNSON, Leslie - age 18; of Upland; last Sat bought license to m Marie Cheek, age 22, of GC (J10/1/15)

JOHNSON, Mary Ann (FURR) - b Louden Co., VA 23 May 1834/1835; of Mill Twp (G8/2/18); dt Newton and Pleasant Furr; m 1858 to William W. Johnson (d 4 Apr 1918); d 21 Sep 1918, bur GC Cem (G9/27/18)

JOHNSON, Ralph - f of Jnsbr; is in US Army at Ft. Thomas, KY; recently m (J8/31/17)

JOHNSON, Solomon - of Jnsbr has resigned as Executor of Jesse Johnson estate (J10/22/15); b Jefferson Twp 14 Dec 1848; m 1st 1873 Elizabeth Russell (d 1889); m 2nd Janet Myers 4 Jan 1894; brother of Mrs. Sol Wise; d 9 Apr 1918, bur Jefferson Cem (G4/12/18)

JOHNSON, William Wetherell - b Burks Co., PA 6 May 1832; of Mill Twp (J8/13/15); 1858 m Mary Ann Furr; lived in GC; d 4 Apr 1918, bur Marion (G4/12/18)

JOHNSON SCHOOL, Jefferson Twp Dist. # 3 Sch - let out last Fri (J4/2/15); tchr is Clarence Nelson (G11/23/17); has box supper 7 Feb 1919 (J1/31/19)

JOHNSTON, F.B.B. - Rector, St. Paul's Episcopal Ch., GC (J4/18/19)

JOHNSTON, Horace - s Mrs. A.J. Johnston (G6/22/17)

JOHNSTON, Lulu - dt M/M A.J. Johnston of GC (G12/28/17) - see L. DANCER

JOHNSTON, Mrs. Mary Ann - b 23 May 1835; of Mill Twp (G7/27/17)

JOLLY, Mrs. M.M. - of GC; dt Mrs. S.M. Crowder (G6/17/98)

JONES, Dr. __ - built large house on W. 6th St., Jnsbr ca 1867; now owned by Thurza Howell of Fairmount and occupied by families of Jesse Thomas, Riley Lyons, and Frank Smith; it burned last Sun (G12/24/97)

JONES, Abijah - lived in Jnsbr; d 30 May 1889 (J6/1/89)

JONES, Alex - s Mrs. Ed Jones; in army in France (J2/21/19)

JONES, Andrew - s Mrs. Eva Jones of Jnsbr (G11/23/17)

JONES, Anna - b Wales, living in GC working at Morewood Tin Plate Works; tried to m William Brennen but her family prevented it; she is less than 18 yrs old (G12/10/97)

JONES, Annie (IRVING) - b NJ 10 Oct 1849; m H.H. Jones 11 Nov 1871; lived in GC; d 19 May 1916, bur Millville, NJ (J5/26/16)

JONES, Anna - age 48; wife of John P. Jones of SW of Fairmount; mbr Friends; d 9 Jul 1920 (J7/16/20)

JONES, Annie B. - GC Welsh person (G3/5/97)

JONES, C.R. - Deer Creek Sch tchr 1898-99 (G8/19/98)

JONES, Carl - mbr/officer, Jnsbr K of P (G1/26/17)

JONES, Mrs. D. - GC Welsh person (G3/5/97)

JONES, David - of GC; and wife are parents of Mrs. Lewis Jenkins of Warren, OH (J10/29/15)

JONES, Daniel - last Wed m Maggie Baker in GC RC Ch.; will live in GC (G5/28/97)

JONES, M/M E.R. - mbrs GC Tribe of Ben Hur (G7/30/97)

JONES, Eaton - brother of Ben and John E. Jones, and of Lizzie (JONES) Davies (G7/30/97)

JONES, Edna - grad, Jnsbr HS 1897 (G5/7/97)

JONES, Elwood - of GC; s R.C. Jones of GC; brother of Ralph E. Jones (G12/28/17)

JONES, Mrs. Elwood - GC Pythian Sisters mbr (J10/6/16)

JONES, Emma (MAJOR) - wife of Louis T. Jones; of GC; given surprise party for 23rd birthday last Tue (J4/16/15)

JONES, Mrs. Eva - of Jnsbr; mother of Mrs. Mary VanHook of Plymouth, and of Andrew Jones (G11/23/17)

JONES, Frank - saloon keeper; brother of William Jones (G8/6/97)

JONES, Georgia - GC Christian Ch. mbr (J10/6/16)

JONES, Hazel E. - Jnsbr M.E. SS officer (J1/12/17); sister of Mrs. Charles Waite of Deer Creek area (J6/1/17); Jnsbr Sch tchr; att Muncie Normal this summer (J8/3/17)

JONES, Harry - Welshman living in GC (G1/14/98)

JONES, Hattie - is divorced from her husband, Thomas E. Jones of Jnsbr (G11/?/09)

JONES, Henry - mbr GC Tigers football team; last Sun in a game with Upland, had shoulder dislocated (J10/6/16)

JONES, Jack - of GC; now in US Army (J6/29/17)

JONES, Miss Jeanette - 1919-20 Candy Sch tchr (J4/30/20)

JONES, Jesse A. - Truant Officer for GC, Jnsbr, and Marion (G8/27/97; G9/23/98)

JONES, Mrs. Jim - of Radley; dt of Mrs. Katharine Milholland of near Lake Galatia (J10/6/16)

JONES, John A. - is GC truant officer (G3/15/18); Mill Twp octogenarian (J8/1/19; J8/27/20)

JONES, Mrs. John - GC Welsh person (G3/5/97)

JONES, Mrs. John A. - lived 2 mi N of Fairmount; d 12 Mar 1918 (G3/15/18)

JONES, Lewis N. - farmer near Upland, S of Taylor Univ; age 72; m Mary Fallis; brother of John W. Jones of Fairmount, of Thomas E. Jones of CA, and of G.W. Jones of Upland; d 12 Nov 1919 (J11/14/19)

JONES, Lida - fall 1876 assisted Uriah S. Candy teaching at Harrisburg Sch (J6/1/17)

JONES, Lucille - b GC 12 Feb 1898; grad, GC HS 1915 (J5/21/15)

JONES, Miss Maggie - GC Welsh person (G3/5/97)

JONES, Margaret - dt Mrs. Dan Jones of GC (J1/16/20); grad, GC HS 1918 (G5/10/18)

JONES, Mrs. Maria - of W of Fairmount; sister of Mrs. Malinda Goodykoontz (J2/28/19)

JONES, Marion - s Mrs. W.E. Jones; is soldier now in Belgium on way home from France (J12/27/18)

JONES, Mary E. (STEWART) - age 18; dt Charles Stewart of GC; m Floyd Jones; d 23 Dec 1918, bur GC Cem (J12/27/18; J1/3/19)

JONES, Murl - Lake Sch tchr 1918-19 (J3/28/19)

JONES, Nora - sister of Floyd and Lloyd Jones of Upland (J3/2/17) - see T. TROUT

JONES, Ollie - mbr GC Baptist Ch. (J7/23/15)

JONES, Opal - 8th grade grad, Jnsbr Sch 1919 (J4/18/19)

JONES, Ora L. - of GC; age 36; has license to m Nettie Nelson, age 26 (G12/27/18)

JONES, P.I. - and family of GC have moved to Toledo, OH (J10/22/15)

JONES, Paul - s Thomas E. and Hattie Jones of Jnsbr (G11/?/09)

JONES, Ralph E. - s R.C. Jones of GC; brother of Elwood Jones of GC; mbr Canadian army in France, has been wounded (G12/28/17)

JONES, 'Lizzie' (PAGE) - age ca 17; dt Mrs. Ella Page; m 8 Aug 1894 W. Jones at age 14; sues husband for divorce and custody of their child; couple work at Tin Plate Works; he is a drunk who abandoned family (G7/23/97)

JONES, Suzie (YOUNG) - lived in Upland; age 67; m Samuel Jones; mbr Upland MM; d 2 Dec 1919 (J12/5/19)

JONES, Thomas E. - of Jnsbr is granted divorce from his wife, Hattie Jones (G11/?/09)

JONES, W.O. - mbr/officer in GC K of P (G7/14/11)

JONES, Wilda - dt M/M W.C. Jones of Jnsbr (G1/26/17)

JONES, William - brother of Frank Jones, the saloon keeper (G8/6/97)

JONES, Rev. Winston - New Light/Christian preacher who sometimes preached in Candy Sch House ca 1860 (J6/8/17)

JONESBORO - in mid-1850's there were no river bridges here, people forded river below the mill dam then forded Back Creek to go to Jnsbr from Harrisburg or they used canoes to cross the river; there were no RR's in Grant Co. in May 1861 (J5/4/17); Pennsylvania RR came through Harrisburg in 1867/8 and the RR Station was called Jnsbr until 1892 when GC was organized (J4/13/17); Ben Rothinghouse had a cooper shop in hollow in rear of his home on Main St.; Alex Coyne hauled hoop rolls to this cooper shop prior to 1871 from his father's sawmill in Madison Co. near Hackleman (hoop rolls are small round hickory saplings that in a cooper shop are split in half with outside shaved and smoothed, the ends notched for joints; barrel staves were cut by hand with drawknife); 1871, Harry Wiley had a planing mill on the riverbank just N of where streetcar bridge was later built; Jnsbr and Harrisburg were joined by a covered bridge (burned Nov 1901) (J4/6/17); in 1874 Jnsbr had four churches: one Friends, two Methodists & one Presbyterian (J4/20/17); 1st gas well in this area, and 3rd in state, was drilled Apr 1887 on E side of Big Four RR 1 blk. S of RR Station (G5/25/17; J6/8/17); Min Murphy owns barbershop, and E.C. Fort is the barber; W.S. King & Co. buy hides/pelts in their butcher shop; Samuel Moore is Attorney with office on N. Main St.; F.S. Lucas has Meat Market on S. Main St. (J7/1/87); B.F. Burk & Co. are retail/wholesale druggists; J.L. Whitson has harness shop on High St.; Jnsbr Flour & Meal Mill is owned/operated by S.R. Fankboner; Lew Switzer has hardware store, John Eichar is his gas fitter (J7/22/87); Jack Futrell opens saloon in Meek Blk. (J9/2/87); in 1889, A.P. Harvey has St. John Sewing Machine Office that also sells Waterbury watches; 8 Apr 1889, James K. Barkalow sold his bakery/grocery store to D.W. Hayworth; Jnsbr's gas well is called "Excelsior", it roars and gushes; E.N. Pierce & Co. have Dining Hall/Ice Cream Parlor/Bakery in Moore Blk.; F.M. Lottridge has a blacksmith shop; M/M F.J. Clark have

Photograph Gallery on S. Main St.; Amos Cray, Justice of Peace, is an insurance agent, having his office at corner of High & Water St. in B.F. Wiley's Furniture Store; A.J. Rogers is the City Expressman; Mrs. James Simpson is "Fashionable Dressmaker" on N. Main St.; Dr. J.C. Knight, Physician/Surgeon has office on S. Main; R.T. Ellis has barbershop in Clark Bldg. on S. Main (J6/8/89); Mrs. Hodupp, a widow, manages Jnsbr Hotel efficiently (J8/10/89); Dr. E.B. Tyler has a dentist office upstairs in Jnsbr's Hussey Bldg.; Dr. G.W. McKinney, Physician/Surgeon, is 2nd office S of Jnsbr Post Office on W side of Main St.; Dr. E.M. Whitson, Physician/Surgeon, has office in Stewart's Blk.; Dr. S.S. Horne office is in Barkalow Bldg. on High St.; Dr. Vance & Dr. Knight have Jnsbr office on Main St. near Post Office and GC office in Thompson Blk. (G4/28/93); has new jail; Jack Stradley, Town Marshall (G9/22/93); Dr. G. W. McKinney & Dr. S.S. Horne, Physicians/Surgeons, offices in Jnsbr Bank Bldg. and in GC Bank Bldg.; J.R. West & Co. has hardware store (G6/24/95); Hodupp Hotel/Restaurant is purchased by H.B. Liming of Kosciusko Co. (G1/8/97); James Cunningham moved his drugstore from Jnsbr to Home Corner; Spence's Barbershop is here; Ben Pemberton, Town Marshall (G1/15/97); Central Union Telephone Co. will soon connect GC, Jnsbr & Marion (G1/22/97); Ruley & Courtney's Hall is used for plays and theatre; Ed Pierce has a grocery store (G2/5/97); Noah Harris has a plant nursery; I.M. Hoagwood will establish drug store on Main St., James McPherson will run it (G2/12/97); Jnsbr policemen include Loran Pemberton and B.F. Richardson; B. Fowler appointed Justice of Peace taking place of William Shepard who resigned (G3/12/97); Central Hotel is here (G5/7/97); A.J. Miller is on Town Board (G6/18/97); ca 150 Jnsbr families are supplied with gas from well on Zimri Richardson's farm (G6/25/97); George Young runs River Saloon (G7/16/97); 24 Jul 1897, Jnsbr Bicycle Race won by Jack Hill in 15 min., 51 sec.; Homer Howell came in 2nd (G7/30/97); H.B. Liming closed Hodupp Restaurant and abandoned the Hotel (G8/13/97); L.D. Smith is a Jnsbr jeweler (G8/20/97); work begun on new bridge (G8/27/97); Zeek & Co. Grocery/Restaurant at NW corner of 4th & Main St. burned (G10/1/97); Elam H. Neal, Postmaster; G.W. Wilson, Big Four RR agent (G10/29/97); Frank B. Hannan tailor business failed (G11/12/97); Charles Campbell sold his saloon to George Meekins and Joe Brown (G11/26/97); W of Jnsbr is Schrader's Brick Yard (G12/3/97); Robert Corder gas well in S. Jnsbr burst a pipe; there is a Jnsbr Brass Works (G12/10/97); Toll Road between here and Fairmount, now property of Ind. Traction Co., toll is abolished (G12/24/97); Ind. Traction Co. track almost complete between Fairmount and Jnsbr; average width of right-of-way is 21.5' (G1/14/98); Wm. Zeek sold Jnsbr Feed Mill to John King (G3/11/98); Chris Hill is a Jnsbr butcher (G4/1/98); Charles Sisson is prop., Jnsbr Hotel (G5/13/98) 29 May 1898, Jnsbr-Fairmount Electric Car Line 1st operated (G6/3/98); D.H. Beard opens Jnsbr blacksmith shop (G8/19/98); Jnsbr & GC City Councils take option to buy river dam from S.R. Fankboner for $450; Ben Pemberton, night Marshall (G9/2/98); Alt Hiatt and Jack Futrell run bowling alley located next to the bank (G9/9/98); Jnsbr Mining Co. is putting down another gas well S of town (G9/16/98); Independent Telephone System serv Jnsbr, E.A. Neal, mgr.; A.P. Harvey sells his "New Machine" sewing machine sales/repair shop, retires to Curtisville (J3/4/04); Neill & VanValer own Jnsbr Flour Mills and Elevator, will remodel flour mills (G7/14/11); Jnsbr Post Office in Schrader Bldg nearly 10 yrs (J4/16/15); Charles Shatto of Shatto & Frederick Grocery bought out George Frederick (J10/8/15); Hattie Craw is Asst. Postmistress; Jnsbr Flour Mill owned by Neill and VanValer until J.S. Neill sold out to VanValer; John Adams, Prop., Royal Movie Theatre (J10/22/15); up to 1,000 autos will pass through Jnsbr Nov 3rd on Dixie Highway driving entire length of the highway; autos from Jnsbr and GC may join the procession (J10/29/15) Jnsbr Town Bd. voted to buy its first motor fire truck and to install electric street lights (J6/15/17); soon to have street lights (G7/13/17); has new fire truck (J12/28/17)

JONESBORO ADVENTIST CHURCH - a funeral recently held here (G10/28/98); D.S. Hammond is the Elder (J7/9/15)

JONESBORO ANTLERS FOOTBALL TEAM - last Sun beat Marion All-Stars 4 to 0 (J10/13/16)

JONESBORO BRASS BAND - recently formed; gave concert at 4th & Main St. (G4/8/98); 18 Jun 1898, holds social to raise money (G6/24/98); band ordered red and black uniforms (G8/5/98)

JONESBORO CHAPTER OF NATIONAL WAR MOTHERS - 28 Mar 1919 a charter is issued to Mrs. A.F. Seiberling who organized this chapter (J4/18/19)

JONESBORO CITIZENS' BANK - 19 Dec 1898 begins; Cashier, B.F. Barze will continue as Cashier of First National Bank of GC, also; stockholders are B.F. Barze, L.C. Bond, W.A. Gorby, George S. Harris, Capt. J.M. Maring, and T.K. Sheldon (G12/16/98); Amos L. Cray is Asst. Cashier (G12/23/98)

JONESBORO MONTHLY MEETING OF FRIENDS - Charles D. Hiatt, pastor (G4/30/97); has revival (G10/15/97); Rev. Hiatt and Miss Maud had the revival (G10/29/97); Elwood O. Ellis will preach Sun (G5/20/98); Rev. Charles D. Hiatt, pastor (G5/27/98); Oct 1908, Rev. Milo S. Hinkle, pastor (G7/14/11); begin new MH at cost of $10,000, on Water St. site where the present MH has been for 33 yrs; C.S. Dudley, pastor (J8/13/15); progress is made on new MH (J9/3/15); M/M Allen Robinson, Mrs. Frank Smith, Mrs. John Smith, Jack Marshall, John Thomas are mbrs (J10/8/15); choir sang at Harvey Kirkpatrick's funeral 2 Jul 1916 (J7/7/16); mbrs include Will Moorman, James Massey, Dorothy Coppock, and Mrs. F.C. Miller; Rev. Axton, new pastor; Will Thomas, mbr of Charles Pitt's SS class; hosted Grant Co. WCTU convention (J10/6/16); 7 Jan 1917 Rev./M Franklin Meredith begin revival here (J1/5/17); SS mbrs include Charles Pitt, Mildred Howe, Zela Hall, Fern Wiley, Genevieve Walker, Winifred and Dorothy Coppock, Ada Gray, Frederick Gordon, Naomi and James Macy, Mildred and Hazel Thomas, Lola and Vera Rhodes, Ruth King, Pansy Butler, Earl Sutphin, Ernest Arnett, Leonora Wilson, Ethel Smith, Nellie Moon, Emeline and Nathan Hill, and Carl Neal (J7/27/17); pastor is Charles Axton (J3/7/19); M/M Bernard Thomas and Mrs. O. Gordon are mbrs (J4/25/19)

JONESBORO FOOTBALL TEAM - defeated Marion Normal team 14 to 0 last Sun (J10/6/16)

JONESBORO HIGH SCHOOL - Miss Helen Osborne is a tchr (G3/12/97); 1897 grads include Elmer Coomler, Charles Cray, Nina Ditmer, Don Elleman, Ethel Evans, Roxie Herron, Edna Jones, and Lizzie Marks; Helen Osborne is f Principal (G5/7/97); W.F. Gilchrist, Supt. of Schs (G8/20/97); Jesse A. Jones is Truant Officer for GC, Jnsbr, and Marion (G8/27/97); is commissioned by State of Indiana 17 Jan 1898 (G1/21/98); 1898 grads are Dar Dailey, Mamie Retts, Bayard Ruley (G4/22/98); HS hopes to get gym (J10/1/15); Lawrence Bloom, soph (J10/8/15); 1916 grads included Wayne Tucker, Faye Brumley and Grace Brumley (J1/5/17); 1919 grads were Earl Weimer, William Bourie, Fay Scott, Irene Brighton, Francis Craig, Clysta Smith, Ruby Wersing, Fannie Spangler, Lucille Wright and Georgia McKeever (J4/18/19)

JONESBORO HIGH SCHOOL FOOTBALL TEAM - last Sat beat GC HS 6 to 0 (G1/1/97)

JONESBORO - THE INDEPENDENT - James Pinkerton, publisher; Vol 1 in 1887 (J7/22/87)

JONESBORO KNIGHTS OF PYTHIAS LODGE No. 102 - mbrs include J. Harter, E.E. Friedline, Dr. Knight, Wm. Lester, Elam Neal, Ode Roush, Wm. Young (G10/7/98; G11/19/97); mbr/officers: Pearl Robinault, Wm. Cragun, Albert Brindle, Guy Brumley, Harry Brannen, Watt D. Jay, J.N. Harter, Carl Jones, Charles Clark, and John Addelberger (G1/26/17)

JONESBORO LIBERTY GUARDS - may be disbanded next month (G11/29/18)

JONESBORO MASONIC LODGE No. 109 - mbrs include R.D. Beck, Richard Ashcroft, George Crow, J.S. Harvey, Robert Ruley, A.W. Meadows, D.W. Roush, and W.A. Taylor (G12/24/97); mbrs in the army include I.L. Bothwell, Park Gillespie, Corp. A.R. Lazure, Sergt. Frank W. Russell, and Pvt. Wayne S. Tucker (G11/29/18)

JONESBORO METHODIST EPISCOPAL (M.E.) CHURCH - officers include P.B. Wright, Dr. J.C. Knight, Dr. E.M. Whitson, E.L. Zeis,D.W. Winslow (G1/29/97); Rev. J.F. Radcliff of Sharpsville is f pastor (G3/12/97); Rev. W.R. Suman, pastor (G1/15/97); Rev. L.A. Retts, pastor (G4/2/97); pastor, Rev. W.R. Suman (G5/27/98); pastor, Rev. L.A. Retts (G9/2/98); Oct 1909, pastor is W.W. Kent who is married (J10/10/19); pastor, Walter W. Kent (G7/14/11); Rev. J.W. Walters, pastor replaces Rev. E.E. Lutes (J4/16/15); Ethel and Esther Watson (J10/8/15), and M/M J.S. Neill are mbrs (J10/22/15); SS officers include Harry Brannen, Ode Roush, Mae Bourie, Frank Wright, Mrs. Elmer Kethcart, Hazel Jones (J1/12/17); W.R. Faber, mbr (G11/30/17); pastor is Charles E. White (J3/7/19); new pastor is W. Earl Pittinger (J4/11/19; J4/18/19); Mrs. Elvie Whitson is mbr (J12/24/20)

JONESBORO METHODIST PROTESTANT (M.P.) CHURCH - Rev. M.F. Iliff is pastor (G5/21/97); church has a new steeple (G7/23/97); H.V. Sharp, pastor (G7/14/11); Mrs. W.H. Green is mbr (J10/22/15); SS mbrs include Robert, Lucille and Dora Himelick; Russell Eiler; Pauline Massey; William McDowell; Lucille Norris; James and Janet Baskett; Katherine Babb; Bill Coates; William McCaslin; Marie Lancaster; Thelma Fisher; Ossie Long; and Ruth Lineberry (J6/29/17); Rev. George L. Farrow, pastor for last 4 yrs leaves; Rev. James L. Barclay comes as pastor (J8/24/17), and is still pastor (J3/7/19); Mrs. Earl Himelick, Mrs. Merle Lancaster, Mrs. Frank Leazenby are mbrs (G11/12/20)

JONESBORO ODD FELLOWS LODGE - mbrs include Percy and Earl Nicholson, Harvey Buzbee, James Glass, T.M. Ruley, Amos Cray, Oscar Phillips and Louis Lewis (J1/14/16)

JONESBORO PRESBYTERIAN CHURCH - organized 31 May 1839 as HOPEWELL PRESBYTERIAN CHURCH at home of Robert Wilson near Ink Ford on Mississinewa River 4 mi. E of Jnsbr, was in frame bldg. until 1865 when it was torn down and moved to Jnsbr; 1867 it was moved to its present location; after a fire in 1892 a brick church was built on site (G6/7/18); L. Harold Forde, pastor (G9/22/93); Rev. M.E. Beall, pastor of both GC and Jnsbr churches (G2/12/97); Rev.

M.E. Beall came in 1895, now is resigning (G3/26/97); Mrs. Al Rothinghouse is a mbr (G10/1/97); Rev. J. Ambrose Dunkel, pastor (G12/31/97; G5/27/98); pastor is Rev. J.W. Hunter (G7/14/11); the dec pastor, Rev. Dr. James Omelvena funeral was Sat, bur Delphi, IN (J3/19/15); M/M George Neill and Mrs. Adam Hoyer are mbrs (J10/22/15); Rev/M J. Roger Sillers leaves pastorate here to be pastor of Crawfordsville Presbyterian Ch. (J10/13/16); pastor, Rev. George J. Donnell (J1/19/17), resigned (G7/20/17); Carl Neal had service (G6/22/17); Mrs. Charles Ashwell, mbr (G7/13/17); John Welsh, pastor (J3/7/19); Mrs. A.J. Keever is mbr (G11/5/20)

JONESBORO RAMBLERS FOOTBALL TEAM - beat Lake Galatia Football Team last Sun 6 to 0 (G11/?/09)

JONESBORO REBEKAHS - mbrs include Mrs. Lola M. Ruley, Mrs. Linda Press, Mrs. Eva Miller, Mrs. Mary Polk, and Mrs. Henry Miller (J1/14/16)

JONESBORO SCHOOLS - A.C. Highley, Supt. (J3/4/04); 1919 8th grade grads are Everett Bannon, Everd Barker, Orville Clark, Harold Coppock, Ina Diltz, Nina Freeman, George Iiams, Opal Jones, Raymond Pilcher, Lola Rhodes, Clara Sutphin, Lyle Trotter, Harriett Wright, Hazel Trotter, and Palmer Little (J4/18/19)

JONESBORO SONS OF VETERANS, VICKSBURG CAMP - Loran Pemberton is a mbr (G7/15/98); Commander is E.E. Friedline; mbrs include H.O.P. Cline, N.J. Coppock, and C.C. Gray (J3/4/04)

JONESBORO SPIRITUALIST SOCIETY - organized ca 1896 with eight mbrs, now has 80 mbrs (G1/14/98)

JONESBORO STATE BANK - I.N. Roush is a Bank Officer (G1/1/97); Robert Corder is President (G1/7/98); E.L. Zeis is Cashier; bank goes out of business (G12/2/98)

JONESBORO WILDCATS FOOTBALL TEAM - will play GC All-Stars next Fri PM (J10/29/15); last Sat lost 12 to 0 to GC All- Stars (J10/6/16)

JONESBORO WOMEN'S CHRISTIAN TEMPERANCE UNION - met at Mrs. Rose Rush home; mbrs include Mrs. Mattie Gibson, Mrs. Lula Marshall, Mrs. Ethel Smith, Mrs. J.S. Neill, Mrs D.M. Bell (J4/16/15), Mrs. Charles Petty (J10/6/16), Mrs. Nathan Hill (G6/22/17), Mrs. W.W. Linesberry, Ida McDowell, Mattie Gibson, Viola Fowler, Elsie Sutphin, Rachael Axton, Eva Pearson, Ethel Smith, Elizabeth Johnson, Mattie Bailey, Hannah Loughridge, Mrs. Linda Press, Bessie Stock (J12/27/18), Mrs. A.F. Leffingwell, Mrs. Cyrus Coppock, Mrs. Alice Henderson (J2/20/20)

KAUFMAN, Joe - is GC Asst. Fire Chief (J4/16/15)

KAUFMAN, Junietta (LIVENGOOD) - b 29 Oct 1868, dt Julia Livengood, sister of Mrs. Charles Rothinghouse; m Joseph Kaufman, mbr M.E. Ch., d 11 Jan 1917, bur GC Cem (G1/12/17; J1/12/17)

KAUFMAN, Miss Maude - lives in Jnsbr (G11/?/09)

KAUFMAN, Ruth Elizabeth - dt M/M J.F. Kaufman of GC (G11/?/09)

KEARNS, Grace A. - grad, GC HS 1897 (G5/21/97)

KEARNS, Thomas - age 75; b in Ireland; lived just N of GC; mbr RC Ch.; d 3 Feb 1898 (G2/11/98)

KEEGAN, Mrs. Bridget - of Marion; age 81; grandmother of Mrs. Oscar Howard; d ca 17 Sep 1915, bur Crown Hill Cem, Indianapolis (J9/24/15)

KEEGHLER, W.C. - funeral at Matthews last Wed (J4/9/15)

KEENEY, __ - young man who drowned in Mississinewa River N of Harrisburg at an early date (J6/8/17)

KEEVER, A. Jay - of Jnsbr; is Co. Prosecuting Attorney candidate in Republican primary (J1/14/16)

KEEVER, Mrs. A. Jay - mbr Jnsbr Presbyterian Ch. (G11/5/20)

KEEVER, Sarah E. - age 61; m William Keever; mother of Mrs. Bernard Allred of Fairmount, and of Jay Keever of Jnsbr; d 30 Apr 1920, bur Park Cem (J5/7/20)

KELLEY, Jonathan - age ca 70; of Van Buren; killed on RR 23 Jul 1918 (G7/26/18)

KELLEY, Mrs. Susannah - b 18 Dec 1833; of Mill Twp (G7/27/17; J8/27/20)

KEMP, Edwin Cary - b Alton, IL 31 May 1858; s James and Rachel Kemp; m Anna Raps 3 Mar 1880; mbr GC Christian Ch.; d 15 Jun 1919, bur Riverside Cem (J6/20/19)

KENDALL, Abe - Trustee, GC Christian Ch. (J1/7/16)

KENDALL, Mrs. Abe - mbr GC Christian Ch. (J10/8/15)

KENDALL, Orman Russell - age 4 months; s M/M Abe Kendall; d 25 Dec 1915, bur Riverside Cem (J12/31/15)

KENNEY, William - mbr GC Fire Dept. (J3/4/04)

KENT, Walter W. - m; Oct 1909, is pastor of Jnsbr M.E. Ch. (J10/10/19); pastor of Jnsbr M.E. Ch.(G7/14/11)

KERCHEVAL, Lula (PIERCE) - dt M/M J.E. Pierce; m 14 Sep 1893 L.C. Kercheval of Sheridan; live in Sheridan (G9/22/93)

KERNS, Thomas - ca 1870 owned 80-acre farm in Harrisburg S of Main St. from RR to 3rd or 4th St.; his farmhouse/home is on S. B St. near 1st St. (J4/13/17); brother of John and Joseph Kerns; Thomas was killed at a RR crossing in Harrisburg at an early date (J4/20/17)

KERR, __ - dt M/M James Kerr; b recently (G4/9/97)

KERTH, Myrtle (ROUSH) - dt Mont Roush; m Jan 1905 Leonard Kerth, oil operator (J1/16/20)

KESTER, Emerson - of Jnsbr; m __ Pemberton, dt Elisha Pemberton; recently was injured (G6/10/98)

KETHCART, Mrs. Elmer - Jnsbr M.E. SS officer (J1/12/17)

KIDNER BRIDGE over Mississinewa River - contract was let for 180' bridge at Kidner's Ford; cost is $2,385 (G10/28/98); Charles Klick drowned near there (J6/25/15); was a big crowd at the baptizing at Kidner Ford last Sun (J8/3/17); Methodists had baptism service at Kidner Ford 8 Jun 1919 (J6/13/19)

KIDNER, Clone - b 9 Nov 1879 five mi. E of Jnsbr; s Mrs. Adam Hoyer; widower; d 14 Apr 1917, bur GC (G4/20/17)

KIDNER, George - age 60; d 21 Nov 1916, bur Matthews Cem (J11/24/16)

KIDNER, Rev. Reuben - New Light/Christian who often preached in Candy Sch House at an early date (J6/8/17)

KIERSTEAD, May - 8th grade grad, Mill Twp 1898 (G5/13/98)

KIMBALL, __ - s M/M Evan Kimball; b 16 Dec 1897 (G12/24/97)

KIMBALL, Mrs. Evan - dt Mrs. Phoebe Daugherty (G1/14/98)

KIMBALL, Frank - unmarried; f Jnsbr Supt of Schs; d Sat in OH, bur Converse, IN (J5/14/15)

KIMBROUGH, Eli W. - Jnsbr Liberty Guards mbr (G9/20/18)

KIMBROUGH, Fern (ENGLISH) - dt William H. English (J1/12/17)

KIMBROUGH, Flora (ENGLISH) - dt William H. English (J10/1/15)

KIMBROUGH, Thomas J.- with wife, two children, and Clark Kimbrough, all of Elk City, KS are visiting his brothers, John and Owen Kimbrough of Fairmount (J8/20/20)

KIMES, F. - last wk purchased marriage license with Carrie A. Ringo (G12/24/97)

KIMES, L.H. 'Jack' - b ca 1884; lived in Fairmount; m; d 12 Feb 1919, bur Park Cem (J2/14/19)

KING, __ - dt Mrs. Ben King of GC (J4/30/20); - see F.L. MILLER

KING, Bert - age 5; s John B. King of Jnsbr; 3 Jun 1898 injured in feed mill accident (G6/10/98)

KING, John B. - bought Jnsbr Feed Mill from William Zeek (G3/11/98)

KING, Reuben - Feb 2nd, party for his 27th birthday at home of his sister, Mrs. Lewis Best (G2/9/17); s Mrs. Ben King of GC; has enlisted in US Army (G7/27/17)

KING, Ruth - mbr Jnsbr MM SS (J7/27/17)

KING, Stephen - his Fairmount harness shop was wrecked when saloon next door was dynamited 25 Jun 1887 (J7/1/87)

KING, W.S. - & Co. are Jnsbr butchers who buy hides and pelts (JI7/22/1887)

KINGIN, Samuel - grandfather of Mrs. T.S. McKee; d last Fri in Greenfield (J10/6/16)

KINNEY, Edward - age 37; d 9 Sep 1915 in GC (J9/10/15)

KIRBY, Mrs. Lydia - Deer Creek Sch tchr 1916-17 (J9/1/16)

KIRBY, Rictor - m 11 Aug 1917 May Roush, dt M/M Omer Roush; will live in GC (J8/17/17)

KIRKPATRICK, Basil Leo - b 6 Nov 1918; s Lindley and Elsie (G11/8/18)

KIRKPATRICK, Bessie - att W.E. Mason wedding anniv party with parents, James and Samantha Kirkpatrick (G7/2/97); - see A. PATTISON

KIRKPATRICK, Emory - att W.E. Mason wedding anniv party with parents, James and Samantha (G7/2/97); m Gladys Gregg at home of her mother, Clara Gregg (J6/11/15)

KIRKPATRICK, Harvey Monroe - 8th grade grad, Zeek Sch 1915 (J6/18/15); b 2 Jul 1899; accidently shot while squirrel hunting on Osage Farm ca 3:30 PM, d ca 10:30 PM (J6/30/16); funeral at Jnsbr Friends MH 2 Jul 1916, Fred Carter preached, music by East Bethel PM and Jnsbr MM choirs, bur Park Cem (J7/7/16)

KIRKPATRICK, James H. - att W.E. Mason wedding anniv party with his children and his wife, Samantha (G7/2/97); purchased new Overland car (J6/9/16); house and farm bldgs were damaged by a cyclone, Eldo Patterson is repairing them (G5/31/18); moved to new home on Muncie Pike, which was f known as Mrs. E.T. Moore Farm (J5/9/19); had barn roof blown off and small out-buildings destroyed by wind Sat 29 Nov 1919 (J12/5/19); kicked by horse 20 Dec 1919, unconcious for awhile but not seriously hurt (J12/26/19); hired Zahn Sharon to help put up hay (J7/23/20)

KIRKPATRICK, Lindley - att W.E. Mason wedding anniv party with parents, James and Samantha (G7/2/97); severely bruised hip due to kick by horse (G6/15/17); party and shower given for him and his new wife, 50 people att (G3/15/18); and wife are parents of 9 lb. dt (J5/28/20)

KIRKPATRICK, Nora Belle - att W.E. Mason wedding anniv party with her parents, James and Samantha Kirkpatrick (G7/2/97); - see E. OSBORN

KIRKPATRICK, Samantha F. (MASON) - att W.E. Mason wedding anniv party with family (G7/2/97); wife of James Kirkpatrick, was in car passing horse and buggy near Zeek Sch when horse's head broke her arm (J6/30/16)

KIRKPATRICK, William 'Willie' - att W.E. Mason wedding anniv party with parents, James and Samantha (G7/2/97)

KITSELMAN, Mrs. Mattie - of GC; dt Mrs. E. Niswonger (G4/15/98)

KLICK, Charles - age 22; lived in Dunkirk; drowned in river near Kidner Bridge, bur in KY (J6/25/15)

KNAPP, Frank, Sr. - b France 9 Jul 1863; m Mary Bechler; of GC; d 22 Jun 1918, bur Riverside Cem (G6/21/18)

KNAPP, Frank James - b 3 Nov 1920; s M/M Frank Knapp of GC (G11/5/20)

KNIGHT, Charles - age ca 22; s T.W. Knight of Jnsbr; was soon to m Miss Lizzy Carey; d 28 Jul 1897 (G8/6/97)

KNIGHT, Miss Clara - dt Mrs. Anna Rook (J8/24/17)

KNIGHT, F. Bennett - grad, Mill Twp Sch 1898 (G5/13/98)

KNIGHT, Ira - of Upland; m Bertha Himelick, dt M/M George Himelick; 12 Aug 1915; will live in Upland (J8/20/15)

KNIGHT, Dr. J.C. - Physician/Surgeon office on S. Main St., Jnsbr (J6/8/89); & Dr. Vance have Jnsbr office on Main St. near Post Office and GC office in Thompson Blk. (G4/28/93); officer in Jnsbr M.E. Ch. (G1/29/97); & Dr. Vance operated on Syms Scott of Jnsbr (G4/9/97); offers services as Vol. Army Surgeon to Indiana Gov. Mount (G4/29/98); mbr Jnsbr K of P (G10/7/98)

KNIGHT, Thomas - Candy Sch tchr prior to CW (G6/1/17; J6/1/17)

KNIGHT, Thurlow - grandson of M/M E.H. Howell (J7/11/19)

KNOPP, Jesse - officer, GC K of P (G7/14/11; J4/25/19)

KNOPP, Roy M. - b 2 Dec 1917; s M/M J.C. Knopp of GC (G12/7/17)

KNORRE, Anna Louise - local 6-yr old (J4/2/15)

KNORRE, W.J. - owner/operator, GC bakery (J3/23/17)

KNOX, James - lives in Harrisburg; is advertising for return of his lost dog (J9/2/87)

KYLE, Will J. - of Brashear, Lay & Kyle, have a GC store selling wallpaper (G9/22/93); of GC (G3/12/97); of Kyle & Beggs (G5/28/97); not m (G7/9/97); came to GC from Hagerstown ca 1892 (G3/18/98)

LAKE GALATIA FOOTBALL TEAM - lost 6 to 0 last Sun to Jnsbr Ramblers (G11/?/09)

LAKE SCHOOL, Fairmount Twp Dist. No. 6 - was let out 26 Mar 1915 (J4/2/15); Miss Davis, tchr 1916-17 (J9/15/16); last day of sch 9 Apr 1918 (G4/12/18); last day of sch 21 Mar 1919, Murl Jones, tchr 1918-19 (J3/28/19)

LAKE GALATIA - neighborhood will have 4th of July celebration at the lake; Rev. A.C. Reynolds of OH will give oration; GAR Posts and bands are requested to att (J6/8/89); has three 1919 8th grade grads: Gladys Hewitt, Americanus Weimer, and Webster Lewis (J5/23/19)

LAMBERT, Mrs. Ed - sister of Charles Campbell of LaPorte (G2/5/97)

LAMPKINS, William - cook at Mississinewa Hotel (G1/1/97)

LANCASTER, Charles - Jnsbr painter/wallpaper hanger; broke his arm when thrown out of his wagon, broke same arm 1 yr ago when he fell off a house (G5/14/97)

LANCASTER, Ferrol - grad, Jnsbr HS 1918 (G5/10/18); Wise Sch tchr 1918-19 (G9/6/18); dt M/M Corbin Lancaster of Jnsbr;

student at John Herron Art Institute, Indianapolis (J12/31/20); - see F. SIMONS

LANCASTER, Harlie - age 10; broke through ice of Mississinewa River near old wooden bridge, was rescued (G1/1/97)

LANCASTER, Marie - mbr Jnsbr M.P. SS (J6/29/17)

LANCASTER, Mrs. Merle - mbr Jnsbr M.P. (G11/12/20)

LANDESS, Wyeth - Puckett Sch tchr 1914-15 (J5/7/15)

LANDRETH, Howard - b 6 Dec 1895 near Georgia, IN; grad, GC HS 1915 (J5/21/15)

LANE, Mrs. A. - sister of Mrs. Thurlow Lung of Marion (J10/1/15); dt M/M A. Abernathy of Marion; of GC (G11/12/20)

LANE, Raymond - s M/M Aaron Lane; in army (G11/30/17)

LARKIN, Jane (VanCANNON) - b Randolph Co., NC 15 Mar 1851; dt Martin and Lida VanCannon; m Samuel Larkin 5 Aug 1871; sister of Ira VanCannon of near Fairmount; mother of Emma Larkin; mbr Jnsbr M.P. Ch.; d 10 Aug 1917, bur GC Cem (G8/17/17; J8/17/17)

LARKIN, Moses - age 76; f of S. Jnsbr; d 17 Sep 1898 (G9/23/98)

LARRABEE, Ethel (MASON) - awarded Diploma of Chiropracty (G9/20/18)

LARRABEE, Hal J. - engaged to Ethel Mason (J4/2/15); Sun m Ethel Mason (J6/18/15); will study chiropractic in Davenport, IA; awarded Diploma in Chiropracty (G9/20/18)

LAWRENCE, Guy - Mill Twp 8th grade grad 1917 (G6/15/17)

LAWRENCE, Helen (HOFGENS) - dt M/M Henry Hofgens of GC; 21 Jun 1917 m Morton J. Lawrence, s M/M William C.

Lawrence of Huntington Co.; will live in Detroit, MI (G6/22/17)

LAWSON, John H. - of Sims Twp; age 71; m; d (G2/16/17)

LAY, James H. - of Brashear, Lay & Kyle; have GC store that sells wallpaper (G9/22/93); m; is GC "cash" grocer (G7/16/97); is elected GC Mayor (G5/6/98)

LAYMAN, Dora (LAMB) - age 18; dt Thomas Lamb; m Oscar Layman (age 21) of GC 19 Sep 1915 (J9/24/15)

LAYTART, George - of GC; b Pendleton Co., KY 13 Feb 1861; s Jacob and America; m 1908 Sarah Ann Fogle; mbr Christian Ch.; d 13 Mar 1916, bur Walnut Creek Cem (J3/17/16)

LAZURE, A.R. - Jnsbr Mason; army Corp. (G11/29/18); Chairman, Jnsbr Division of Mill Twp Fifth Liberty Loan Drive (J4/18/19)

LAZURE/LEISURE, Mrs. Harry - of Jnsbr; dt J.W. Sellers of OH (G7/30/97)

LAZURE, Ronald - s M/M Harry Lasure; joins US Marine Band (G7/20/17)

LEACH, Charles M. - lives 4 mi. S of Jnsbr on Muncie Pike (G11/12/97); of near Fowlerton; d 11 Jul 1918 (G7/19/18)

LEACH, Miss Ethel - raised 3 mi. SW of Fairmount; US Army nurse; d in MD army camp of flu, bur Harmony Cem (G10/11/18)

LEACH, Corp. Harry D. - s Mrs. A.E. Leach; is soldier in France (J12/27/18)

LEACH, Hazel B. - of GC; 28 Oct 1898 was given party for 12th birthday (G11/4/98)

LEACH, John - f resident; d Sat at home near Hartford City (J4/23/15)

LEACH, Margaret - dt M/M Walter Leach of GC (G11/26/20)

LEACH, Mrs. Verlie - of Converse; dt Mrs. Allie Carroll of Lake Galatia area (J2/2/17)

LEACH, Mrs. Walter L. - dt of Mrs. Margaret Culp of Greensburg, PA (J3/26/15); sister-in-law of Enoch Davis who d recently in AL (G1/11/18); father, Samuel Culp, d 20 Mar 1918 (G3/22/18)

LEACH, William A. - is replaced as manager of Lovett's Opera House by W.P. Garthwait (G1/15/97)

LEACH, Mrs. William A. - mbr '97 Club (G12/31/97)

LEAMON, William - of Jnsbr; age 54; d 25 Apr 1917, bur GC Cem (GJ4/27/17)

LEAZENBY, Mrs. Frank - mbr Jnsbr M.P. Ch. (J10/8/15; G11/12/20)

LEAZENBY, Howard - 8th grade grad, Jnsbr Sch 1918 (G5/10/18)

LeBOLD, Leonard - local 11-yr old (J4/2/15)

LeBRUN, Donald - local 7-yr old (J4/2/15); s M/M Jess LeBrun of GC (G12/28/17)

LECKLIDER, Mrs. Levina - b 27 Jul 1838; of Mill Twp (J8/15/19); of GC; m Simon Lecklider; d 25 May 1920, bur Riverside Cem (J5/28/20)

LECKLIDER, Martha (BOOKOUT) - dt Reuben and Nancy (Terrell) Bookout of North Jnsbr; m __ Lecklider; lives in LaFontaine (G1/26/17)

LECKLIDER, Simon J. - b 15 Jan 1834; of Mill Twp (G7/27/17; J8/27/20)

LEE, Karry - brother of Mrs. S.B. Davis of GC; is in US Army (G7/20/17)

LEER, James M. - of Marion; b 1845 near Pt. Isabel; farmed in Green Twp; m; d 4 Sep 1916, bur Pt. Isabel Cem (J9/8/16)

LEER, Mrs. James - dt Wesley and Malinda Conguer (J2/28/19)

LEER, Mrs. Mant - of North Grove area; is mother of Mrs. Orlo Griffith (G11/30/17)

LEES, Eunice - age 13 mon; dt M/M Bert Lees; d 14 Jan 1918, bur Jefferson Cem (G1/18/18)

LeFEVER, Dr. H.H. - f of Jnsbr; s M/M Samuel LeFever of Jnsbr; d 9 Jan 1897 in Union City (G1/15/97)

LEFFINGWELL, Mrs. Albert F. - mbr Jnsbr WCTU (J2/20/20)

LEISURE, Orange - of Green Twp; age 40; s Nate Leisure (dec); d 1 Aug 1920 (J9/10/20)

LEMON, John P. - age 39; lived N of Jnsbr; m; d 24 Sep 1916, bur GC Cem (J9/29/16)

LEMON, Mrs. Leslie G. - sister of Mrs. Rinta Wimpy of W of Jnsbr (J10/1/15); sister of Chester Buffington (G11/30/17)

LEMON/LEMMONS, William - of N. Jnsbr had foot amputated recently (J7/23/15)

LEMON, Mrs. William - of Jnsbr; age 60; d 16 Mar 1916, bur GC Cem (J3/24/16)

LENFESTY, Elden E. - s Robert Lenfesty of near Puckett; m 28 Jul 1897 Ludella Sparks, dt John Sparks of near GC (G7/30/97)

LENFESTY, Leonard K. - b Westfield 29 Mar 1908; s L.L. and Ida Lenfesty; nephew of Ora Lenfesty; mbr GC Christian Ch.; d 29 Dec 1918, bur Jefferson Cem (J1/3/19)

LENFESTY, Mrs. Ora - mbr GC Christian (G11/23/17)

LENNEN, Eva Gertrude (ANDERSON) - age 32; of GC; tried to commit suicide by drinking carbolic acid last Fri; was taken to Lapel to home of her sister, Mrs. Sim Lennen; will recover (J7/23/15); b 29 May 1887; dt John and Margaret Anderson; m Guy Lennen 25 Dec 1904; d 23 Mar 1918; bur Lapel Cem (G3/29/18)

LEONARD, Edward - m 30 Dec 1916 Grace Lewis, dt Mrs. E.E. Worley; will live in GC (GJ1/5/17; J1/5/17)

LEONARD, Mrs. J.E. - mbr GC Pythian Sisters (J4/16/15)

LERMINIAUX, Frank - mbr GC Tigers 1916 football team (J10/6/16); is GC Mayor (J4/25/19)

LERMINIAUX, Leonard - s M/M Frank Lerminiaux; is Penn RR agent; accidentally shot himself in leg with his own revolver (G11/23/17)

LERMINIAUX, Louise - local 13-yr old (J4/2/15)

LESLIE, Mrs. N.B. - GC WCTU mbr (J10/6/16)

LESTER, William - mbr Jnsbr K of P Lodge (G10/7/98)

LEWIS, __ - s M/M Evan Lewis of the Fair Store; b 20 Jul 1898 (G7/22/98)

LEWIS, Mrs. __ - mother of Samuel Lewis of Jnsbr; d 12 Jan 1897 in Jnsbr (G1/15/97)

LEWIS, Ben - s M/M Oliver Lewis of Lake Galatia area; is in US Army in KY, will be home soon (J2/21/19; J4/11/19)

LEWIS, Mrs. D.J. - GC Welsh person (G3/5/97)

LEWIS, David T. - of OH; m; s M/M Reese Lewis of GC (G12/27/18)

LEWIS, E.M. - taught at Candy Sch 1914-15 (J6/18/15)

LEWIS, Elizabeth Ann - mbr Welsh Union Congregational Ch., GC (G1/1/97); celebrates St. David's Day (G3/5/97); b Wales, U.K. 13 May 1857; m 1 Jun 1879 Rees T. Lewis; mbr GC M.E. Ch.; d 12 Oct 1920, bur GC Cem (J10/15/20)

LEWIS, Emmaline - of Fairmount; m; d recently (J5/25/17)

LEWIS, Evan - next Wed will m Mabel Florence Maring (G6/11/97); 13 Dec 1897 purchased Fair Store from H.H. Burgess (G12/17/97)

LEWIS, George A. - mbr/officer of GC K of P (G7/14/11)

LEWIS, Helen - Jun 1917, dt M/M Wren Lewis (J6/30/22); North Grove Sch tchr 1920-21 (J8/27/20)

LEWIS, Helen Lucille - age 6 months; dt M/M Roscoe Lewis; d Mon, bur GC IOOF Cem (J6/11/15)

LEWIS, Jacob M. - b 4 Oct 1832; lives in Mill Twp (G7/27/17; J8/1/19)

LEWIS, Mrs. Jacob - given party last Sun for her 73rd birthday (G2/23/17; J2/23/17)

LEWIS, James Andrew - b 6 Jun 1899 in Parker City; grad, GC HS 1917 (G5/18/17; J5/18/17); of Gary is s M/M Wren Lewis of GC (G12/28/17)

LEWIS, Josephine - North Jnsbr Sch tchr 1914-15 (J6/18/15)

LEWIS, Lavina - 1916-17 FFA student (J9/15/16)

LEWIS, Leonard - f of Fairmount; serv in France with US Army, now is oil-field worker in KS; m Millicent Linville (a tchr) of Jnsbr (J12/19/19)

LEWIS, Louis - mbr Jnsbr Odd Fellows Lodge (J1/14/16)

LEWIS, Mabel Florence (MARING) - will m Evan Lewis next Wed (G6/11/97); mbr '97 Club (G12/11/97)

LEWIS, Margaret - dt M/M William Lewis of GC; m Walter James Masters of Detroit, MI yesterday in St. Paul's Episcopal Ch., GC; will live in Detroit (J4/16/15)

LEWIS, Minnie - dt M/M Rees Lewis; m Burr Lloyd Saunders on Sun, will live in GC (J5/21/15)

LEWIS, Rees - celebrates St. David's Day with other GC Welsh (G3/5/97); mbr GC K of P (G7/23/97)

LEWIS, Samuel - recently bought Centre Grocery from Captain McCune (G1/28/98)

LEWIS, Mrs. Samuel - of Jnsbr; celebrates St. David's Day with other Welsh (G3/5/97)

LEWIS, Scott - m 17 Jun 1916 Opal Hayes, dt M/M Nelson Hayes; will farm E of GC (J6/23/16)

LEWIS, Sydney - s M/M William Lewis of GC; brother of Margaret (LEWIS) Masters (J4/16/15); s Mrs. William Lewis of Detroit, MI; will m 14 Apr 1918 Gladys Whybrew, dt Mrs. Charles Ross (G4/12/18)

LEWIS, Virgil - brother of Mrs. Stella Elliott of Chicago Heights, Jnsbr (G6/22/17)

LEWIS, Will - plays clarinet, GC Brass Band (G10/1/97)

LEWIS, William H. 'Billy' - of GC; b Wales, U.K. 19 Dec 1869; m; d 20 Sep 1916, bur GC Cem (J9/22/16)

LEWIS, Wren - mbr GC Christian Ch. (J2/20/20)

LEY, F.J. - has meat market at S. G & 1st St., GC (G11/19/97)

LEY, Lizzie - lives on South F St., GC (G1/1/97)

LIBERTY GUARDS - Companies are organized in Matthews, Fowlerton, Rigdon, Swayzee, Converse, and Fairmount; A.E. Wilson is Major of Battalion that includes these Companies (G7/12/18); a GC Co. will be formed with the assistance of Capt. Charles S. Loy of the Swayzee Co. (G8/2/18); Jnsbr Co. planned (G9/13/18); Jnsbr Co. includes L.Eldo Patterson, Elias Sparks, Webster Cox, Eli W. Kimbrough and Harold Small (G9/20/18); may be disbanded next month (G11/29/18)

LIGHTLE, __ - 5-month old infant of M/M W.H. Lightle; d 6 Oct 1898 (G10/7/98)

LIGHTLE, Levi - age 86; of Monroe Twp; widower; d 9 Oct 1918, bur Jefferson Cem (G10/11/18)

LIGHTLE, Lucille - local 9-yr old (J4/2/15); - see L. DUNCAN

LIGHTLE, W.H. - resigned as GC Postmaster (G6/17/98)

LILLY, Bernice - age 30; m 1st John Coovert, Jr. (d ca 1906); m 2nd Ed Clark Lilly; d 25 May 1916, bur GC Cem beside 1st husband (J6/2/16)

LIMING, H.B. - of Kosciusko Co.; has purchased the Hodupp Hotel and Restaurant, Jnsbr (G1/8/97); closed his Hodupp Restaurant and abandoned the hotel (G8/13/97)

LINEBERRY, Miss Ruth - of Jnsbr; student at Marion Normal (J10/6/16); mbr Jnsbr M.P. SS (J6/29/17)

LINEBERRY, Rev. W.W. - Pres., Indiana M.P. Ch. Conference; is moving to Jnsbr (J10/1/15)

LINEBERRY, Mrs. W.W. - mbr Jnsbr WCTU (J12/27/18)

LINN, Edith - grad, GC HS 1919 (J4/11/19); b Marion 19 Jan 1901 (J5/16/19)

LINN, Mrs. John F. - sister of Jesse Douglas of Logansport (G11/16/17)

LINVILLE, Ann - a schoolmate of Uriah S. Candy at the Candy Sch prior to 1861; still living (J6/8/17)

LINVILLE, Elisha - b Henry Co. 1831; s Jeremiah and Eunice; m Sarah Aburn (dec); lived in Jnsbr; d 6 Dec 1915; bur Mentone (J12/10/15; J12/10/20)

LINVILLE, Elisha 'Lasher' - b 27 Jul 1886; s M/M William Linville (J8/3/17)

LINVILLE, John Milton - b Grant Co. 23 Jan 1854; m 1st 7 Mar 1874 Malinda Parks (d 23 Apr 1912); m 2nd 17 Jul 1915 Elizabeth Morgan; farmer E of GC; d 23 Jun 1917, bur GC Cem (G6/29/17)

LINVILLE, Lee - last Sat was his 35th birthday (J1/7/16)

LINVILLE, Millicent - North Grove Sch tchr 1915-16 (J8/27/15)

LINVILLE, Ralph - s Mrs. Lee Linville; recently given party for 9th birthday (J8/17/17)

LITTLE, Miss Alice - of North Grove area; granddt of M/M Clint Hockett (J1/5/17); mbr North Grove PM SS (J9/7/17)

LITTLE, Leonard - and wife are mbrs North Grove PM SS (J9/7/17)

LITTLE, Palmer - mbr North Grove PM SS (J9/7/17); 8th grade grad, Jnsbr Sch 1919 (J4/18/19)

LITTLE, Rachel - age 79; came to Grant Co., 1852; m Nathan Little; d last wk at home of son in Fairmount (G1/28/98)

LIVENGOOD, Frank - s Julia Livengood of Jnsbr (J1/12/17)

LLOYD, Mrs. Rebecca - age 85; d Wed at County Infirmary, bur Mt. Hope Cem (J6/4/15)

LONG, Frank 'Doc' - of GC; in US Army, stationed in MD (G5/18/17; J6/29/17)

LONG, Harry - of GC; s Mrs. Laura Long of GC (G8/26/98)

LONG, Harv - of Jnsbr; s M/M Samuel Long of Wabash (G11/23/17)

LONG, Harvey D. - grad, Jnsbr HS 1918 (G5/10/18)

LONG, Jessie L. - Dec 1910, Wise Sch student who won Mill Twp Spelling Contest (J12/31/20); b 5 Jul 1897 2.5 mi E of GC; grad, GC HS 1915 (J5/21/15)

LONG, John - Tin Plate employee; captured after a foot race with Jnsbr policemen Pemberton and Richardson; faced with paternity suit, he m Stella Teague of Jnsbr (G3/12/97); age 27; s Mrs. Laura Long of GC; m; employee of Morewood Co.; killed at RR crossing 20 Aug 1898, bur IOOF Cem (G8/26/98)

LONG, Lee - and wife go to Fulton Co., IL (J1/?/87); went to New Bremen, OH this wk (J9/2/87); of Jnsbr; s Mrs. Dianna Long of Wabash (J6/8/89); will have his Flouring Mill built N of American Window Glass Co. Plant and E of Panhandle RR tracks in GC (G1/8/97; G1/22/97); GC Flouring Mill grinds its first batch of wheat (G7/9/97); mills 65 barrels of flour per day; powered by a 35 hp Atlas engine (G7/16/97)

LONG, Ollie (GEORGE) - lived near GC before m 20 Jul 1900 to Thomas L. Long (J12/10/20)

LONG, Ossie - mbr Jnsbr M.P. SS (J6/29/17)

LONG, Philip - m Dianna Roush in the Isaac Roush log cabin; marriage was performed by Rev. __ Minnick; Uriah S. Candy att the wedding (J6/8/17)

LONG, Thomas L. - b Ridgeville 22 Sep 1879; s Joseph and Laura Long; m 20 Jul 1900 Ollie George of near GC; worked in GC Tinplate mills; d 8 Dec 1920; bur GC Cem (J12/10/20)

LONG, Thurman - of GC; s Mrs. Laura Long of GC (G8/26/98)

LOTT, Miss Leota - Cashier, Ed Pierce Grocery, Jnsbr (G2/5/97)

LOTTRIDGE, Francis 'Frank' M. - has Jnsbr blacksmith shop (J6/8/89); was divorced last wk by his wife (G4/2/97); of Biddlecum & Lottridge, opened new carriage/blacksmith shop at South A & Railroad St., GC (G5/28/97)

LOTTRIDGE, Mrs. Francis M. - is sick (J3/4/04); of Jnsbr; age 74; d Aug 1910 (J8/6/20)

LOTTRIDGE, Minta - divorced Francis M. Lottridge; he failed to provide for her and their children; at the trial, temper was displayed between Frank and his wife's mother (G4/2/97)

LOUGHRIDGE, Hannah - mbr Jnsbr WCTU (J12/27/18)

LOVE, Frame - age 76; farmer W of Jnsbr; wife dec; d last wk (J1/31/19)

LOVE, Rev. Laura - age 57; Marion United Brethren Ch. pastor; killed 28 Apr 1917 in train-auto accident (G5/4/17)

LOVETT, J.W. - of Anderson; owns Lovett's Opera House in GC as well as other GC real estate (G2/26/97)

LOWE, __ (WINE) - age 28; m Charles Lowe 8 Aug 1906; d 24 Dec 1916, bur Marion Cem (J12/29/16)

LOWE, Mrs. Walter - of GC; mbr GC WCTU (J10/29/15; G2/9/17)

LOY, Capt. Charles S. - of Swayzee Liberty Guards, will help form a Company in GC (G8/2/18)

LUCAS, August N. - Jnsbr M.P. Ch. mbr (J8/27/15)

LUCAS, Mrs. Belle - dt Dr/M S.S. Horne, Jnsbr (G11/5/97)

LUCAS, F.S.- has Meat Market on S. Main St., Jnsbr (J7/1/87)

LUCAS, Mrs. Newton - 1/2 sister of Mrs. William Duling of near Fowlerton (J7/4/19)

LUCAS, Phil H. - is County Infirmary Physician (J1/5/17)

LUCAS, Will A. - will replace W.E. Squires as motor car (i.e. street car) pilot through GC (G1/1/97); had rubber tires put on his buggy (G10/1/98)

LUCKEY, Rev. J. Thomas W. - recently resigned as pastor of GC Christian Ch. (J10/6/16)

LUDLOW, Edna - Mill Twp 8th grade grad 1917 (G5/11/17)

LUDLOW, Eva - Mill Twp sch 8th grade grad 1916 (J5/12/16)

LUDLOW, Mrs. J.A. - dt of W.W. Worley (J4/9/15)

LUDLOW, Luthur L. - in US Army, s M/M John Ludlow of E of GC; m 5 Jan 1918 Olwin Morgan of GC (G1/11/18); stationed in OH (G7/26/18)

LUDWIG, Mrs. A.K. - mbr GC WCTU (J1/21/16; G11/30/17)

LUGAR, Miss Katharine - sister of Mrs. J.F. Adamson of GC (G3/11/98)

LUNG, Mrs. Thurlow - of Marion; sister of Mrs. A. Lane of GC (J10/1/15); of GC is dt M/M A. Abernathy of Marion (J12/17/20)

LUSHER, __ - of Herrold & Lusher; sells clothing 3 doors W of Mississinewa Hotel, GC (G9/22/93)

LUTES, Rev. E.E. - is Jnsbr M.E. Ch. pastor (J4/16/15)

LYGHTLE, Jacob - purchases GC fire team, coal wagons, harness, feed, and other horse supplies (G2/9/17)

LYNCH, Mrs. James - of College Hill area; dt Mrs. Newton Carter (J3/16/17)

LYNCH, Pearl - College Hill Sch 1918-19 tchr (J2/21/19)

LYNCH, Roscoe - age 25; s William Lynch; Sun d of flu; bur GC cem (G11/29/18)

LYONS, Jesse - mbr GC All-Stars 1916 football team (J10/6/16)

LYONS, Riley - and family lived in 3-family house on West 6th St., Jnsbr; home burned last Sun (G12/24/97)

LYONS, Robert S. - of Marion; with W.W. Coate operating as Coates & Lyons bought Edge Tool Works from Bruce & Marks (5/27/98)

LYONS, Ruby - local 8-yr old (J4/2/15)

MacDONALD, C.L. - and wife are parents of Mrs. Roy May (G10/5/17)

MacDONALD, Will - s M/M C.L. Macdonald of N of Jnsbr; is coming home since his 3-yr enlistment in the 6th Cavalry Band is complete; he serv in TX (J10/8/15)

MACDONALD SOAP AND FERTILIZER CO. - in N. Jnsbr; Roy May has been Supt. of plant for five yrs (J10/6/16)

McCABE, Mrs. Creath - age 96; b KY; d 1 Jun 1920 at home 1 mi. N of GC, bur Riverside Cem (J6/4/20)

McCALLUM, Mrs. John - mbr GC WCTU (J2/21/19); dt Mrs. Edmund Hall of Canada (G11/12/20)

McCALLUM, Sadie - dt Rev/M John McCallum of GC (J11/12/20)

McCASLIN, William - mbr Jnsbr M.P. SS (J6/29/17)

McCLAIN, John - has license to m 'Ada' Wysong (G6/4/97)

McCLARY/McCLEARY, Edward - Aug 1904, is GC Marshall (J8/8/19); is GC night Marshall (G7/14/11)

McCOMBS, Paul - s J.T. McCombs; m Irene Jett 1 May 1920; both are grads of FFA (J5/7/20)

McCONNELL, W.C. - mbr/officer in GC Odd Fellows (J7/9/15); Elder in GC Christian Ch. (J1/7/16)

McCORMICK, Francis - mbr GC All-Stars 1916 football team (J10/6/16)

McCOY, J.C. - last Sat sold Centre Grocery to Capt. W.W. McCune (G7/23/97)

McCULLEY, William - saloon keeper on South 3rd St., GC (G1/8/97)

McCUNE, Isabelle - dt Capt. W.W. McCune (G7/23/97)

McCUNE, Capt. W.W. - Justice of Peace with office in Opera House Blk., GC (G1/1/97); 17 Jul 1897 bought Centre Grocery from J.C. McCoy; dt, Isabelle, will work in grocery (G7/23/97); sold his interest in Centre Grocery to Samuel Lewis and is leaving within a month for the Klondike gold fields (G1/28/98); will organize a company of volunteers if war with Spain is declared (G4/15/98)

McDANIEL, Ethel - grad, Jnsbr HS 1910 (J5/7/20)

McDANIEL, Eula (ZEEK) - dt M/M George Zeek; m Edgar McDaniel (s of James) Apr 10 in Newport, KY; will live in Jnsbr (J5/7/15)

McDONALD, Joe - won the GC 5-Mile Bicycle Road Race (G8/20/97); of South 1st & A St., GC; brother of Mrs. Laura Sullivan (G5/27/98)

McDONALD, William - GC contractor/builder who shares office with Dr. Goodin on Main St. near First St. (G9/22/93)

McDOWELL, Ida - mbr Jnsbr WCTU (J12/27/18)

McDOWELL, John F. - f of GC; now of Canton, OH; wife d last Oct; serv in CW (G12/7/17)

McDOWELL, William - mbr Jnsbr M.P. SS (J6/29/17)

McFEELEY, Joseph - of Marion; elderly; d 18 Jun 1887 (J6/24/87)

McGINNIS, Fred - s M/M Joe McGinnis; is home from Army serv in France (J4/25/19)

McGUIRE, Patrick - b 16 Mar 1825; of Mill Twp (G7/27/17)

McHENRY, Nellie - age 3; dt M/M Thomas McHenry of GC; d of flu last Tue, bur GC cem (G12/28/17)

McHENRY, Mrs. Thomas - lives in GC (G11/23/17)

McKEE, Roy - s M/M Thomas S. McKee (J12/27/18); Mill Twp 1920 8th grade grad (J5/21/20)

McKEE, Perry Z. - s M/M Thomas S. McKee; is in France with US Army (J9/28/17)

McKEE, Thomas S. - GC Water/Light Supt. (J7/23/15)

McKEE, Mrs. T.S. - granddt of Samuel Kingin who d in Greenfield last Fri (J10/6/16)

McKEEVER, Charles - s Mrs. Nancy McKeever of Jnsbr; d 12 Jul 1898 in accident at work on RR in ND (G7/15/98)

McKEEVER, Clarence - s Mrs. Dorey McKeever of Jnsbr (G1/1/97); brother of Nellie (McKeever) Miller (J4/6/17)

McKEEVER, Georgia - grad, Jnsbr HS 1919 (J4/18/19)

McKEEVER, James - 8th grade grad, nsbr Sch 1918 (G5/10/18)

McKEEVER, John - brother of Clarence and of Nellie (McKEEVER) Miller (J4/6/17)

McKEEVER, Nancy (JOHNSON) - of Jnsbr; b VA 7 Jul 1830 (J8/13/15); dt Gabriel and Nancy Johnson; m 4 Sep 1855 John McKeever (d ca 1891); mbr M.P. Ch.; d 29 Mar 1916 (J3/31/16)

McKINNEY, Dr. G.W. - Physician/Surgeon; has 2nd office S of Jnsbr Post Office on W side of Main St.; & Dr. S.S. Horne, Physicians/Surgeons, have offices in Jnsbr Bank Bldg. and in GC Bank Bldg. (G6/24/95); with Dr. Horne, successfully operated on William Swisher's lip cancer (G1/1/97); 14 Oct 1897 with Dr. Conley operated on W.M. Dunlap (G10/15/97); 3 Oct 1898 with Dr. Horne, successfully operated on Mrs. Elisha Jay (G10/7/98)

McKINNEY, Mrs. Lucy - mbr GC WCTU (J10/6/16)

McKINNEY, Mary E. - of Mill Twp; age 56; widow; d 1 Mar 1916, bur Marion IOOF Cem (J3/3/16)

McLERNON, Thomas J. - Aug 1903, GC Councilman recently dec (J8/8/19)

McMANIS, Frank - mbr GC K of P Lodge (J12/17/20)

McMANIS, Harry - mbr GC K of P Lodge (J12/17/20)

McNEAR, J.B. - now lives on his farm in Ontario, Canada after selling his farm near Lawton, OK (J1/14/16)

McPHERSON, James - will run drug store to be established on Main St., Jnsbr by I.M. Hoagwood (G2/12/97)

McPHERSON, Mrs. James - sister of Mrs. Charles Parker of Fairmount (G12/10/97)

McPHERSON, Mildred - Mill Twp 1920 8th grade grad (J5/21/20)

McPROUD, Constance Bliss - of GC; b OH 22 May 1849; m; he d 13 Mar 1916, bur Farmland (J3/17/16)

McQUISTON, Louise - 8th grade grad, Mill Twp 1918 (G5/31/18)

McQUISTON, Mrs. William - of Jnsbr; mother-in-law of Frank Darter (dec) (G11/16/17)

MACY, Helen - mbr Jnsbr MM (J7/27/17)

MACY, James - mbr Jnsbr MM SS (J7/27/17)

MACY, Joseph - s Mrs. Mary Macy of GC (J2/20/20)

MACY, Lydia (THOMAS) - b Grant Co. 16 Apr 1843; of Jnsbr; dt Elijah and Lavina Thomas; m John C. Macy 16 Nov 1861; mbr Friends; d 4 Apr 1917, bur GC Cem (G4/13/17; J4/13/17)

MACY, Naomi - mbr Jnsbr MM SS (J7/27/17; J8/27/20)

MADDEN, Louis Belton - b 1 Aug 1893; s M/M Harry Madden of GC; d 10 Jul 1915, bur Riverside Cem (J7/16/15)

MAGGART, Lon - purchased GC Cycle Co. (G4/8/98)

MAGOTO, Ed - of Stegall & Magoto will run grocery store on Main St., GC (G6/10/98)

MAHAN, Mrs. Achsah - age 51; widow; d Mon, bur Riverside Cem (J3/12/15)

MAIDENBERG, David - of Marion; has GC store; native of Zegowka, Russia; filed for naturalization (J8/13/20)

MAKIN, Charles Griffin - of Fairmount; m Juanita Mullen, dt of Harry Mullen, 1 Aug 1915 (J8/6/15)

MALAY, John - age 62; m Rose; GC grocer; d 11 Sep 1918, bur GC Cem (G9/13/18)

151

MALAY, John - enlisted at Gary in Co. F, 1st Ind. Inf., will enter camp ca Aug 5th (G6/22/17); of GC; now in US Army (J6/29/17)

MALIPHANT, Mr. __ - elected GC St. Paul's Episcopal Ch., Warden at church's organization last Sun (G9/22/93)

MANAHAN, Dora G. (BREED) - m 1st Charles W. Grosscup (d 4 Aug 1902); Mar 1907 m 2nd W.H. Manahan of GC; lives in GC (G6/22/17)

MANN, Delbert - s M/M Roy Mann of Lake Galatia area (J3/2/17)

MANN, Charles - m; s M/M William Mann of Lake Galatia area (G12/7/17)

MANN, James - mbr GC Fire Dept. (J3/4/04)

MAPPIN, Joseph M. - b Johnson Co. 2 Dec 1842; serv 4 yr in Co. I, 70th Ind. Vol. during CW; m 2nd Mrs. Mary Best; Elder in Christian Ch.; f of Jnsbr; d Tue in GC, bur Riverside Cem (J3/12/15)

MARCHAL, __ - dt M/M George Marchal; b 4 Sep 1898 (G9/9/98)

MARCHAL, Eddie - grad, GC HS 1910; att Marion Normal Coll 1910-1911 (J9/24/20); of Gary; s M/M Gene Marchal of GC (J7/9/15)

MARCHAL, Florence Agnes - age 5; dt M/M George Marchal of GC; d 10 Feb 1917, bur Riverside Cem (G2/9/17; G2/16/17)

MARCHAL, Florence E. (HARP) - b Van Wert, OH 26 May 1876; dt Alexander and Dorothy Harp; m 16 Nov 1897 George F. Marchal; d 3 Dec 1917, bur Riverside Cem (G12/7/17)

MARCHAL, Mrs. Frank C. - and husband live at South C & First St., GC (G1/1/97); of GC; sister of John Myers of Versailles, OH (J10/6/16)

MARCHAL, Gene - operated the steamboat, Eureka, on the Mississinewa River ca 1893 (J8/20/15)

MARCHAL, George F. - works in J. Weinstein's Dry Goods Store; m 16 Nov 1897 Florence E. Harp, dt Mr. A. Harp of S. F St., GC (G11/19/97); within past yr has lost, by death, his wife, a dt and a son (G5/17/18); of GC; disappeared 3 Jul 1920 (J7/9/20); b Shelby Co., OH 23 Jan 1873; s Joseph N. Marchal; committed suicide, found in Mississinewa River; bur Riverside Cem (J7/16/20)

MARCHAL, Mrs. Margaret - mother of Mrs. Harry Beers (J8/8/19)

MARCHAL, Nellie - of GC is given party for her birthday last Mon (J9/3/15)

MARCHAL, Verne Franklin - age 15; s George Marchal; d 16 May 1918, bur GC Cem (G5/17/18; G5/24/18)

MARCHAL, Walter - age 18; s M/M F.B.Marchal, f of GC; d of flu in WV Oct 1918 (G10/18/18)

MARCHAL, William - of Gary; s M/M F.C. Marchal of GC (G12/28/17)

MARINE, Alfred - of Marion; brother of Mrs. W.E. Mason (J4/18/19)

MARINE, Charles O. - files for divorce from Carrie L. Marine (G8/26/98)

MARINE, Cora - dt Mrs. Josie Marine of College Hill area (J8/24/17)

MARINE, Daniel - m Mary E. __ (d 4 Sep 1917) (G9/7/17)

MARINE, Glettis A. (LYGHTLE) - b Grant Co. 6 Jan 1895; dt Jacob H. and Mary C. Lyghtle; m 30 Jun 1914 Virgil J. Marine; mbr Marion First Baptist Ch.; d 9 May 1920, bur Jefferson Cem (J5/14/20)

MARINE, Harve - of Hartford City; brother of Mrs. W.E. Mason (J4/18/19)

MARINE, Jack - of Lancaster, OH (J4/18/19); f of GC; m; brother of Mrs. Wm. E. Mason; d last wk, bur Riverside Cem (J12/5/19)

MARINE, Mrs. Jack - dt William VanArsdel of Jefferson Twp; of Jnsbr (G5/27/98)

MARINE, Jesse - 17 Oct 1898, divorced Millie Marine (G10/21/98)

MARINE, Josie - dt Mrs. Rebecca Forehand of College Hill (J1/28/16)

MARINE, Mary E. - age 71; m Daniel Marine; d 4 Sep 1917, bur Jefferson Cem (G9/7/17)

MARINE, Nathan 'Nate' - is very sick (J6/1/89)

MARINE, Rebecca Jane (NELSON) - is ill at home of dt, Mrs. W.E. Mason (G3/1/18); b OH 5 Apr 1844; dt William and Rebecca Nelson; husband d ca 1889; sister of Henderson Nelson; mbr Bethel M.E. Ch. E of GC; d 8 Jul 1918, bur GC Cem (G7/12/18)

MARING, Capt. J.M. - Citizen's Bank of Jnsbr stockholder (G12/16/98)

MARION COURTHOUSE - cave-in at SW corner of block revealed location of a town well; O.M. Middleton, age 87, says he helped dig a well at each corner of the Square at about the time of the CW (J5/16/19)

MARION MONTHLY MEETING OF FRIENDS - Rev. C.E. Hiatt, pastor (J4/13/17); Cornelia Collins is a mbr (G11/23/17)

MARION NORMAL COLLEGE/MARION COLLEGE - will have Law Dept. headed by Dean G.A. Henry this Sep (G7/9/97); Wesleyan Methodists take over in fall of 1920, will close their Theological Seminary at Fairmount where it has operated since ca 1906 (J7/18/19); Marion Coll dedicated 13 Jun 1920 (J6/18/20); repairs cost $21,000 (J7/30/20)

MARION SECOND MM OF FRIENDS/SOUTH MARION MM OF FRIENDS - Rev. DeWitt Foster is pastor (J4/13/17)

MARKER, Mrs. John - of Ligonier; mother of Mrs. Elizabeth Wright of Jnsbr (J3/26/15)

MARKS, __ - of Bruce & Marks Manufacturing Co./Bruce & Marks Edge Tool Works, GC; d 1894 (G1/1/97; G6/18/97)

MARKS, Mrs. Eliza - of Jnsbr; age 97; oldest person in Grant Co. in Aug 1910 (J8/20/20)

MARKS, Lizzie - grad, Jnsbr HS 1897 (G5/7/97)

MARLEY, Elva - mbr Jefferson WCTU (G11/12/20)

MARLEY, James - age 83; of Fairmount; d 30 Aug 1920, bur Park Cem (J9/10/20)

MARSHALL, __ - s M/M Frank Marshall of 1st St., GC; b 26 Jul 1897 (G7/30/97)

MARSHALL, Hazel - mbr GC Christian Ch. (J10/6/16)

MARSHALL, Jack - mbr Jnsbr MM (J10/8/15)

MARSHALL, Lula (TINCHER) - mbr Jnsbr WCTU (J4/16/15)

MARTIN, Mrs. Edwin L. - f of GC; 24 Oct 1917 d at her Lagro home (G10/26/17)

MARTIN, Mrs. Gail - of GC; dt Mrs. Margaret E. Hillman (dec) (J10/22/15)

MARTIN, John A. - GC tailor on Main St. near First St. (G9/22/93); f tailor; 7 Jun 1898 divorced by wife (G6/10/98)

MARTIN, Mary Ann - b Miami Co. 21 Nov 1891; m William Martin 27 Sep 1913; d 29 Nov 1918, bur GC (G12/6/18)

MARTIN, Noah - mbr GC Baptist Ch. (G1/14/98)

MARTIN, Mrs. Noah - 22 Apr 1898, 34th birthday (G4/29/98)

MARTIN, Ralph - s Mrs. E.L. Martin (dec) (G10/26/17)

MARTIN, Robert - officer, GC K OF P Lodge (G7/14/11); s Mrs. E.L. Martin (dec) (G10/26/17)

MARTIN, Stella - dt John and Elizabeth Martin; John beat Stella while in a drunken rage; Elizabeth files for divorce (G4/29/98)

MARTIN, Theron Harry - b GC 23 Aug 1905; s Mrs. Henry Holtzman; grandson Edwin L. Martin of Lagro; d of flu 22 Nov 1918, bur Lagro Cem (G11/29/18)

MASON, Alva - of SE of GC; a party of 40 friends celebrated his 15th birthday 31 Jan 1897 (G2/5/97)

MASON, Catherine - age 75; of Marion; widow of Thomas J. Mason; d 28 Oct 1919 (J10/31/19)

MASON, Charles - age 77; m 2nd in Oct 1916 Sarah J. (age 75); lived in Jnsbr; divorced Sarah J. recently (J3/30/17)

MASON, Charles E. - b Grant Co. 11 May 1897; GC HS grad 1915 (J5/21/15); s M/M W.E. Mason (G1/5/17; J1/5/17); att Purdue Univ 1917-18 (G11/23/17); m 3 Apr 1920 Bessie Ellen Trice, dt M/M John Trice of near Summitville (J4/9/20)

MASON, Chester C. - b 30 Sep 1895; grad, GC HS 1915 (J5/21/15); s M/M W.E. Mason; m Hattie Mae Osborn 15 Sep 1917 (G9/21/17)

MASON, Miss Della - of GC; intends to go to Klondyke gold fields (G8/20/97)

MASON, Ernest J. - US Army cadet in advanced flying sch in IL (G1/18/18)

MASON, Ethel - and Hal J. Larrabee gave a recital (J3/19/15); grad, GC HS 1912; Certificate, Muncie Normal 1913; engaged to Hal J. Larrabee (J4/2/15); m Sun (J6/18/15)

MASON, Hattie Mae (OSBORN) - m Chester C. Mason 15 Sep 1917 (G9/21/17); att Osborn Reunion in Anderson (J8/8/19); moved into her new country home (G11/12/20)

MASON, William E. - of SE of GC; and wife were given party last Sun on 11th wedding anniv (G7/2/97); mbr/Elder, GC Christian Ch. (J1/14/16;J10/6/16); preparing to open sugar camp on his farm, has 100-150 maple trees that haven't been tapped for 9 yrs (G3/9/17; J3/9/17); is East Mill Twp Chairman of 5th Liberty Loan Drive (J4/11/19)

MASON, Mrs. William E. - dt Mrs. Rebecca Jane (NELSON) Marine; injured in an auto accident (G3/1/18); sister of Mrs. Frank Tribby, Mrs. Joe Anson of Huntington, Mrs. Dan Grosscup of Mt. Vernon, OH; Mrs. I.J. Rich of Hartford City, Mrs. Mary Gilson of Marion, Jack Marine of Lancaster, OH; Harve Marine of Hartford City, and Alfred Marine of Marion (J4/18/19)

MASSEY, Ada - mbr Jnsbr M.P. Ch. (J10/22/15)

MASSEY, Emil - att Tri-State Coll (J10/1/15); s M/M Elmer E. Massey of Jnsbr; recent Tri-State Coll grad (J8/24/17)

MASSEY, James - mbr Jnsbr MM (J10/6/16)

MASSEY, Pauline - mbr Jnsbr M.P. SS (J6/29/17); dt M/M Elmer E. Massey of Jnsbr (G7/20/17)

MATHIAS, Mary E. - age 64; m John Mathias; d in Van Buren 17 Apr 1917, bur Union Chapel Cem (G4/20/17)

MATTHIAS, Samuel - GC glass blower at Thompson Glass Factory; was found by his wife raping their 9-yr old dt, Ethel, in AM; his wife notified authorities, he was arrested at work, taken to Marion, sentenced to Michigan City State Prison, and sent to prison by 2:00 PM that same day (G4/9/97)

MAY, __ (MacDONALD) - dt M/M C.L. Macdonald; m Roy May (G10/5/17)

MAY, Miss Cleo - mbr GC Baptist Ch. (J7/23/15); with mother, Mrs. Jesse May, escaped injury when their buggy overturned on Deer Creek hill recently (J10/29/15)

MAY, Lester - s M/M Roy May; living in IL (G10/5/17)

MAY, Roy - resigned after 5 yrs as Supt. of Macdonald Soap and Fertilizer Co. in N. Jnsbr; moves with his wife to Alton, IL where he purchased a fertilizer factory (J10/6/16); has dismantled his IL fertilizer factory and shipped it to Jnsbr; has taken a RR job in PA (G10/5/17)

MAYBERRY, Guy - returned to GC to live (G2/11/98); Capt. of new GC Volunteer Military Co. (G5/27/98); m 19 Sep 1898 Mrs. Maude DeHart of Ridgeville (G9/30/98)

MAYBERRY, Mrs. Guy - age 19; dt Mrs. George W. Ford(e) of Avon, OH; m for 1 year; lived in GC; d 7 May 1897 (G5/14/97)

MEADOWS, A.W. - mbr Jnsbr Masons (G12/24/97)

MEARING, Harold - age 4; s M/M John Mearing f of GC; grandson M/M Charles Mearing of GC; accidently killed 31 Jul 1916, bur GC Cem (J8/4/16)

MEEK, Mrs. Dianna R. (POOL) - b 25 Dec 1839; lives in Mill Twp (J8/1/19)

MEEK, Frank - of Jnsbr; completes a course in telegraphy, the "art of jerking lightning" (G8/30/97)

MEEK, Herman - of Jnsbr; 17 Apr 1897 arrested for stealing $10.00 from George Brumley's Barbershop (G4/23/97); is paroled from Jeffersonville State Reformatory (G8/12/98)

MEEK, Dr. John A. - ca 1870 owned 80 acres E of First St. in Harrisburg (J4/13/17); age 77; recently trampled and injured by his Jersey cow (G6/18/97)

MEEK, Milburn - s Mrs. W.C. Jones of Marion; in US Navy, 1st Jnsbr man to enlist after declaration of war (G4/13/17)

MEEK, William - of Jnsbr; attempted suicide in Marion prostitute's house recently (G2/12/97)

MEEKINS, __ - dt M/M George Meekins; b 6 Jul 1897 (G7/9/97)

MEEKINS, George - and Joe Brown bought Jnsbr saloon from Charles Campbell (G11/26/97)

MEEKINS, Harry - mbr GC K of P Lodge (G7/23/97)

MENDENHALL, Otway 'Otto' - Mill Twp sch pupil; passed exam for teaching license (G5/14/97); graduated in Mill Twp Commencement held in Deer Creek Friends MH (G6/1/97)

MENGES, Rev. Melvin - becomes GC Christian pastor Nov 1st (J10/6/16); leaves GC Christian Ch. pastorate (J3/9/17)

MEREDITH, Franklin - retired Friends Minister; has moved to Jnsbr (J9/29/16)

MEREDITH, Fred C. - 3rd grader, Zeek Sch 1915-16 (J5/5/16); 1916-17 Zeek Sch student (J3/30/17); Mill Twp 1920 8th grade grad (J5/21/20)

METCALF, __ - of Bandy & Metcalf, Props. of Park Meat Market on W side of First St. between North D & E St., GC (G9/22/93)

METCALF, Robert - is brother of Mrs. Ace Highley of W. Jnsbr (J9/3/15)

MIDDLETON, O.M. - age 87; helped dig a well at each corner of the Grant Co. Courthouse square at about the time of the CW (J5/16/19)

MILHOLLAND, Catherine - dt M/M Clarence Milholland (J7/9/15)

MILHOLLAND, Clarence - and sister Etta are children of Mrs. Katherine Milholland (J10/22/15)

MILHOLLAND, Mrs. Katherine - mother of Mrs. Jim Jones of Radley (J10/6/16)

MILL TWP - Trustee Hubert O.P. Cline has office in Jnsbr Bank Bldg (G1/1/97); Assessor is J.E. Ward (G5/20/98)

MILL TWP SCHOOLS - students that passed exams for teaching licenses include Ina and Grace Coggeshall, Emma Gulick, George and Frank Carter, Charles Woodruff, Otto Mendenhall (G5/14/97); 1897 Commencement held in Deer Creek Friends MH; grads include George E. and Frank Carter, Otway Mendenhall, Ina and Edna Grace Coggeshall, Emma Gulick, Charles Mendenhall (G6/1/97); four 8th grade students who passed exams for County Diplomas are Bessie Molton and Carl Jay of Dist. 3, Lucy Allen of Dist. 4, Lillie Wise of Dist. 6 (G4/29/98); other 8th grade 1898 grads are May Kierstead and F. Bennett Knight (G5/13/98); 10 Jun 1898, 8th grade commencement was held in North Grove Friends MH; Bessie Molton of Dist. 3 had best essay (G6/17/98); begins 13 Sep 1915 (J9/10/15); began 2 Sep 1918 (G9/6/18); all county schs closed due to flu (G10/11/18), schs closed until 28 Oct 1918 (G10/25/18); county schs closed again due to flu (G11/29/18); schs re-opened 9 Dec 1918 (G12/13/18)

MILL TOWNSHIP SCHOOL Dist. No. 1, CANDY SCHOOL - district originally went from river E to Twp Line and was 2 mi. wide N to S; first sch bldg. was of logs and was at W end of Walnut Creek Cem, prior to 1855 it burned; 1855 a frame sch was built on SW corner of the Candy farm and thus was known as Candy Sch; in this sch, Maggie Boles held summer 1855 term; Mahala Moreland held summer 1856 term; Josiah

Boles taught 1855-57, the 1st two winter terms; next tchr was Thomas Knight followed by Amanda Ink for 2 terms; then Eli Wright before CW, David Bowers was next but he left for army before his term ended (J6/1/17); Candy Sch bldg often used for church services: early Candy Sch preachers were Reuben Kidner, New Light; Rev. Depo, New Light; Winston Jones, New Light; Rev. Rammels, Methodist; and Samuel Sawyer, Presbyterian (J6/8/17); U.S. Candy, Mary Smith, Albert Candy, Arminta Eviston, and Elwood Ellis all taught their 1st terms as tchrs in this sch (J6/1/17); 1897-99 tchr is Miss Alice Sheffield (G9/3/97; G8/19/98); Miss Jeanette Jones is 1919-20 tchr (J8/29/19)

MILL TOWNSHIP SCHOOL Dist. No. 2, NORTH JONESBORO SCH/"FROG COLLEGE" - is 1 mi. W of N. Jnsbr; was a frame built while George Fankboner was Trustee (J6/1/17); built 0.5 mi. W of present North Jnsbr Sch (G6/1/17); A.N. Wimpy is 1898-99 tchr (G8/19/98); Dec 1910, students Earl Pearson and Goldie Shaw won 3rd and 2nd places in the Twp Spelling Contest (J12/31/20); E.W. Tucker and Miss Merle Conelley are 1919-20 tchrs (J8/29/19)

MILL TWP SCH Dist. No. 3, DEER CREEK SCHOOL - Bessie Molton and Carl S. Jay passed exam for County 8th Grade Diplomas (G4/29/98); Bessie Molton had best essay at 10 Jun 1898 commencement (G6/17/98); C.R. Jones is 1898-99 tchr (G8/19/98); new sch will be built to replace the old sch (G8/19/98); closed Fri for summer (J5/7/15); Miss Lucille Shugart is 1919-20 tchr (J8/29/19)

MILL TWP SCH Dist. No. 4, NORTH GROVE SCHOOL - was frame built while George Fankboner was Trustee (J6/1/17); Lucy Allen passed Co. 8th Grade Diploma exam (G4/29/98); Gulie Harvey, 1898-99 tchr (G8/19/98); sch starts 2 Sep 1918, Mrs. Murvel Garner, 1918-19 tchr (G9/6/18); Murvel Garner took over teaching for his wife (G12/13/18); has been closed for past wk due to flu (J1/10/19); Murvel Garner will be 1919-20 tchr (J8/29/19)

MILL TWP SCH Dist. No. 5, ZEEK SCHOOL- was frame built while George Fankboner was Trustee (J6/1/17); 2 mi. SE of

GC; Miss Alice Sheffield, tchr 1897-98 (G12/10/97); Robert Clayborn will build new brick sch for $782 (G6/17/98); E.E. Heal, 1898-99 tchr (G8/19/98); lets out 23 Apr 1915 (J4/2/15); Maude Smith 1915-16 tchr; last day of sch is 2 May 1916 (J5/5/16); 1916-17 Maude Smith, tchr; students include Edna Petty, Laura and Jason Corn, Charles Osborn, Fred Meredith, Marion Howell, Nolia Patterson (J3/30/17); sch year ends 27 Apr 1917 (G4/27/17), and 26 Apr 1918 (G4/19/18); Miss Ruth Jones is 1919-20 tchr (J8/29/19); will have box social 21 Nov 1919 (J11/21/19)

MILL TWP SCH Dist. No. 6, NORTH BETHEL SCHOOL/ WISE SCHOOL (located on NW corner of junction of Co. Roads 500 E & 600 S) - was frame built while George Fankboner was Trustee (J6/1/17); Lillie Wise passed Co. 8th Grade Diploma exam (G4/29/98); box supper Oct 20 with proceeds used to purchase organ for sch (J10/13/16); 2 mi E, 2 mi S of GC; 1920-21 tchr is Miss Merle Conelley; will have box social Nov 19th (G11/12/20); student Jessie Long won the Twp Spelling Contest (J12/31/20)

MILLER, __ - s M/M Jesse Miller; b recently (G1/15/97)

MILLER, A.J. - is on Jnsbr Town Board (G6/18/97)

MILLER, Cecil - s M/M William Miller of Fairmount; m 8 Jan 1918 Pearl A. Corn, dt M/M Esom Corn (G1/11/18)

MILLER, Donald - s M/M A. Miller of GC; is Franklin Coll student (J12/24/20)

MILLER, Dorothy - local 10-yr old (J4/2/15)

MILLER, Ervin - s Mrs. Frank L. Miller of Indianapolis; grandson Mrs. Ben King of GC (J2/20/20)

MILLER, Eva - m; mbr Jnsbr Rebekahs Lodge (J1/14/16)

MILLER, Mrs. F.C. - mbr Jnsbr MM (J10/6/16)

MILLER, Mrs. Frank L. - of Indianapolis; dt Mrs. Ben King of GC (J2/20/20)

MILLER, Mrs. Henry - mbr Jnsbr Rebekahs (J1/14/16)

MILLER, J.A. - has Livery Stable one-half block W of RR Depot in GC (G9/22/93)

MILLER, Mary A. - age 13; dt M/M Henry Miller; d Fri, bur Riverside Cem (J4/23/15)

MILLER, Nellie (McKEEVER) - of OH; f of Jnsbr; age 44; m 1st __ Meadows; m 2nd __ Miller; sister of Clarence and John McKeever of Jnsbr; d 30 Mar 1917, bur GC Cem (J4/6/17)

MILLER, Vern - mbr GC Tigers football team (J10/6/16)

MILLIKAN, Walter - b ca 1888; s M/M J.B. Millikan of near Fairmount; m; in US Army in Germany, d of disease (J3/14/19); did not d 17 Feb 1919 but is alive and well in Germany (J4/11/19)

MILLNER, Miss Maud - of Leesburg, OH; held revival at Jnsbr Friends MH with Rev. __ Hiatt (G10/29/97)

MILLS, Clarence - b near Veedersburg 14 Oct 1890; s Thomas J. Mills of Crawfordsville; m 30 Nov 1918 Edith Eakins of Jnsbr; brother of Edward L. Mills of GC; d of flu 21 Feb 1919, bur GC Cem (J2/28/19)

MILLS, Frank T. - b in Jnsbr; age 68; m; d at his Marion home last Sun (J2/6/20)

MILLS, Otto - s Jasper Mills of Canada; f of GC; now in Canadian army in France (G11/30/17)

MINNICK, Rev. __ - lived S of Co. Infirmary near the Ink sawmill in early 1850's; New Light/Christian preacher who sometimes preached at the Walnut Creek Log Ch.; he m Philip Long to Dianna Roush (J6/8/17)

MITCHELL, Newt - was engineer on first train in Grant County (J8/24/17)

MITTANK, Michael - b ca 1834; lived in Fairmount Twp; d 15 Feb 1920 (J2/20/20)

MOLTON, Bessie M. - Deer Creek Sch student, passed exam for a County Diploma (G4/29/98); 8th grade grad Mill Twp sch (G5/13/98); given award for best essay 10 Jun 1898 at Mill Twp Schs Commencement at North Grove MH (G6/17/98)

MONROE, Ida (SEXTON) - b Grant Co. 14 Jun 1870; dt Edmond and Mary Sexton; m 1st Lona Lucas ca 1889; m 2nd Claude Monroe of Upland 9 Aug 1900; d 11 Sep 1915 at home in GC, bur Cumberland Cem (J9/17/15)

MONTGOMERY, Miss Estella - of Jnsbr; granddt of William Schriber (J3/7/19)

MONTGOMERY, Irving - b 25 Oct 1872; mbr Jnsbr Presbyterian Ch.; d 4 Jul 1889 (J8/10/89)

MONTGOMERY, Velda - age 19; s M/M Samuel Montgomery of SE of GC; killed by lightning 26 Sep 1920, bur Howe Cem (J10/1/20)

MOODY, James T./F. - of Moody & Sons; opened new meat market in Commercial Hotel Bldg on Main St. W of 1st St. (G12/10/97); GC butcher; age 44; injured while crossing RR tracks (G1/7/98); injured foot is amputated (G1/14/98)

MOON, Nellie - mbr Jnsbr MM SS (J7/27/17)

MOON, Mrs. Rebecca - b 5 Jan 1819; of Fairmount; oldest woman in Grant County; d last wk at home of dt, Mrs. Sarah Allred (G9/20/18)

MOORE, Dr. Charles - of Fairmount; d 26 Apr 1897 (G4/30/97)

MOORE, Miss Della - mbr GC Christian Ch. (G2/12/97)

MOORE, Edward - local 10-yr old (J4/2/15)

MOORE, Eldon T. - age 40; lived S of Jnsbr; m; mbr Christian Ch.; d 5 Jan 1917, bur Anderson (G1/12/17)

MOORE, Mrs. Floyd - of Fowlerton; dt Mrs. __ Plyly of GC (G11/?/09)

MOORE, Howard - of Otisco; s Park Moore of W. Jnsbr (J7/23/15); recently d in Jeffersonville (J2/6/20)

MOORE, Miss Jennie - mbr GC Christian Ch. (G2/12/97)

MOORE, Mary E. (HALL) - dt Louis and Jane (Loop) Hall; d Dec 1911 (J11/26/15)

MOORE, Meredith - 4th grader, Zeek Sch 1915-16 (J5/5/16)

MOORE, Nina Ray - young dt of Mrs. Floyd Moore of Fowlerton (G11/?/09)

MOORE, Samuel - Attorney; office is on Main St., Jnsbr (J7/1/87)

MOORE, Sarah - f of GC; age 77; husband d ca 1908; d 26 Sep 1916, bur Jericho Cem near Winchester (J9/29/16)

MOORMAN, Will - mbr Jnsbr MM (J10/6/16)

MORELAND, Mahala - taught at Candy Sch summer 1856 (G6/1/17; J6/1/17)

MORGAN, A.D. - had grocery store in Harrisburg prior to 1892; he now operates a shoe repair shop on Third St., GC (J3/23/17); Elder, GC Christian Ch. (J1/14/16)

MORGAN, Anna - local 10-yr old (J4/2/15)

MORGAN, Burr O. - f GC Marshall (G1/15/97); age 48; s A.D. Morgan; wife d 3-4 yrs ago; d 20 Feb 1917, bur Walnut Creek Cem (G2/23/17)

MORGAN, Dan - GC Welsh person (G3/5/97)

MORGAN, David 'Dai' - officer, GC Odd Fellows (J7/9/15); mbr GC Baptist Ch. (J7/23/15); lives in GC (G2/9/17); "Dai" means "Dave" in Welsh; is Independant Candidate for GC Clerk (G10/26/17; G11/2/17)

MORGAN, Dwight - of GC; now in US Army (J6/29/17)

MORGAN, Everett - last evening m Annie Griffin in GC (G2/9/17)

MORGAN, Frank - s M/M A.D. Morgan; m; is moving to near Fowlerton (J4/25/19)

MORGAN, George - and brother John are sons of Mrs. Ross Morgan of GC (G11/12/20)

MORGAN, Jeanette - local 11-yr old (J4/2/15)

MORGAN, Joseph - GC Welsh person (G3/5/97)

MORGAN, Maggie - GC Welsh person (G3/5/97)

MORGAN, Olwin - mbr GC Baptist Ch. (J7/23/15); - see L. LUDLOW

MORGAN, Paul - of GC; now in US Army (J6/29/17)

MORGAN, Rees J. - of Mexico, IN; bought Jnsbr Grain Elevator and C&O Coal Yards from W.R. Brock (J6/13/19)

MORGAN, Richard - GC Welsh person (G3/5/97)

MORGAN, Mrs. Sam - mbr Welsh Union Congregational Ch., GC (G1/1/97)

MORGAN, William - s A.D. Morgan; m Lizzie; 8 Feb 1898 committed suicide by drinking carbolic acid; bur Walnut Creek Cem (G2/11/98)

MORRIS, George S. - of N. Jnsbr; burned badly when his home burned 22 Feb 1917; m (J3/2/17)

MORRIS, Jasper - and wife live near Kidner Bridge (G7/20/17)

MORRIS, Mrs. John C. - 1st husband, John Hayes, d 5 yr ago; she d Thur at home in GC, bur in Elwood (J5/28/15)

MORRIS, Luther - opened saloon in Fairmount 8 Mar 1897; 17 possums were eaten by patrons at the opening (G3/12/97)

MORRIS, Pina - m Jasper Morris; d 13 Jun 1920; bur Jefferson Cem (J6/18/20)

MORRIS, Rebecca J. - age 65; widow of A.N. Morris; d 24 Dec 1916, bur Jefferson Cem (J12/29/16)

MORRISH, John - East Bethel PM SS Supt. (J4/2/15); has new 5-passenger Overland auto (G4/20/17; J4/20/17)

MORRISH, W.H. - barn, shed and 85-ton silo burned 16 Sep 1920 on his farm SE of Jnsbr (J9/17/20)

MORROW, H.L. - mbr/officer GC Odd Fellows (J7/9/15)

MORROW, Joseph - and family were first residents of Harrisburg ca 1868 (J6/8/17)

MORROW, R.H. - mbr/officer GC Odd Fellows (J7/9/15)

MORROW, Russell - grad, GC HS 1910; att Marion Normal Coll fall 1910 (J9/24/20); of GC; brother of Frank Morrow of Ft. Wayne (J7/23/15)

MORROW, William A. - killed in GC RR yard 14 Dec 1910; widow is Minnie; father of Harry, Walter, Russell (J3/19/15)

"MORTON RIFLES" 34TH IND. INF. REGMT. - 36th annual reunion was held 10 Sep 1918 in Marion; 50 vets registered (G9/13/18)

MULL, Mrs. Kathryn - of Jnsbr; mother of Otis Mull of TN (G11/23/17)

MULLEN, Charles - clarinetist in GC Brass Band (G10/1/97)

MULLEN, Hildreth - local 10-yr old (J4/2/15)

MULLEN, Jehu - age 73; s Mrs. Achsah Mullen (age 97, prob oldest person now living in Grant Co.); wife d ca 1915; serv in CW; was watchman at Tinplate Factory; d 15 Nov 1917, bur GC Cem (G11/23/17)

MULLEN, Juanita - dt of Harry A. and Gertrude (THOMAS) Mullen; m Charles Griffin Makin of Fairmount 1 Aug 1915 (J8/6/15)

MULLEN, Lester - mbr GC Christian Ch. (G11/23/17)

MULLEN, Nelle - dt Jehu Mullen; GC HS grad; tchr in GC West Ward Sch (G11/23/17); - see T. HEAL

MURPHY, Albert - charged his step-brother, Elias Reel with assault; Reel was acquitted because it "was a family affair" (G8/6/97)

MURPHY, Blanche (BAIRD) - b Jnsbr ca 1890; dt M/M W.O. Baird, now of Gary; m Allen Ray Murphy; lived in Jnsbr; d last Fri, bur Riverside Cem (G11/5/20)

MURPHY, Min - owns a Jnsbr barbershop (J7/1/87)

MURRAY, Mrs. Charles - mbr '97 Club (G1/14/98)

MURRAY, Mrs. Walter - m; is very ill in home in Mississinewa Hotel (G7/16/97)

MYERS, Alex - traded 70-acre farm 2 mi SE of Jnsbr to Dr. Whitson for stock in Jnsbr Bank (G3/5/97)

MYERS, Pvt. Earl O. - brother of John Myers of Jnsbr and of James Myers of Detroit, MI; age 25; d in France 30 Nov 1918 of pneumonia (J12/27/18)

MYERS, George E. - Elder in GC Christian Ch. (J1/14/16)

MYERS, Miss Hazel - violinist with Marion Philharmonic Orchestra; sister of Mrs. Vera Harter (J4/16/15)

MYERS, Lige - of GC; s Mrs. Lucinda Myers (J1/16/20)

MYERS, Mrs. Lucinda - husband d ca 1902; lived in GC since ca 1904; age 68; d last Sat; bur Riverside Cem (J1/16/20)

MYERS, Mary Elizabeth - age 7; dt M/M Harry Myers of Jnsbr; d 1 May 1916, bur Marion IOOF Cem (J5/5/16)

MYERS, William D. - ex-Indiana Secretary of State; he and wife recently adopted Mabel Jenkins, youngest child of M/M Thomas Jenkins (both dec) of GC (G1/15/97)

MYERS, Zadock 'Doc' - of GC; age 25; s Lucinda Myers; m; d 28 Jan 1916, bur GC Cem (J2/4/16)

NEAL, Carl - att Earlham Coll 1914-15 (J7/9/15); s M/M Joseph R. Neal of Jnsbr; grad, Jnsbr HS 1909; grad, Marion Normal, grad, Earlham Coll 1916; won scholarship to Hartford Theological Seminary (J5/5/16); preached at Jnsbr Presbyterian Sun (G6/22/17); mbr Jnsbr MM SS (J7/27/17); will preach at Back Creek MH this Sun in the absence of pastor Mattie Cammack-Gibson (J8/3/17); grad, Hartford, CT Theological Seminary 1919; is sailing to India as missionary for 7 yrs; mbr Friends (J9/26/19); twin brother is Harl Neal of Warsaw, sister is Mary Neal of Jnsbr; serv under Congregational Church Mission Board, d in India of typhoid fever 4 Jun 1920 (J6/11/20)

NEAL, Charles E. - b Marion ca 1848; father of Albert Neal; m; d 26 Jan 1920 (J1/30/20)

NEAL, Cyrus - of Marion; Edgar Baldwin m Myra Rush at his residence last wk (J9/2/87)

NEAL, E.A. - manager of Independent Telephone System, Jnsbr (J3/4/04)

NEAL, Elam H. - Jnsbr's new Postmaster (G10/29/97); mbr Jnsbr K of P Lodge (G10/7/98)

NEAL, George - att DePauw Univ 1910-12 (J9/24/20)

NEAL, Gladys - grad, Jnsbr HS 1910 (J5/7/20); mbr Jnsbr MM Young People's group (J8/27/20); 1913-14 Earlham Coll student (J6/15/17)

NEAL, Harl - s M/M Joseph Neal of Jnsbr; lives with wife in Warsaw (J10/29/15)

NEAL, Luna (EVISTON) - b May 1865; dt George W. and Sarah A. (Craw) Eviston; m Elam H. Neal; d 19 Apr 1909 (J11/19/20)

NEAL, Mary Jeanette (SHUGART) - of Jnsbr; dt William Shugart (J1/21/16)

NEELY, Icile - local 11-yr old (J4/2/15)

NEELEY, Lester - s M/M P.O. Neeley of GC (J1/21/16)

NEILL, George - brother of J.S. Neill; and wife are Jnsbr Presbyterian Ch. mbrs; worked in Jnsbr Flour Mill 10 yrs; moving to a farm near Bloomington (J10/22/15)

NEILL, J.S. - came to Jnsbr in 1902; senior mbr of Neill & Van Valer, owners/operators of Jnsbr Flour Mill; has sold out his interest, bought large farm near Bloomington; mbr Jnsbr M.E. Ch.; moves his family to near Bloomington (J10/22/15)

NEILL, Mrs. J.S. - mbr Jnsbr WCTU (J4/16/15); mbr Jnsbr M.E. Ch. (J10/22/15)

NELSON, Anna - age 19; wife of Dallas Nelson of E of GC, d of typhoid 24 Oct 1898, funeral at Jnsbr Adventist Ch. (G10/28/98)

NELSON, Ardene Elizabeth (KING) - age 31; dt Mrs. Elizabeth King; m Harley Nelson; d 18 Apr 1916, bur GC IOOF Cem (J4/21/16)

NELSON, Charlotte (COLEMAN) - dt Daniel and Mary Ann Coleman (J3/26/15); m Henderson Nelson 30 Mar 1865; 60th wedding anniv in GC (J4/2/15); b Grant Co. 6 Jul 1844; mbr GC M.E. Ch.; d 28 Apr 1916 in GC (J5/5/16)

NELSON, Clarence E. - b 6 Dec 1897 in N. Jnsbr; grad, GC HS 1915 (J5/21/15); Johnson Sch tchr (G11/23/17)

NELSON, E.O. - GC Chief of Police (J10/6/16)

NELSON, Elmer - s Jesse Nelson of GC (J10/29/15)

NELSON, Eugene - age 54; of GC; s Jesse Nelson; d 28 Nov 1919, bur NE of GC (J12/5/19)

NELSON, Glen H.- grad, Jnsbr HS 1918 (G5/10/18)

NELSON, Henderson - 53rd birthday 22 Mar 1897 (G3/26/97); m Charlotte Coleman 30 Mar 1865, 60th wedding anniv in GC (J4/2/15)

NELSON, Jesse W. - owns a farm and considerable GC property; his son, Elmer tried in court to prove him incompetent because of his age, court denied Elmer's petition (J10/29/15); Mill Twp octogenarian (J8/27/20)

NELSON, Johnson - b Grant Co. 5 Oct 1847; s William and Rebecca Nelson; brother of Henderson Nelson of GC; m 4 Jul 1868 to Sarah Johnson (dec 13 Feb 1891); 1878-90 he operated a sawmill and hoop factory in Harrisburg; later went west; d in Dakota 6 Mar 1919 (J3/21/19)

NELSON, Mary Jane (BENNINGTON) - b Adams Co., OH 12 Oct 1844; m ca 1868 Joel R. Nelson (dec); d 28 Jul 1918, bur Howe Cem (G8/2/18)

NELSON, Merle - dt Mrs. S.W. Nelson of GC (G7/13/17)

NELSON, Nettie - of GC; age 26; dt Sylvester Nelson; has license to m Ora. L. Jones of GC (G12/27/18)

NELSON, S.W. - opens new Meat Market on North 1st St. between D & E Streets, GC (G2/5/97)

NELSON, Mrs. Sarah H. (ENTSMINGER) - b 30 Nov 1851 E of GC; dt John Entsminger (G3/4/17); raised on farm just S of Co. Infirmary (J5/4/17); was Uriah S. Candy schoolmate at Candy Sch prior to CW (J6/1/17); still living (J6/8/17)

NELSON, Stephen - age 18; lives E of GC; injured by broken pitchfork while working in hay field (G7/14/11)

NELSON, Ves - age 55; s Jesse Nelson; farmer N of GC; widower; d 10 Sep 1918, bur Marion Cem (G9/13/18)

NELSON, Will - b Grant Co., lived in Grant Co. and in Jnsbr; recently sent to penitentary for 2 yrs for robbing an old soldier (G1/8/97)

NESBITT, Cyrus - age 80; d 20 Jan 1918, bur Thrailkill Cem (G1/25/18)

NESBITT, Lucille - b 8 mi. E of Marion 19 Oct 1895; lives with grandfather John L. Thompson; grad, GC HS 1915 (J5/21/15)

NEWBY, Arthur - s Mrs. Laura Newby (J1/7/16); purchased new Ford car (J10/24/19)

NEWBY, Harmon J. - s Mrs. Laura Newby; m (J1/7/16); of 5 mi. E of Jnsbr; struck by lightning while feeding livestock, he was burned and rendered unconcious for several hours but is now recovering (J6/6/19)

NEWBY, Mrs. Laura - is mother of Arthur and Harmon J. (J1/7/16)

NEWHOUSE, James Thomas - of Green Twp; age 68; m; d 21 Oct 1916, bur Knox Chapel (J10/27/16)

NEWSOM, Mary Lucas - dt M/M Frank Newsom; was given party for 13th birthday last Tue (J4/30/20)

NEWSOME, Paul G. - Mill Twp 1920 8th grade grad (J5/21/20)

NICHOLS, John - from Wales; lives in GC (G1/14/98)

NICHOLSON, Anna C. - lived in GC ca 1910; moved to Marion (J10/1/15); age 37; m Harry Nicholson; d 25 Sep 1915; bur GC Cem (J10/1/15)

NICHOLSON, Earl - and his brother, Percy are mbrs Jnsbr Odd Fellows (J1/14/16)

NICODEMUS, Horace Milton - s Isaac Nicodemus; m 24 Jan 1897 Amanda L. Gosnell of Marion; live in Jnsbr (G1/29/97)

NICODEMUS, Isaac - lives in Jnsbr; serv 57th Ind. Vol. Inf. during CW (J10/8/15); mbr Jnsbr GAR (J4/2/20)

NOBLE, Margaret Alice - b Pittsburg, PA; age 37; m L.A. Noble; d 10 Mar 1917, bur GC Cem (G3/16/17)

NOBLE, Ralph - of GC; now in US Army; s Mr. Allie Noble of GC (J6/29/17; G12/28/17)

NORDYKE, Lora - dt Mrs. Rhoda Nordyke (dec) (G12/7/17)

NORDYKE, Mrs. Rhoda - of Wabash; f of GC; widow for less than a yr; d 5 Dec 1917 (G12/7/17)

NORRIS, Lucille - mbr Jnsbr M.P. SS (J6/29/17)

NORTH GROVE PM OF FRIENDS (BCMM of Friends) - Rev. Elwood O. Ellis preaches Sun (G5/20/98); Mill Twp Schs 8th grade commencement held in MH 10 Jun 1898, best essay is by Bessie Molton of Deer Creek Sch (G6/17/98); Rev. David Harris of Deer Creek preached Sun (J3/16/17); SS mbrs include M/M Leonard Little, Ethel and Gordon Howell, Irene Jett, Alice and Palmer Little, Goldie Pattison, Verlou Allen (J9/7/17); homecoming will be Sun Jul 14 (G7/12/18); after 50 yrs of existence, the Meeting is laid down due to easy travel to other churches by auto (J9/24/20)

NORTON, Albion - b Suffolk, England in 1830; s M/M James Norton; 1848 came to Grant Co. with parents, settled across road from Thomas Newby farm S of Jnsbr; m 1860 Elizabeth Weeks; 13 Sep 1918, baptised in Mississinewa River by Rev. A.S. Bash, joined GC Christian Ch.; d 9 Jan 1919, bur GC Cem (J1/17/19)

NORTON, Alfred - of GC; age 62; m; d 13 Apr 1917, bur Howe Chapel Cem (G4/20/17)

NORTON, Ben - of Lake Galatia area; has new Ford touring car (G12/7/17)

NORTON, Fred - age 94; b England; serv in CW; d 12 Apr 1916, bur GC IOOF Cem (J4/21/16)

NORTON, George - of Jnsbr; d last Wed (J1/?/87)

NORTON, Ralph - s Mrs. Phoebe Norton; brother of Mrs. Al Rothinghouse (G1/1/97)

NOTTINGHAM, Hannah - aunt of Mrs. Leslie Lemon; d at home near Fowlerton (J9/24/15)

NOTTINGHAM, Mrs. Mary - b ca 1839; of Fowlerton; d 6 Mar 1920 (J3/12/20)

NOTTINGHAM, Mrs. Sarah J.- age 78; came to Jnsbr ca 1868; lived on N. Water St.; mbr Jnsbr M.E. Ch.; d 17 Sep 1898, bur IOOF Cem (G9/23/98)

O'BRIEN, Elsie - dt Mrs. James O'Brien of GC (G7/13/17)

O'BRYANT, H.W. - is GC jeweler (G7/30/97)

OCKERMAN, James A. - b Wyandotte Co., OH 13 Feb 1854; m ca 1875 Anna Anderson; father of Garnet Ockerman of Jnsbr; d 1 May 1919; bur Riverside Cem (J5/9/19)

ODER, Mrs. Elizabeth - age 77; d 5 Feb 1898, bur Walnut Creek Cem (G2/11/98)

OLDS, Mrs. Hattie - of GC; dt Mrs. Sarah Griffin of Marion (G11/12/20)

OLINGER, __ - b Sullivan Co. 6 Oct 1852; m 30 May 1871 Philip Olinger (d 22 Feb 1916); mbr Christian Ch.; d 7 Mar 1920, bur NE of GC (J3/12/20)

OLIVER, __ and __ - infant twins b last wk, d same day; dts M/M Jesse Oliver; bur Walnut Creek Cem (J2/20/20)

OLIVER, C.H. - of E of GC; s Wemburn Oliver; came here with parents in 1861 from Kenton Co., OH; to Muncie on the RR then to Jnsbr on the old board stage road; in 1862 they moved to farm where he lives; W.M. Price had farm across road from them (G6/1/17; J6/1/17)

OLIVER, Carl 'Peggy' - lost right leg and 3 toes on left foot 1 yr ago in GC RR accident; is now telegrapher in GC Penn. RR Office (G2/19/97); arrested for selling booze to 6 boys (J3/26/15)

OLIVER, Mrs. Ed - of E of GC; d Jan 1905 (J1/16/20)

OLIVER, Harvey - mbr GC Christian Ch. (J12/24/20)

OLIVER, Hartson - 1871 had Harrisburg barrel shop (J4/6/17)

OLIVER, Henderson - s Hartson Oliver (J4/6/17); has his Law Office in Jnsbr, lives in Marion (G1/8/97)

OLIVER, Mrs. Henderson - lives in Jnsbr (G2/11/98)

OLIVER, Jerry - s Hartson Oliver (J4/6/17); d at his home in Bluffton last wk (G12/16/98)

OLIVER, John - of Marion; s Wemburn Oliver (J6/1/17)

OLIVER, Robert - killed on RR in early Harrisburg (J4/20/17; J6/8/17)

OLIVER, William - s Hartson Oliver (J4/6/17); had a store in Harrisburg in fall of 1890 (J3/30/17)

O'NEAL, Rebecca - of Marion; age 93; widow; d 16 Oct 1916, bur in MI (J10/20/16)

O'NEAL, Susan - of Somerset; age 87; widow of Dr. L. O'Neal; d, bur LaFontaine Cem (J9/1/16)

OREN, Elihu J. - age 81; lived 3.5 mi. N of Upland; m; d 17 Oct 1916 (J10/20/16)

OSAGE FARM - [name applied in 1967 to the Lindley and Elsie Kirkpatrick farm of 110 acres located on N side of Co. Rd. 800 S and on W side of Co. Rd. 350 E; ca 1980 the 14.5 acres owned 1919-41 by James and Samantha Kirkpatrick was repurchased and added to Osage Farm as Osage Farm NW, it is located on the S side of Wheeling/Muncie Pike and on E side of Co. Rd. 275 E] - Osage Farm NW was f known as the Mrs. E.T. Moore farm; James Kirkpatrick has purchased it and has moved into the main house on Muncie Pike at the NE corner of the farm (J5/9/19)

OSBORN, Charles - 3rd grader at Zeek Sch 1915-16 (J5/5/16); 1916-17 Zeek Sch student (J3/30/17)

OSBORN, Clarice - dt M/M Otis Osborn (G6/22/17)

OSBORN, Ed - lives S of Jnsbr; was given party for 38th birthday; relatives att were James and Samantha Kirkpatrick, Lindley and Elsie Kirkpatrick with son, Basil (J7/11/19)

OSBORN, George A. - 1875-76 Harrisburg Sch tchr, following William Owens and preceding Uriah S. Candy (J6/1/17)

OSBORN, Merl - s M/M Otis Osborn (G6/22/17)

OSBORN, Mrs. Otis - dt M/M Sam Hammond of GC (G6/22/17)

OSBORNE, Miss Helen E. - Jnsbr HS Principal/tchr (G3/12/97); ex-Principal of Jnsbr HS; leaves for her home in MI (G5/7/97)

OVERMAN, Allen J. - b near Marion IOOF Cem/Mississinewa Friends MH 18 Feb 1853; m; father of Mrs. Don Dailey of Jnsbr; mbr Friends; d 26 Aug 1919 (J8/29/19)

OVERMAN, Amos - lives 2 mi. E of GC (G4/2/97); a schoolmate of Uriah S. Candy ca 1860; still living (J6/8/17)

OVERMAN, Elisha - a schoolmate of Uriah S. Candy ca 1860; still living (J6/8/17)

OVERMAN, Frances Rebecca (CANDY) - b Wayne Co. 8 Jan 1850; dt Jacob and Hannah Candy; moved to Mill Twp site of GC in 1853; m 1st 4 Mar 1869 John Wesley Kidner (d 13 Mar 1890); m 2nd 2 Apr 1900 James Overman (d 9 Nov 1910), a farmer living near Jnsbr; mbr Jnsbr Presbyterian Ch.; d 20 Aug 1919, bur GC Cem (J6/8/17; J8/22/19)

OVERMAN, Mary J. - age 84; of Marion; d 16 Dec 1919 (J12/19/19)

OVERMAN, Roy - s Elisha Overman of GC; now in US Army; m 27 Dec 1918 Malinda N. Brewer, dt M/M Lindsey Brewer of GC (J1/3/19)

OVERMAN, Thomas - age 84; 27 Mar 1898 d in Marion (G4/1/98)

OWEN, R.C. - mbr/officer in GC Odd Fellows (J7/9/15)

177

OWENS, Seigle Charles - of Fowlerton; s M/M Henry Owens; d 25 Apr 1917, bur East Bethel Cem (G4/27/17)

OWENS, William 'Billy' - first Harrisburg Sch tchr 1874, according to U.S. Candy (G4/13/17; J6/1/17)

OWINGS, Nina - 1915 8th grade Mill Twp grad (J6/18/15)

PACE, John - local 12-yr old (J4/2/15)

PACE, M/M William - are Mill Twp octogenarians (J8/1/19)

PARKER, Myron - age 28; s M/M Charles T. Parker of Fairmount; d of TB 3 Aug 1919 (J8/8/19)

PARKER, William - fined last Fri by GC Mayor Brashear for public intoxication (G1/1/97)

PARKS, __ (ATKINSON) - of near Kidner Bridge; sister of Lewis Atkinson; m Chester Parks (J3/30/17)

PARKS, C.A. - of College Hill area; d of flu last Thur; bur Atkinson Cem (J12/20/18)

PARKS, Miss Echo - of Jefferson area, is Purdue Univ student (J1/7/16); 1916-17 Farmington Sch tchr (J4/6/17)

PARKS, Lee - ca age 30; s Eli Parks; horse threw him into baler, d 11 Nov 1898 at his home 3 mi S of Jnsbr (G11/18/98)

PARKS, Pearl E. - writes to his mother 31 Jul 1917 from Fort Adams, Newport, RI; transferred from Fort Moultrie to Fort Adams last wk on way to France; is getting series of 3 typhoid shots "remember the time I took an over-dose of kerosene? Well, I feel just like that" (J8/10/17); was in Coast Artillery for 3 yrs (J8/17/17); in Battery H, 8th Regmt. in France, can hear big guns firing day and night, sees scores of aeroplanes, his steel helmet weighs 3.5 lbs, British gas mask is better than French mask (G3/22/18); is in Battery H, 53rd Artillery, has seen hard fighting (G6/14/18); in letter to his Uncle James H. Kirkpatrick, he relates that in France 14 Dec 1918, enroute home, he was attacked by a soldier while out walking; he is in hospital with scalp cut (J2/7/19); back from 22 mons serv in France, scheduled to sail from Presidio, CA to the Philippines 15 Sep (J9/19/19); in letter to his mother, Ida (MASON) Stonebraker: he is stationed at Fort Mills, Corregidor, Philippine Is.; has seen Negritos who hunt with bow and arrows, a volcano crater, a snake over 20 ft. long (J5/7/20)

PARKS, Rev. Silas - a Christian/New Light minister; preached at Walnut Creek Log Ch. sometimes; lived E on Farmington Road just across Twp Line; d ca 1855; his funeral procession in two-horse wagons and horseback riders, his body was hauled in a two-horse wagon and was lowered into the grave on harness lines (J6/8/17)

PARSON, Charles A. - of West Marion; age 43; m; killed on RR by train (G3/23/17)

PARSONS, Mrs. Glenn - dt John Brown (G2/8/18)

PARSONS, Harper Franklin - b NC 19 May 1843; m 1st 1868 Nancy Pettigrew; m 2nd 1907 Mrs. Olive Wise (d 16 Feb 1908); Dec 1908 m 3rd Mrs.Josephine Shultz; serv CW in Co. F, 147th Ind. Inf.; d 12 Feb 1918, bur GC Cem (G2/15/18)

PARSONS, Josephine - of GC, is mother of Mrs. Charles Clary of Indianapolis (J1/7/16), Mabel Schultz of Indianapolis (J2/4/16), Harrison Pleasant Shultz (dec), and of Galen Shultz of Toledo, OH (J10/6/16)

PARTRIDGE, William - s-in-law of M/M James Fort of Jnsbr; bartender in a Marion saloon; d 5 Jun 1898 at home of James Fort (G6/10/98)

PATTERSON, Mrs. __ - mother of John Patterson of Trask; age 77; d last wk, bur Walnut Creek Cem (G6/18/97)

PATTERSON, __ (HUTCHINSON) - of Deer Creek area; dt M/M __ Hutchinson of GC; m Alex Patterson (J6/1/17)

PATTERSON, Billy - barber in Oliver Shady Barber Shop, 3rd St., GC (G8/6/97); left town owing money (G5/20/98)

PATTERSON, Forrest Robert - b during past wk; s M/M L.E. Patterson (G1/4/18)

PATTERSON, Hazel - dt M/M Alex Patterson of Deer Creek (J8/24/17); 8th grade grad, Mill Twp Sch 1918 (G5/31/18)

PATTERSON, Mrs. John - age 61; mother of Eldo Patterson; d 8 Jan 1916, bur Jefferson Cem (J1/14/16)

PATTERSON, Lemon Eldo - is repairing cyclone damage on James Kirkpatrick farm bldgs (G5/31/18); mbr of Jnsbr Liberty Guards (G9/20/18)

PATTERSON, Mrs. Eldo - dt M/M Leroy Horner (G11/30/17)

PATTERSON, J.H. - brother of Eldo Patterson; is Marion policeman (G11/30/17)

PATTERSON, Nolia - 1916-17 Zeek Sch student (J3/30/17)

PATTERSON, Robert H. - Harrisburg Sch tchr following Uriah S. Candy, 1877 or later (J6/1/17)

PATTERSON, Stella - and Lilly are dts M/M Alex Patterson of Deer Creek (J8/24/17)

PATTISON, M/M Alva - parents of 8 lb. boy (J5/14/15)

PATTISON, Cleo (ARNETT) - Wise Sch tchr 1916-18 (J9/1/16; G8/31/17)

PATTISON, Goldie - mbr North Grove PM SS (J9/7/17); Mill Twp Sch 8th grade grad 1920 (J5/21/20)

PATTISON, Walter - will m Cleo Arnett Apr 29 (J4/30/15)

PATTON, O.M. - bought Wilson Barber Shop from J.O. Austin (G8/6/97)

PAYNE, Alonzo - farmer near Fairmount; committed suicide 20 Aug 1919 (J8/22/19)

PAYNE, M/M Dan - last wk became parents of a dt, Melba Louise (J5/28/20)

PAYNE, Jim - of Fairmount; has secured a lot in Guthrie, OK (J6/8/89)

PEACE, M/M William - Mill Twp octogenarians (G8/2/18)

PEACOCK, John - farmer S of Jnsbr in Fairmount Twp; had 12 head of cattle killed by lightning last Tue, $800 loss; all 12 were under one tree (J7/18/19)

PEARSON, Addie - mbr Jnsbr WCTU (J12/27/18)

PEARSON, Earl - Dec 1910, Deer Creek Sch student, won 3rd place in Twp Spelling Contest (J12/31/20); m Bethel Carroll 9 Oct 1915; live E of GC (J10/15/15); and wife will soon move to their Jefferson area farm (J1/7/16)

PEARSON, Eva - mbr Jnsbr WCTU (J12/27/18)

PEARSON, John C. - age 60; m twice; d Sat at his home 2 mi. NE of GC, bur Marion IOOF Cem (J3/12/15)

PEARSON, Leona - Mill Twp 8th grade grad 1916 (J5/12/16); grad, Jnsbro HS 1920 (J4/16/20)

PEARSON, Mrs. Mary N. - b 15 Mar 1829; lives in Mill Twp (G7/27/17; J8/27/20)

PEARSON, M/M Shad - of Jefferson area will soon move to a farm on Soldier's Home Pike (J1/7/16)

PEARSON, Winnifred - lives on farm NE of GC; filed suit for divorce from husband, Shadrack Pearson (G6/14/18)

PEEL, __ - of Garthwait & Peel; sells real estate in Mississinewa Hotel Blk. (G6/24/95)

PEELE, Anna - m Richard Elliott 18 Jul 1915 (J7/23/15)

PEELE, Mrs. E.B. - of 409 North A St., GC is mbr GC Baptist Ch. (G2/26/97); mbr '97 Club (G2/4/98); 27 Apr 1898 given 34th birthday party (G4/29/98)

PEEL(E), Edna - twin of Esse; 3 Jun 1897, they had 9th birthday party (G6/4/97)

PEELE, F.H. - of Jnsbr; 62nd birthday last wk (G3/11/98)

PEELE, George - of Jnsbr; s Holliday and Susan Peele; m (wife dec); d 12 Jul 1915, 1st funeral procession in Jnsbr composed entirely of autos (J7/16/15)

PEELE, John - young son of M/M Haliday Peele of Jnsbr; d 6 Dec 1897 (G12/10/97; G1/21/98)

PEELE, Susan (HOOVER) - of Jnsbr; brother, John/ Jonathan Hoover of Blountsville, d Jul 1917 (G7/20/17; G3/29/18)

PEELE, Willis - a Jefferson Twp Sch tchr, had to close sch when he became ill; sch has now reopened with Amos Dubois as tchr (J1/?/87); m Lizzie Duling 24 May 1889 (J6/1/89)

PEERY, Pete - Captain, GC All-Stars football team (J10/29/15)

PEERY, Raymond D. - b Monroe Twp 5 Sep 1901; s Oliver F. and Angie Peery; killed 7 Apr 1916 by auto while riding bicycle; bur GC Cem (J4/14/16)

PEGDEN, Charles - and wife of GC have 29th wedding anniv next Sun (J4/30/20)

PELL, Rev. Millard - GC M.E. pastor (G1/15/97; G4/2/97)

PEMBERTON, Ben - Jnsbr city Marshall (G1/15/97); with fellow Jnsbr policeman Richardson, captured John Long who then married to avoid a paternity charge (G3/12/97); Jnsbr night Marshall (G9/2/98)

PEMBERTON, E.M.- was Mill Twp Trustee when first Harrisburg Sch was built, prob in 1874 (J6/1/17)

PEMBERTON, E.W. - 28 Nov 1897, 61st birthday (G12/3/97)

PEMBERTON, Elisha - father-in-law of Emerson Kester of Jnsbr (G6/10/98)

PEMBERTON, John - his house burned recently (G1/15/97); new brick house is almost completed (G2/5/97)

PEMBERTON, Loran M. - Jnsbr Marshall; mbr Vicksburg Camp, Sons of Veterans, Jnsbr (G7/15/98); with Charles Hodupp, bagged 40 quail within 3 mi. of GC 14 Nov 1898 (G11/18/98)

PEMBERTON, Mrs. Lottie - d 29 Jun 1889 (J6/1/89)

PEMBERTON, Rolland/Rollin N. - living in Detroit, MI (J8/3/17)

PENN, Samuel - fined last Fri by GC Mayor Brashear for public intoxication (G1/1/97)

PERKINS, Mrs. W.H. - of GC; mbr GC M.E. Ch.; d 19 Feb 1920 (J2/20/20)

PERSINGER, James - is struck by Jesse Street while trying to assist Olin Gordon who was being assaulting by Sam Holmes last Mon evening on a GC Street; Gordon is a "dry" and Holmes is a "wet" (J7/23/15); charges of assault were brought against him but a jury acquitted him last Fri (J10/1/15)

PETTY, __ (PHILLIPS) - mbr Jnsbr WCTU (J10/6/16)

PETTY, Ben - of Jnsbr; att Purdue Univ 1910-12 (J12/24/20)

PETTY, Mrs. Ben - of Dayton; dt M/M W.D. Holmes of Jnsbr; has a young son (J10/29/15)

PETTY, Henry H. - of Indianapolis; s M/M Charles E. Petty of Jnsbr (G2/9/17); m 12 Nov 1920 Dorotha Owen of Vincennes (G11/12/20)

PETTY, Marcus/Marquis - his barn burned on N side of Muncie Pike 2.5 mi SE of Jnsbr (G2/9/17); wife Iva is dt George W. and Sarah Ann (SMITH) Baker of Swayzee (G5/4/17; G2/8/18); bought a new Maxwell car at Christmas (J12/28/17)

PHERSON, Lawrence - Mill Twp 8th grade grad 1916 (J5/12/16)

PHILLIPS, Alice - dt M/M William Phillips of GC (G6/22/17); student, Terre Haute Normal Coll (G10/5/17)

PHILLIPS, Mrs. Ann - b 23 Feb 1837; lives in Mill Twp (G8/2/18; J8/27/20)

PHILLIPS, Anne - dt M/M William Phillips of GC (G6/22/17)

PHILLIPS, Daisy - GC Welsh person (G3/5/97)

PHILLIPS, Earl - s M/M Oscar Phillips; m 24 Jul 1915 Mona Rush, dt Jasper Rush; live on farm S of Jnsbr (J7/30/15)

PHILLIPS, Edith - GC Welsh person (G3/5/97)

PHILLIPS, Ethel - local 7-year old (J4/2/15)

PHILLIPS, Oscar - mbr Jnsbr Odd Fellows (J1/14/16)

PHILLIPS, Polly - GC Welsh person (G3/5/97)

PHILLIPS, Walter - a cripple who was struck by Jesse Street when he tried to intervene in assault of Olin Gordon by Sam Holmes on a GC street; Gordon is a prominant "dry" and Holmes is a "wet" (J7/23/15) charges were brought against him but a jury aquitted him last Fri; lives in GC (J10/1/15)

PHILLIPS, William H. - s M/M William Phillips of GC; m 16 Jun 1917 Metta P. Street of Swayzee, dt Washington Brown of Swayzee; will live in Marion (G6/22/17)

PHILPOT, Mansford - purchased license to m Minnie Frazee (G12/24/97)

PICKERING, __ - s Frank and __ (Lawson) Pickering; b 16 Nov 1897 (G11/19/97)

PIDDOCK, Mary Ann (BECHLER) - b OH 7 Oct 1832; dt Peter and Sarah Bechler; m 1st 2 Sep 1849 Jeremiah L. Manley (dec); m 2nd 7 Aug 1886 Aaron Piddock (d 7 Apr 1912); d Jnsbr 29 Oct 1920 at home of dt, Mrs. Maude M. Friedline; bur Pennville Cem (G11/5/20)

PIERCE, Bruce - of Jnsbr; s E.N. and Rachel Pierce of Jnsbr (G7/14/11; J7/9/15)

PIERCE, Mrs. Bruce - granddt of William Schriber (J3/7/19)

PIERCE, Bynum - retired farmer of Monroe Twp; age 87; d 28 Jun 1920 (J7/2/20)

PIERCE, E.N. - and Co. has a Jnsbr restaurant/ice cream parlor/bakery in the Moore Blk. (J6/8/89); living in Jnsbr (G12/24/97)

PIERCE, Ed - has a grocery store in Jnsbr (G2/5/97)

PIERCE, Elmina - of Fairmount; age 77; widow of William Pierce; d 21 Mar 1920 (J3/26/20)

PIERCE, F.P. - of Jnsbr; s Dr. Levi D. Pierce (b 4 Jul 1816) and Matilda (ENTSMINGER) Pierce; Matilda (b 1820), dt Capt. John Entsminger (serv War of 1812); several of family are bur Walnut Creek Cem (J7/18/19)

PIERCE, Gertrude - lived 3.5 mi. E of GC; m William Pierce; d at age 40 yr, 4 mon, 17 da; funeral 11 May 1917 at BC Friends MH (Ruth Carey preaching), bur Back Creek Cem (G5/18/17)

PIERCE, J.E. - lives in Jnsbr (G12/24/97)

PIERCE, Mrs. J.E. - of Jnsbr; sister of Mrs. Walter Parker of Anderson (G11/19/97); 51st birthday last wk (G2/11/98)

PIERCE, Lula - dt M/M J.E. Pierce; m 15 Sep 1893 L.C. Kercheval; will live in Sheridan (G9/22/93)

PIERCE, Maybelle - local 8-yr old (J4/2/16)

PIERCE, William M. - of Upland; b Clinton Co., OH 10 Dec 1852; s James H. and Mary E. Pierce; d 1 Sep 1920, bur Puckett Cem (J9/10/20)

PIERSON, __ - dt M/M David Pierson of Jnsbr; b 10 Nov 1897 (G11/12/97)

PILCHER, Raymond - 8th grade grad Jnsbr Sch 1919 (J4/18/19)

PINKERTON, James - Jnsbr Independant owner/publisher (J6/8/89)

PITT, Rev. Charles - Jnsbr MM SS tchr (J10/6/16; J7/27/17)

PITTENGER, Rev. W. Earl - Jnsbr M.E. pastor (J4/18/19)

POLK, Mrs. Mary - mbr Jnsbr Rebekahs Lodge (J1/14/16)

POLLEN, Edna - mbr GC Christian Ch. (J10/6/16)

POLLEN, Emma - local 3-yr old (J4/2/16)

POLLEN, W.E. - mbr/officer, GC Odd Fellows (J7/9/15)

POND, Magdalene - of GC; dt D.R. Pond (dec) of Terre Haute (G10/5/17)

PONTIOUS, Harrie - Mississinewa Hotel prop. (G9/23/98)

POTTS, Rollie 'Roy'- age 15; orphan; nephew of George Zent; GC Western Union messenger boy; PHOTO; 7 Aug 1897 won GC kid bicycle race (G8/30/97); accepts telegrapher job in South Bend (G1/7/98); his job was eliminated, he returns to GC (G2/4/98)

POWELL, Dr. A.A. - of Mississinewa Hotel; s Mrs. M.L. Powell of New Castle (G3/26/97); Dentist, leaves to take postgrad Harvard Univ course (G7/2/97); returned from Harvard Univ dental course (G8/27/97); sold GC dental practice; has new one in Mattoon, IL (G12/9/98)

POWELL, Cecil A. - 1919 Mill Twp 8th grade grad (J4/4/19)

POWELL, Joe - of Zeek area; bought a new Overland auto (G10/26/17)

POWELL, Mrs. Joe - of Zeek area; sister of John Stewart (d 28 Jun 1919) of Fairmount (J7/4/19)

POWELL, Nina Faye - Mill Twp 8th grade grad 1916 (J5/12/16)

POWELL, Vern - s Mrs. Leah Powell (G10/8/97)

POWERS, Frank 'Shorty' - of GC; age 51; m; killed on RR by train 2 Mar 1917 (G3/9/17; J3/9/17)

POWERS, Von - age 9 mons; s M/M Mark Powers of Liberty Twp; declared prettiest baby in Grant Co. (J7/1/20)

PRATHER, Marguerite (SHADY) - f of GC; b GC 19 Feb 1897; dt Oliver and Clara Shady; moved to Anderson with parents ca 1905; m Karl Prather 4 Nov 1916; mbr M.E. Ch.; d 21 Jan 1917, bur Anderson cem (G1/26/17)

PRATT, Harold - s M/M Ora Pratt of GC (G11/12/20)

PRATT, Ora - is a GC Constable (J7/23/15)

PRESS, Albert Kellogg - owns new Grant auto (J4/16/15)

PRESS, Mrs. Charles - Nov 1910, d, bur in NJ (G11/5/20)

PRESS, Linda (HARRIS) - mbr Jnsbr Rebekahs Lodge (J1/14/16); mbr Jnsbr WCTU (J12/27/18; J2/20/20)

PRICE, Irene - of GC; age 64; m David Price; d 15 Jan 1918, bur Jefferson Cem (G1/18/18)

PRICE, L.K. - of Marion; will manage GC Bruce & Marks Manufacturing Co. for Mr. Bruce, plant owner (G1/1/97)

PRICE, Michael - age 91; d Grant Co. Infirmary 5 Feb 1917, bur Mt. Hope Cem (G2/9/17)

PRICE, Mrs. R. - GC Welsh person (G3/5/97)

PRICE, Rich - helped rescue Wood Huff and Belle Whitson when they fell through the ice into the Mississinewa River (G1/1/97)

PRICE, Robert - mbr GC Baptist Ch. (G1/14/98)

PRICE, Mrs. Robert - 20 Nov 1917 was given party in her GC home for her 70th birthday (G11/23/17)

PRICE, W.M. - ca 1862 had farm E of Harrisburg across road from Wemburn Oliver family farm (J6/1/17)

PRICKETT, Jacob W. - b Tipton Co. 4 Feb 1856; s Jacob and Martha; wife d ca 1901; d 19 Feb 1918, bur GC Cem (G2/22/18)

PRICKETT, L.A. - officer, GC K of P (G7/14/11); of GC; mgr, Custer Lumber Co.; a leader of "drys"(i.e., persons wishing to rid area of alcoholic drink by legal prohibition); gave beating to Dr. Brose Horne, "wets" speaker (J7/23/15)

PRICKETT, Mrs. L.A. - dt of Mrs. Nancy Sharon of Sweetser; sister of Mrs. Albert Stevens of Sweetser (J4/2/15)

PRICKETT, Martha H.G. - dt M/M L.A. Prickett (J7/23/15); grad GC HS 1919 (J4/11/19); b GC 28 Jun 1902 (J5/16/19)

PRICKETT, Richard - s M/M L.A. Prickett (J2/20/20)

PRITCHARD, Charles Ed - f of GC, now of Montezuma; 1892 established First National Bank of GC (G5/21/97); grad, Earlham Coll; convicted of embezzlement from his Montezuma Bank (G12/17/97)

PRITCHETT, Clarence - 8th grade grad, Mill Twp Sch 1918 (G5/31/18)

PRUITT, Otis Pleasant - b Howard Co. 21 Oct 1879; s Isaiah and Margaret Pruitt; m Elsie Hinkle 4 Jan 1905; lived in GC; d 8 Nov 1918, bur GC Cem (G11/15/18)

PUCKETT SCHOOL - session closed Fri, Wyeth Landess was 1914-15 tchr (J5/7/15)

PUGH, Serg. James L. - s M/M O.W. Pugh of Upland; m 14 Jun 1918 Cora Conelley of E of GC; is now discharged from army; both are tchrs; will live in Grant Co. (J12/27/18)

PYETTE, Jacob Brenton - age 85; lived in Marion as a small boy; one of 1st Grant Co. CW enlistees, serv 8th Ind. Inf.; d at Soldier's Home recently (J1/16/20)

QUAIL - season is Nov 10 - Dec 20; 15 bird daily bag limit; 45 bird possession limit (G11/12/20)

QUIRK, Miss Anna - replaced her sister, Agnes, as Western Union telegrapher in GC (G10/8/97)

QUIRK, Miss Agnes - is Western Union telegrapher in GC (G2/19/97); has left GC for a similar position in South Bend (G10/8/97)

RABBIT - Al Dye and 3 other men shot 75 rabbits in 3 days hunting along the Kankakee River near Lowell (J1/3/19); hunting season closes 10 Jan 1920 (J1/9/20)

RADAMAKER, Edward - local 6-yr old attempting to win a pony and cart in GC merchants contest (J4/2/15)

RADCLIFF, Rev. F. - s Mrs. L. Radcliff of England (G4/30/97)

RADCLIFFE, Rev. J.F. - Jnsbr M.E. Ch. pastor; was in carriage with his wife just N of Back Creek Friends Cem when 2 men with revolvers took his watch and $2.50 on 14 Sep 1893 (G9/22/93); now of Sharpsville (G3/12/97)

RADER, Matilda - of Roseburg; age 75; killed on RR, 9 Mar 1918 (G3/15/18)

RAMMELS, Rev. __ - Methodist preacher who sometimes preached in the Candy Sch house ca 1860 (J6/8/17)

RANDALL, C.W.- Editor, GC Weekly Journal; m 17 May 1898 Eula Alford, dt Rev./M G.W. Alford of Elwood (G5/20/98)

RANKIN, Mrs. W.C. - mbr '97 Club; lives on South A St., GC (G3/11/98)

RATLIFF, Rev. Harvey - Bethel MM pastor (G1/26/17; J1/26/17)

RATLIFF(E), Sue (THOMAS) - mbr Deer Creek WCTU (G10/22/97)

RAY, Mrs. Clinton - of GC is mbr GC Baptist Ch. (G11/5/20)

RAY, Robert - mbr GC K of P Lodge (J12/24/20)

READING, Helen Devonne - b last Sat to M/M Edwin O. Reading of GC (J1/21/16)

REASONER, Edward - is drilling water well at College Hill Sch house (J10/13/16)

REECE, Maria (EGBERT) - age 85; b OH; dt Henry and Phebe (THORNSON) Egbert; m 1st 1848 John W. Moore (d 1860); m 2nd 1864 Charles Reece (d 1906); mbr Marion Christian Ch.; d 22 Feb 1916, bur Marion (J2/25/16)

REEL, Mrs. Anthony - age ca 50; of GC; fell from wagon driven by her drunken husband, broke collarbone (G4/22/98)

REEL, Elias - small boy, was run over by a wagon and injured (G7/2/97); tried on charge of assault on his step-brother, Albert Murphy; acquitted since it was "family affair" (G8/6/97)

REEL, Elizabeth K. - m James E. Yeager last Mon at GC home of her parents, M/M Charles W. Reel (J4/2/15)

REEL, Geneva - 1919 Mill Twp Sch 8th grade grad (J4/4/19)

REEL, Lula Belle - age 35; m Elias Reel; d 24 Mar 1917, bur GC Cem (G3/30/17)

REESE, David - and Harry are GC Welsh (G1/14/98)

REESE, John O. - is discharged as night policeman because of his problems with the Mayor (G11/26/20)

REEVES, Alma - of Grant Co.; age 84; mother of Horace Reeves of Fairmount, and of David and George Reeves of Matthews; d 26 Feb 1917 at Matthews (G3/2/17; J3/2/17)

REEVES, Homer - age 18; s M/M Horace Reeves of Fairmount; 11 Jul 1911 drowned in Ancil Winslow gravel pit (G7/14/11)

RELFE, Ruth - of College Hill area; enters nurse's training in Indianapolis (J5/16/19)

RENN, Henry, Jr. - s Mrs. Mary Renn of GC; now in US Army in NJ (G5/18/17; G6/22/17; J6/29/17); is in Delaware army camp (G10/5/17)

RENN, Mary Elizabeth (AHLHEIT) - b Germany 31 Aug 1868; dt B. and Helena Ahlheit; m Henry Renn 27 Feb 1892 at Logansport; mbr German Lutheran Ch.; lived in GC; d 30 Sep 1917 of TB, bur GC Cem (G10/5/17)

RETTS, Rev. L.A. - Jnsbr M.E. pastor (G4/9/97; G4/2/97)

RETTS, Mamie - grad, Jnsbr HS 1898 (G4/22/98)

REYNOLDS, Rev. A.C. - of OH; will give oration at 4th of July celebration at Lake Galatia (J6/8/89)

REYNOLDS, Louis - age 73; Liberty Twp farmer; d recently at his home near Weaver (J8/24/17)

REYNOLDS, Nelva - grad, GC HS 1917 (J5/18/17)

REYNOLDS, Ray - of GC; now in US Army (J6/29/17)

REYNOLDS, Rev. S.R. - elected GC Christian Ch. pastor (G8/6/97); 27 Aug 1897 brought his bride from Logansport to GC (G8/30/97); resigns as of 1 May 1898 from pastorate of GC Christian Ch. (G4/15/98)

RHOADS, John A. - has lived in Jnsbr 23 yrs (G3/26/97)

RHOADS, William - b near Harrisburg; is oil well driller in Rangoon, India; is visiting his cousin, Milo Burgess of GC (J1/16/20)

RHODEHAMEL, Ruby (HARRIS) - dt D.W. Harris; sister of Phil J. Harris (dec) (G10/5/17)

RHODEHAMEL, Mrs. S.A. - of Marion; mother of Mrs. C.E. VanValer of GC (G11/16/17)

RHODES, Lola - mbr Jnsbr MM SS (J7/27/17); 8th grade grad, Jnsbr Sch 1919 (J4/18/19)

RHODES, Vera - mbr Jnsbr MM SS (J7/27/17)

RICH, Mrs. Eri - d at her home near Fairmount 27 Mar 1915 (J4/2/15)

RICH, Mrs. I.J. - of Hartford City; is sister of Mrs. W.E. Mason (J4/18/19)

RICH, Sylvester - m last wk Ethel (WRIGHT) Baskett, dt M/M J.M. Wright (J1/2/20)

RICHARDS, Mrs. J., Jr. - lived near New Cumberland; d 21 Sep 1893 (G9/22/93)

RICHARDSON, Benjamin Franklin - Jnsbr policeman (G3/12/97); Jnsbr night Marshall; is ill (G8/5/98)

RICHARDSON, Hop - 10 Mar 1897 shot/killed a mad dog in Jnsbr (G3/12/97)

RICHARDSON, Marie - dt Benjamin F. and Susan A. (NELSON) Richardson of Jnsbr (G11/16/17)

RICHARDSON, Martha J. - of Jnsbr; b Hancock Co. 8 Feb 1840; m 1st 20 Feb 1859 Aaron Tweedy (d 17 Oct 1865); m 2nd 4 Jan 1875 G.S. Richardson; d 13 Apr 1917, bur GC Cem (G4/20/17)

RICHARDSON, William - age 63; farmer near Rigdon; d 26 Jul 1920 (J7/30/20)

RICHARDSON, Zimri - gas well on his farm supplies 150 Jnsbr families; 21 Jun 1897 gas was shut off to drill well deeper in search of oil (G6/25/97); well is flowing 25 barrels of oil per day (G7/9/97); well was "shot", no oil now but lots of gas (G7/16/97); Singer Oil Co. derrick over well is taken down (G7/30/97)

RICHCREEK, __ - of Richcreek & Burgess; purchased well drilling/repairing rig from Ed Buford (G5/28/97)

RICKS, George H. - age 23; of Jnsbr; and Ethel Crabb, age 18, of Marion obtained marriage license recently (J8/3/17)

RIDDLE, William - of GC; 19 Oct 1915 m Gladys Griffin of GC; will live in GC (J10/22/15)

RILEY, Elizabeth - age 72; f of Fairmount; widow; d in Upland 17 Dec 1919, bur Fairmount cem (J12/26/19)

RILEY, William - age 54; b Ireland; mbr RC Ch.; d last Wed at home of son-in-law, John Hanahan (7/9/97)

RITTER, Jacob - age 83; of 2 mi SE of Jnsbr; d 13 Apr 1898 (G4/15/98)

ROBB, Martha (WHITE) - dt M/M Marion White of GC; last Sat m John Robb of Marion (G7/13/17)

ROBBINS, J.E. - of Frank & Robbins; have a Furniture Store in Opera House Blk., GC (G6/24/95); undertaker (G1/15/97); sold undertaking business to J.E. Ward; retiring to f home in Troy, OH (G10/8/97)

ROBERTS, __ - s M/M John Roberts; b 28 Jul 1898 (G8/5/98)

ROBERTS, Alice - GC Welsh person (G3/5/97)

ROBERTS, Frank - of Jnsbr; arranged to have a prize fight with Gayle Ruley next Sun; Deputy Sheriff Bradford stopped it (G4/22/98)

ROBERTS, George - age 66; farmer E of GC; m; d 6 May 1917, bur Matthews Cem (G5/11/17)

ROBERTS, John - GC Welsh person (G3/5/97)

ROBERTS, Rev. Phineas - lived on a farm S of Farmington; New Light/Christian who preached sometimes in the Walnut Creek Log Ch. at an early date (J6/8/17)

ROBERTS, Samuel - b GC 4 Aug 1898; lived in Wales 15 mons.; grad GC HS 1917 (J5/18/17); is in US Army (J6/29/17)

ROBINAULT, Pearl J. - officer, Jnsbr K of P (G1/26/17)

ROBINSON, M/M Allan - of Jnsbr; mbrs Jnsbr MM (J10/8/15)

ROBINSON, Mahala (SKEEN) - b KY 30 Jul 1897; dt Elijah (dec) and Mary Skeen; m William Robinson; d 17 Nov 1919, bur Jefferson Cem (J11/21/19)

ROE, Everett - of Jnsbr; m 28 Apr 1917 Nellie Stone of Grant Sch area near Fairmount (G5/4/17)

ROGERS, A.J. - is Jnsbr City Expressman (J6/8/89)

ROGERS, Elmer - ex-conductor of Marion Car Line; fell through ice into Mississinewa, was rescued (G1/1/97)

ROMINGER, Floyd - Mill Twp 8th grade grad 1916 (J5/12/16)

ROMINGER, Isaac J. - age 74; retired in Jnsbr; has license to m Rachel Edna Carter, age 62, of Jnsbr (J10/6/16)

ROOK, Mrs. Anna - mother of Bennett Knight and of Clara Knight; sister of Mrs. Jesse Overmyer of Kansas City, KS (G11/23/17; J8/24/17); broke hip (G10/5/17)

ROOK, Jack - ca 1871 in Harrisburg, owned factory which made tow from flax straw for making rope (J4/6/17; J6/8/17)

ROOK, John H. - appointed administrator of estate of Daniel Winslow (dec) (J6/8/89)

ROSS, Mrs. Elizabeth - b 22 Mar 1828; of Mill Twp (G7/27/17; J8/1/19)

ROSS, Dr. J.C. - of GC; until recently was the County Infirmary physician (J1/5/17)

ROSS, Maggie - lives on South H St., GC; 27 Jul 1898 given party for her 11th birthday (G7/29/98)

ROTHINGHOUSE, Mrs. Al - dt Mrs. Phebe Norton; sister of Ralph Norton (G1/1/97); mbr Jnsbr Presbyterian Ch. (G10/1/97); mbr '97 Club (G1/14/98; G2/11/98)

ROTHINGHOUSE, Ben - was operating, prior to 1871, a cooper shop in the hollow back of his home on Main St., Jnsbr (J4/6/17)

ROTHINGHOUSE, C.H. - seriously ill in a Martinsville hospital (G4/2/97)

ROTHINGHOUSE, Mrs. Charles - dt Mrs. Julia Livengood of Jnsbr; sister of Frank Livengood and of Juniette Kaufman (J1/12/17)

ROTHINGHOUSE, Ernest - s M/M Charles Rothinghouse of Jnsbr (J7/9/15)

ROTHINGHOUSE, Fred - s Ben Rothinghouse of Jnsbr (J4/6/17); and wife are given 4th wedding anniv party 26 Sep 1898 (G9/30/98)

ROUSH, Catharine - a schoolmate of Uriah S. Candy; still living (J6/8/17)

ROUSH, Charles - young s of John Roush of 2 mi. E of GC; injured last wk while playing (G4/8/98)

ROUSH, Mrs. Clem - good friend of Mrs. Sallie Stevens, f of Jnsbr then missionary in India; Mrs. Clark Bateman of Bombay, dt of Mrs. Stevens, visited Mrs. Roush for 2 wks recently (J8/1/19)

ROUSH, Daniel W. - mbr Jnsbr Masons (G12/24/97)

ROUSH, Fred - 24 Jan 1898 was 27th birthday (G1/28/98)

ROUSH, Garr A. - BA-Ind Univ, Jun 1905 (J7/2/20); Nov 1905, chemist; accepted position in NJ laboratory of Thomas A. Edison (G11/12/20)

ROUSH, Isaac - m Mary Miller 27 Mar 1834; moved to Grant Co. in 1842; lived 55 yrs on same farm; d a few months ago (G4/9/97); had the log cabin home where Dianna Roush m

Philip Long; Rev. __ Minnick performed the marriage; the cabin later burned (J6/8/17)

ROUSH, Isaac 'Ike' N. - officer in Jnsbr Bank (G1/1/97); bought livery stable at N. 3rd & A St., GC from E. Buford (G7/29/98)

ROUSH, John - of Otisco, Clark Co.; brother of Mrs. George Ryder (G11/23/17)

ROUSH, Mary (MILLER) - b Miami Co., OH 28 Jun 1816; m 27 Mar 1834 Isaac Roush; 1842 moved to Grant Co.; lived 55 yrs on same farm; parent of 6 boys and 5 girls, all now living; d 3 Apr 1897, bur IOOF Cem (G4/9/97)

ROUSH, O.P. - of South B St., GC; is employee of GC Roller Mills (G12/24/97)

ROUSH, Ode - Jnsbr M.E. SS officer (J1/12/17); mbr Jnsbr K of P (G10/7/98)

ROUSH, Mrs. Omer - mother of May (ROUSH) Kirby (J8/17/17); dt Benjamin J. (d 1903) and Martha J. (NELSON) Ice; her mother d 13 Jun 1919 (J6/20/19)

ROUSH, William - ca 1855 had farm immediately W of the Candy farm (J6/1/17)

ROUSH, William P. - b 31 Jul 1836; of Mill Twp (J8/1/19); was a schoolmate of Uriah S. Candy (J6/8/17)

ROWE, Joseph P. - of N. Jnsbr; age 75; m; d 27 Apr 1917, bur Marion IOOF Cem (G5/4/17)

ROWNEY, M/M Thomas - of E. James St., Jnsbr; 14 Feb 1897 celebrated 4th wedding anniv (G2/19/97); Irene and Roy are their children (G6/11/97)

RULEY, __ - dt M/M Robert Ruley of Jnsbr; b last wk (G11/5/97)

RULEY, Bayard - grad, Jnsbr HS 1898 (G4/22/98); s Mrs. Maggie Ruley of Jnsbr; age 30; d Nov 1910 (G11/12/20)

RULEY, Claude L. - f of Jnsbr; m May Miller (dt M/M A.J. Miller); d 9 Oct 1915, bur Anderson (J10/15/15)

RULEY, D.K. - has a grocery store in GC (G9/22/93)

RULEY, Mrs. David - aunt of Iva (FEAR) Stokes (J1/7/16)

RULEY, David Winston 'Wint'- s Zachariah A.T. and Edith Ellen (WALTHALL) Ruley; of 2.5 mi. SE of GC (G10/19/17)

RULEY, Gail - of Jnsbr; fought Pearl Fowler last Sun in prize fight at Schrader's Brick Works W of Jnsbr; he won (G12/3/97); 28 Dec 1897, in prize fight in Fairmount (G12/31/97); arranged to fight with Frank Roberts; Deputy Sheriff Bradford stopped it (G4/22/98); of Milwaukee, WI; visited mother, Lizzie Ruley of Jnsbr (G7/14/11)

RULEY, John Taylor - age 5 mons.; won 1st prize in baby show in Goldthwait Park (J7/9/15); child of M/M Wint Ruley; won baby contest at Grant Co. WCTU convention held at yesterday at Jnsbr Friends MH (J10/6/16)

RULEY, Lizzie - of S. Main St., Jnsbr; visited by s, Gail Ruley of Milwaukee, WI (J5/16/19)

RULEY, Lola M. - m; mbr Jnsbr Rebekahs (J1/14/16)

RULEY, Margaret 'Maggie' (MOON) - b Clinton Co., OH 21 Mar 1852; dt Thomas and Sarah Moon; m 1873 Burtney W. Ruley (d 1905); mbr M.E. Ch.; d 30 Mar 1920 (J4/2/20)

RULEY, Paul - s M/M Thomas Ruley; grad Jnsbr HS; m 20 Apr 1918 Eva Barker, dt M/M Edward Barker; will live in Jnsbr (G4/26/18)

RULEY, Robert - mbr Jnsbr Masonic Lodge (G12/24/97)

RULEY, Mrs. Robert - sister of Miss Mary Lovett North of Milford (G2/12/97)

RULEY, Taylor - his farm is 2.5 mi. SE of GC; baler set straw afire recently (G7/14/11)

RULEY, Thomas Mallen - m Sarah J. Bacy/Basye 27 Jun 1887 (J7/1/87); and wife are belled at home (J7/22/87); of SE of Jnsbr (J10/22/15); mbr Jnsbr Odd Fellows (J1/14/16)

RULEY, Will - recently erected gas light in front of his Jnsbr store (J6/24/87)

RULEY, Zachariah Amos Taylor 'A.T.' - b Rockbridge Co., VA 19 Feb 1849; s William W. and Rebecca G. Ruley; m 1st 1879 Edith Ellen Walthall (of Back Creek MM, d 11 Jan 1880); m 2nd Lida Parks in Dec 1880; mbr Jnsbr M.P. Ch.; d 15 Oct 1917 (G10/19/17)

RUSH, Mrs. Ben - lives near North Grove; was a Baldwin (J11/21/19)

RUSH, Bertha - grad, Jnsbr HS 1910 (J5/7/20)

RUSH, Charles - of Jnsbr; Muncie sch tchr (J10/22/15)

RUSH, Mrs. Mary (HARVEY) - Jnsbr octogenarian (J6/18/19)

RUSH, Minnie M. (TINCHER) - b 6 Oct 1873 near Jnsbr; dt William H. and Mary Tincher; m Jasper A. Rush 31 Aug 1895; mbr Jnsbr MM; d 16 May 1915 (J5/21/15)

RUSH, Rose/Rosa (BRADFORD) - Jnsbr WCTU mbr (J4/16/15)

RUSH, Walter - Mill Twp farmer whose sheep have been killed by dogs this spring (G5/7/97)

RUSH, Walter C. - of near Fairmount; has quit Quakers and all other churches because of their "worldlyness" (G8/26/98)

RUSSELL, Frank W. - Jnsbr Mason who is a Sergt. in army (G11/29/18)

RUSSELL, Mrs. Perry - of Jnsbr; sister of Miss Myrtle Northam of Walkerton (G1/14/98), and/or sister of John Nathan of South Bend (J10/1/15)

RUTHERFORD, Mrs. Charles - of GC; dt William Bless of Kokomo (G11/5/20)

RUTHERFORD, Mrs. Cora - of GC; dt Mrs. C.H. Brown (G11/23/17)

RYDER, Courtney - of Detroit, MI; s M/M George Ryder (G11/30/17)

RYDER, Mrs. George - of Zeek Sch area is mother of Mrs. Ora Campbell of Dayton, OH (J10/22/15); sister of Mrs. Kate Duling of Matthews (G11/16/17), and of John Roush of Otisco, Clark Co, (G11/23/17)

SAMMS, Aaron - b 30 Aug 1828; of Mill Twp (J8/13/15); b IN; wife d ca 1892; d 4 Jun 1917, funeral at North Grove Friends MH, bur North Grove Cem (G6/8/17; J6/8/17)

SAMON, Jesse - lives in Central Hotel, Jnsbr (G5/7/97)

SANDERS, Ida - charged with prostitution last spring, is fined $67.95 (G12/10/97)

SANFORD, Rev. Arthur W.- lived N of Harrisburg ca 1850's; New Light/Christian who sometimes preached in Walnut Creek Log Ch.; moved to Marion where he was the Teacher Examiner of U.S. Candy for Candy's first teaching license; father of Amanda (J6/8/17)

SANFORD, Clyde W. - age 19 mons.; s M/M A.B. Sanford; d 22 Sep 1915, bur Marion IOOF Cem (J9/24/15)

SAPP, Lydia - f of Zeek Sch area; m 1st __ Wright; m 2nd Joseph Sapp, moved to Grand Rapids, MI; d Sat (J12/10/20)

SAUNDERS, Ben, Jr. - 1915-16 att Ind Univ (J1/7/16); of GC; is now 2nd Lieut. in US Army (J6/29/17)

SAUNDERS, Burr - is GC Fire Chief (J10/6/16)

SAUNDERS, Burr Lloyd - s M/M B.H. Saunders; Sun m Minnie Lewis, will live in GC (J5/21/15)

SAWYER, Rev. Samuel - Presbyterian who sometimes preached in Candy Sch House in late 1850's (J6/8/17)

SCHAUM, Bertha - dt Jesse Johnson (J4/2/15)

SCHMITKIN(S), Charles - s Mrs. H.S. Schmitkin; att Hanover Coll (J8/3/17); sch tchr in Madison, IN (J12/31/20)

SCHMITKIN, Hazel - dt Mrs. H.S. Schmitkin (J8/3/17)

SCHOOLEY, Blodwin (BARRETT) - dt George and Isabelle (THOMAS) Barrett; m Edward Schooley (G11/2/17)

SCHOOLEY, Ephraim Charles - b 14 Mar 1913; s Edward and Blodwin; d 25 Oct 1917, bur GC Cem (G11/2/17)

SCHRADER, Fred - b Germany 8 Oct 1847; m at Batesville 1871 Elizabeth Hoyer; father of Dr. O.H. Schrader of Jnsbr; had W. Jnsbr brick factory 1875-97 (G12/3/97)

SCHRADER, Fred, Jr. - of Jnsbr; m 20 Jan 1917 Rhea, dt M/M William Shuttleworth of Jnsbr (J3/23/17)

SCHRADER, Dr. Otto H. - of Jnsbr; m Anna Johns 8 Feb 1917 (G2/16/17)

SCHRADER, William - of Jnsbr; m 30 May 1896 Blanche Brumley, dt George Brumley the barber; now he wants a divorce (G3/5/97)

SCHRIBER, William - of Jnsbr; age 87; m; serv CW; mbr Jnsbr Presbyterian Ch.; d 28 Feb 1919, bur GC Cem (J3/7/19)

SCHULTZ, Jennie (ISENHART) - b Jay Co. 23 Feb 1857; m 8 Jul 1895 James Schultz of GC; d 31 Oct 1916, bur GC Cem (J11/3/16)

SCHWANN, __ (GARTHWAIT) - dt M/M W.P. Garthwait of GC; m Rev. Henry W. Schwan; lives WV (G7/13/17)

SCHWAN, William - s Mrs. Henry W. Schwan (G7/13/17)

SCOTT, Alvin B. - of Fairmount; d (G10/4/18)

SCOTT, Clyde E. - age ca 35; s M/M Will Scott of Fairmount; Pvt., US Army in TX; murdered 26 Feb 1918 (G3/1/18)

SCOTT, Fay - 1916-17 att FFA (J9/15/16); grad, Jnsbr HS 1919 (J4/18/19)

SCOTT, Glen - of Fairmount; d in US Army in TX (G6/21/18)

SCOTT, Helen - 2nd grader, Zeek Sch 1915-16 (J5/5/16)

SCOTT, John - farmer of SW of Jnsbr, had several bushels of oats stolen (G9/22/93)

SCOTT, Syms - of Jnsbr; recently operated on by Dr. Vance and Dr. Knight (G4/9/97)

SCOTT, Thelma - mbr GC Christian Ch. (J10/6/16)

SCOTT, Tom - is moving his family back to Jnsbr from the Riley Cranford farm (J10/6/16)

SEAL, Charles - plays alto trombone in GC Brass Band (G10/1/97)

SEBASTIAN, C.J. - pastor, GC Christian Ch. (G7/14/11)

SEIBERLING, A.F. - of Jnsbr; stockholder in GC Land Co. (G3/12/97)

SEIBERLING, Mrs. A.F. - organized Jnsbr Chapter of National War Mothers on 28 March 1919 (J4/18/19)

SEIBERLING, Mrs. Elizabeth (BAUGHMAN) - b 27 Aug 1838; lives in Mill Twp (J8/1/19)

SEIBERLING, James H. - of Indiana Rubber Works; building finest residence in Jnsbr (G7/23/97); J.H. Evans has contract for stone work on house (G7/30/97)

SELBY, John - of Fairmount; age 71; serv in CW; d 1 Dec 1917 (G12/7/17)

SETSER, Lucy - 8th grade grad, Jnsbr Sch 1918 (G5/10/18)

SEWARD, __ - s M/M Thomas Seward; b 24 May 1898 (G6/3/98)

SEWARD, Miss Amanda - dt Mrs. Elizabeth Seward (J3/4/04)

SEXTON, Edith - age ca 25; of GC; not m; d 29 Dec 1915, bur GC Cem (J12/31/15)

SEYFORT, Lee - mbr GC K of P (G7/23/97)

SHADY, Clara (BAINBRIDGE) - dt P.M. Bainbridge of GC; m Oliver Shady; moved to Anderson ca 1905 (G1/26/17)

SHADY, Oliver - owns City Barber Shop on 3rd St., GC (G8/6/97; G7/15/98); m Clara Bainbridge; moved to Anderson ca 1905 (G1/26/17)

SHAFER, Burtney W. - from Rockbridge Co., VA; s Burtney W. and __ (Ruley) Shafer; grand-s of Burtney W. Shafer (d age 90); gr-grand-s of Philip Shafer (d age 88) (J7/18/19)

SHAFER, William D. - b Rockbridge Co., VA 30 Nov 1847; s Philip and Catherine Shafer; m 1st 3 Nov 1870 Nancy Jane Ruley (d 29 Jul 1892); m 2nd 30 Sep 1898 Mrs. Sarah E. (RULEY) Wilson (widow of Henry P. Wilson); mbr M.E. Ch. (G9/30/98)

SHARON, Mrs. Nancy - of Sweetser; has 80th birthday; mother of Mrs. L.A. Prickett (J4/2/15)

SHARON/SHERON, Zahn - is helping Jim Kirkpatrick put up hay (J7/23/20)

SHARP, H.V. - pastor of Jnsbr M.P. Ch. (G7/14/11)

SHATTO, Charles - of Shatto & Frederick Grocery in Jnsbr has bought out Frederick (J10/8/15)

SHAW, Goldie - Dec 1910, student in Mill Twp Dist. # 2 Sch; won 2nd place in Twp Spelling Contest (J12/31/20)

SHEARER, Andrew 'Sandy' - m; 14 Apr 1898 committed suicide (G4/15/98)

SHEARER, Mattie - of Jnsbr; files for divorce from Clifford Shearer for his drunkenness; were m 26 Jul 1896 (G12/31/97)

SHEEHAN, James - of GC; now in US Army, Officers Reserve Corps (G5/18/17; J6/29/17)

SHEEHAN, John T. - s John Sheehan; is soldier in France (J12/27/18)

SHEFFIELD, Miss Alice - tchr, Candy Sch (G9/3/97), or Zeek Sch (G12/10/97); 1898-99 Candy Sch tchr (G8/19/98)

SHELDON, R.K. - ca 1897 was Pres., Sheldon Glass Co.; built 18 room house on 6 acres on South H St., GC; had a stable of blooded driving horses, a Negro groom, and fine carriages; ca 1901 natural gas supply gave out and his glass Co. left GC; house was sold and is now, 1915, standing empty awaiting auction (J4/16/15)

SHELDON, T.K. - stockholder in Citizens' Bank of Jnsbr (G12/16/98)

SHEPARD, William - resigns as Justice of Peace (G3/12/97)

SHERON, Cecil (STACKHOUSE) - b 10 Dec 1897; dt M/M Alva Stackhouse; m ca 1915 Cord Sheron; lived in Jnsbr; d 13 May 1919, bur Summitville Cem (J5/16/19)

SHIELDS, Corwin - 1915 grad 8th grade Mill Twp (J6/18/15)

SHIRK, J.E. - s M/M George A. Shirk (G1/28/98)

SHOEMAKER, Charles W. - pastor, GC M.E. (G7/14/11)

SHOOK, Mrs. Elmo - of N. Jnsbr; age 60; d 10 Nov 1916, bur GC (J11/24/16)

SHUGART, __ - b recently; s Pearl and Stella (DAVIS) Shugart of Jnsbr (J10/8/15)

SHUGART, __ (WIMMER) - dt M/M A. Wimmer; m Frank Shugart of Deer Creek; recently had a baby (G11/16/17)

SHUGART, Bennett - Dec 1905, barn on his farm W of Jnsbr burned (J12/24/20)

SHUGART, Charles Roger - s Mark and Elma Shugart of Deer Creek neighborhood (J8/10/17; J8/17/17)

SHUGART, George Cornelius - baby s M/M Harold Shugart of North Grove area (J2/21/19)

SHUGART, Harold - of North Grove; bought new Dodge auto (G4/26/18)

SHUGART, Henry - b Grant Co. ca 1846; farmer on Deer Creek; accidentally run over by horse-drawn wagon; d 6 Feb 1920 (J2/13/20)

SHUGART, Irene - Mill Twp 8th grade grad 1916 (J5/12/16)

SHUGART, Lehman - 1919 Mill Twp 8th grade grad (J4/4/19)

SHUGART, Miss Lucille - Deer Creek Sch tchr 1919-21 (J8/29/19; J8/27/20)

SHUGART, Mabel - dt M/M Albert Shugart of Deer Creek; d of flu last wk (J4/4/19)

SHUGART, Thurlow - farmer W of Jnsbr on Deer Creek; age 32; s M/M Bennett Shugart; grad, FFA; att Earlham Coll; rec Friends Minister; brother of Mrs. Harold Cooper, a missionary in Madura, India; brother of Mrs. Nellie Davis of Deer Creek; d 21 Mar 1918 (G3/29/18)

SHUGART, William C. - age 86; farmer; 1st wife d ca 1897; m 2nd ca 1912; father of Mrs. Addie Pearson of Jnsbr; mbr Friends; d 9 Apr 1920, bur Marion cem (J4/16/20)

SHULTZ, Galen - of Toledo, OH; recently visited mother, Mrs. H.F. Parsons, and bought marker in GC Cem for grave of his brother, Harrison Pleasant Shultz (J10/6/16)

SHULTZ, John - of Lancaster, OH; s James Shultz of GC (G11/12/20)

SHULTZ, Mabel - f of GC; divorced from William Girt, has resumed her maiden name of Schultz (J1/7/16); of Indianapolis; dt Mrs. H.F. Parsons of GC (J2/4/16)

SHULTZ, Mrs. William - dt Mrs. Thomas Dove (dec) (J4/30/20)

SILLERS, Rev. J. Roger - m; leaves Jnsbr Presbyterian pastorate to be Crawfordsville Presbyterian pastor (J10/13/16)

SILLS, W.M. - elected Sect.-Treas., GC St. Paul Episcopal Ch. last Sun at the organization of the church (G9/22/93)

SIMMS, Charles - s M/M Henry Simms; mbr Co. C of 139th Field Artillery; recently returned from France; will soon be mustered out (J1/10/19)

SIMMS/SIMS, Henry - elderly man employed by Custer Lumber Co., GC; struck by Jesse Street when he tried to intervene in an assault on Olin Gordon by Sam Holmes on a GC street last Mon evening; Gordon is a "dry" and Holmes is a "wet" (J7/23/15)

SIMONS, Francis - age 5 mon.; s M/M Frank Simons; d 26 Sep 1916, bur GC Cem (J9/29/16)

SIMONS, Malinda J. (SNETHEN) - b 24 Feb 1837; of Mill Twp (J8/15/19); b Miami Co., OH; m 1858 Abraham Simons (dec); d 11 Apr 1920, bur Logansport cem (J4/16/20)

SIMONS, Will - while driving a load of hay through N. Jnsbr, was shot in back with .38-cal. revolver by Will Carter, Jr.; Carter was shooting at a dog who was killing his chickens; Simons was only blistered by the spent bullet that penetrated his clothing; the dog escaped (G3/5/97)

SIMONS, William P. - of GC; in US Army (J6/29/17)

SIMONSON, W.H. 'Uncle Billy' - of Marion; drove 1st mule-powered street cars in Marion ca 1890 (J1/23/20)

SIMPKINS, Mrs. D.B. - mbr GC WCTU (J2/21/19); mbr GC Baptist Ch. (G11/12/20)

SIMPSON, Mrs. James - is "fashionable dressmaker" on N. Main St., Jnsbr (J6/8/89)

SINGER OIL CO. - 21 Jun 1897 shut off gas well on Zimri Richardson farm in order to drill deeper to find oil; 150 Jnsbr families are supplied with gas from this well; well is flowing ca 25 barrels of oil per day (G7/9/97); well was "shot"; no oil now but lots of gas (G7/16/97); derrick on Richardson farm is taken down (G7/30/97)

SIPE, Rollie - of New Castle; s J.O. Sipe of GC (J10/22/15)

SIPE, Mrs. Samuel - of GC; dt Rev. A.S. Fields (G7/13/17)

SIPE, Virgil - of GC is 1915-16 Ind Univ student (J1/7/16); is 1917-18 Ind Univ student (G12/7/17)

SISSON, Charles - prop., Jnsbr Hotel (G5/13/97)

SISSON, George H. - local 15-yr old (J4/2/15)

SISSON, John - of Gary; s M/M Charles Sisson of GC (G2/9/17)

SKEEN/SKEENS, Daniel R. - s Mrs. Mary Skeen of Jnsbr (G7/13/17); of Jnsbr; brother of Nancy Forehand of College Hill area (J2/6/20)

SLATER, John - of near Matthews; drove 2-horse wagon into Mississinewa River at Richards Ford; river was high and the wagon bed floated off of rear hounds which then sunk to bottom; he drove team out then went back on horseback with hook and chain, secured the back half of his wagon, and drug it out of the river on 4 Mar 1897 (G3/12/97)

SMALL, Enoch - m Mary Coleman, sister of Bennett B. Coleman; built early river mill at Jnsbr (J12/15/16)

SMALL, Harold - m Maud Horner 24 Nov 1916 (J12/29/16); their parents, M/M Ashton Horner and M/M Oliver Small, gave them the 70-acre Harry Davis farm on Muncie Pike as a wedding gift, it cost $9,600 (G1/5/17; J1/5/17); mbr Jnsbr Liberty Guards (G9/20/18)

SMALL, Kenneth Donald - b last Fri to M/M Harold Small (G10/5/17)

SMALL, Quincy - of Franklin Twp; m 18 Jan 1916 Hazel Roe of Jnsbr (J1/21/16)

SMALL, Reuben - m Betsey Shugart, sister of Cornelius Shugart; built early river mill at Jnsbr (J12/15/16)

SMALL, William - b Grant Co. ca 1841; farmer in W. Marion; d 30 Dec 1919 (J1/2/20)

SMITH, A. Estella - mbr GC Christian Ch. (G2/12/97)

SMITH, Allen Franklin - b Kempton 13 May 1882; s William and Hannah; m Marie E. Johns 6 Dec 1905; d 4 Dec 1915, bur Marion IOOF Cem (J12/10/15)

SMITH, Arthur - of Jnsbr; m 23 Jun 1917 Jeanette Gibbony of Marion (J6/29/17); sold his farm SE of Jnsbr (J1/2/20)

SMITH, Burr - s George W. and Mary Emma (HIATT) Smith (J1/7/16)

SMITH, Calvin J. - of Marion; age 73; father of Jesse Smith of Jnsbr; d 3 Apr 1916 (J4/7/16)

SMITH, Clysta - grad, Jnsbr HS 1919 (J4/18/19)

SMITH, Colene - dt D.H. and Belle Smith of Jnsbr (G7/13/17)

SMITH, Dee - is operating threshing machine for Zeek Sch neighborhood threshing ring (J8/3/17)

SMITH, Dorothy - 15th birthday last Tues (J4/18/19)

SMITH, E.L. - hired to drill gas well on Ras Hiatt farm N of Jnsbr to secure gas for Crosley Paper Co./North Marion Strawboard Works; 2 Feb 1897 a good gas well came in (G1/15/97; G2/5/97)

SMITH, Edna - b Marion 8 Nov 1901 (J5/16/19); grad, GC HS 1919 (J4/11/19)

SMITH, Eli - GC policeman; city paid him $6.00 to bury part of the 105 unlicensed dogs he and O.F Griffin killed (G6/18/97)

SMITH, Ethel - m; mbr Jnsbr WCTU (J4/16/15; J12/27/18); mbr Jnsbr Friends SS (J7/27/17)

SMITH, Frank - and family lived on W. 6th St., Jnsbr in large Dr. Jones house built ca 1867; it burned Sun (G12/24/97)

SMITH, Mrs. Frank - dt Aaron Samms; sister of Mrs. Ed Dailey (J6/8/17); mbr Jnsbr MM (J10/8/15)

SMITH, Fred - s George W. and Mary Emma (HIATT) Smith (J1/7/16)

SMITH, George Washington - b Grant Co. 15 Apr 1855; s Charles H. and Beulah (HAINES); m Mary Emma Hiatt 26 Aug 1880; gave GC Library the Indian stone collection he had picked up on his farm during past 40 yrs; d 30 Dec 1915 (J1/7/16)

SMITH, Gladys - Zeek Sch 8th grade grad 1916 (J5/5/16); att FFA 1916-17 (J9/15/16)

SMITH, Guy - s George W. and Mary Emma (HIATT) Smith (J1/7/16)

SMITH, Harold Guy - of GC; in US Army (J6/29/17); s M/M William Smith; in Army hospital in OH due to being gassed in France (J3/21/19); b Kempton 19 Oct 1895; d at home in GC 30 Mar 1919, bur GC Cem (J4/4/19)

SMITH, Henry - is operating threshing machine for Zeek Sch neighborhood threshing ring (J8/3/17)

SMITH, Herbert - serv 3 yrs in US Army; chosen Capt. of Jnsbr Liberty Guards (G9/20/18)

SMITH, Ira J. - leased Fairmount bldg to open a saloon, it was dynamited 25 Jun 1887 by Fairmount men including Nixon Winslow, J.P. Winslow, H.M. Crilley, Dr. Henley, and J.H. Harrington; Mr. Boland, a Quaker, had instigated this at a meeting held at the Fairmount Wesleyan Church on 23 Jun 1887; the blast destroyed the saloon, the adjacent Fairmount News office and Stephen King's harness shop (J7/1/87)

SMITH, J.E. - joined army recently (G7/22/98)

SMITH, James - m Margaret Jones, dt M/M Charles Jones of Jnsbr; father of Warren and Ethel Smith; d ca 1915 (J1/10/19)

SMITH, Jeanette (GIBBONY) - Marion sch tchr; m 23 Jun 1917 Arthur Smith of Jnsbr (J6/29/17)

SMITH, Jess - of Jnsbr; buys new Ford auto (G6/22/17)

SMITH, Mrs. John - mbr Jnsbr MM (J10/8/15)

SMITH, Joseph L. - 1915 grad 8th grade Zeek Sch (J6/18/15); 1916-17 FFA student (J9/15/16); had eye injured playing football (J10/3/19)

SMITH, L.D. - is Jnsbr jeweler (G8/20/97); has organized a baseball team (G9/3/97)

SMITH, Miss Maggie - 21 Jul 1897, 15th birthday (G7/30/97)

SMITH, Mary - began her teaching career at Candy Sch many years ago (J6/1/17)

SMITH, Maude - Zeek Sch tchr 1914-19 (J4/16/15; J8/27/15; J9/1/16; J3/30/17; G8/31/17; G9/6/18)

SMITH, Rev. Moses - a Missionary Baptist; held first Harrisburg church services in Harrisburg Sch, later built a church on S side of Main St. E of RR (J6/8/17); m; was Harrisburg Baptist pastor ca 1883; now lives with wife in MO (G9/9/98)

SMITH, Pascal B. - b Scott Co., VA 24 Feb 1853; m Elizabeth Gardner 4 Jul 1875; d 19 Oct 1918, bur GC Cem (G10/25/18)

SMITH, Pauline - Jnsbr Sch 8th grade grad 1918 (G5/10/18)

SMITH, Ray - of GC; now in US Army (J6/29/17)

SMITH, Roland - age 81; of Fairmount; m; CW vet; d 2 May 1920 (J5/7/20)

SMITH, Ruby Mildred - one of twins; age 5 mon; dt M/M Dee Smith of E of GC; d 18 Jun 1917, bur GC Cem (G6/22/17)

SMITH, Samuel - b Decatur ca 1879; s Eli Smith; m Anna Alexander; f of GC; worked as a linesman, killed on an electric line 26 Sep 1916; bur GC Cem (J9/29/16)

SMITH, Sarah (SELBY) - b Grant Co. 16 Mar 1848; dt Otho and Jane C. (ALLEN) Selby; m Jan 1865 Sylvester Smith; mbr Jnsbr Presbyterian.; d 9 Mar 1918, bur Park Cem (G3/15/18)

SMITH, Steve - lives E of GC; right leg broke when kicked by a horse (J9/8/16)

SMITH, Rev. T.C. - pastor, GC Baptist Ch. (G9/22/93)

SMITH, Virgil - age 6; s M/M Charles Smith of NE of GC (J7/23/15)

SMITH, Virginia - dt Mrs. Dee Smith; given party for 5th birthday last Sat (J1/28/16)

SMITH, Walter - s George W. and Mary Emma (HIATT) Smith (J1/7/16)

SMITH, Warren - s James (dec ca 1915) and Margaret (JONES) (dec 3 Jan 1919) Smith; brother of Ethel Smith (J1/10/19)

SMITH, William - farmer who in 1871 owned farm E of Mississinewa River that included what became new part of Jnsbr (now GC) IOOF Cem (J4/6/17)

SMITH, William - 17 Apr 1897 had hand cut off at work at Morewood Tin Plate Works; is sueing for $10,000 (G5/27/98), and is awarded $800 (G6/3/98)

SMITH, William 'Nigger' - fined for consorting with a GC prostitute (G2/19/97); moved household goods of Ida Sanders, alleged prostitute, to Alexandria last Tue (G5/14/97)

SMITH, William Russell - b Henry Co. 17 May 1858; his wife d 16 Jan 1920; lived in Jnsbr; d 2 Feb 1920 (J2/6/20)

SMITH, Woodrow 'Woodie' - honorably discharged from US Army (J1/31/19)

SMITHSON, Dewey - age 22; s M/M S.C. Smithson; his brother, Guy, d 3 mons. ago of TB; Dewey d of TB 22 Jun 1920 at his home S of Jnsbr (J6/25/20)

SMITHSON, Glenn - s M/M Guy Smithson of Jnsbr (J10/1/15)

SMITHSON, Isaac - b Grant Co. 28 Mar 1842; m; his son, William Smithson lives in GC; d 26 Jul 1917, bur Marion Cem (G8/3/17; J8/3/17)

SMITHSON, Mrs. Isaac - dt Enoch VanWye (G4/5/18)

SNYDER, Mrs. Bertha - mbr Jefferson WCTU (J2/11/16; G11/23/17)

SOLMS, George Adams - b in Germany; 26-yr old farmer of E of GC; recently filed papers to be US citizen (J3/23/17)

SOLMS, Jacob - purchased the George W. Villars grocery last wk (J4/16/20); bought stock of the John Perkins grocery and is putting it into his store (J6/4/20)

SOLMS, Joseph - local 13-yr old (J4/2/15)

SOLMS, Peter - of GC; b Germany 24 Nov 1842; m; mbr RC Ch.; d 16 Mar 1916, bur GC Cem (J3/17/16)

SOUTH MARION MONTHLY MEETING OF FRIENDS - Eva Stoddard is a mbr (G11/23/17)

SOUTHWOOD, Earl - Mill Twp 8th grade grad 1917 (G5/11/17)

SOUTTOR, Miss Lula - dressmaker on 2nd floor, Opera House Blk., Main St., GC (G1/1/97)

SPANGLER, Clarence - of North Grove area, receives honorable discharge from US Army (J5/16/19); m 6 Mar 1920 Bertie Atkinson, dt (and stepdt?) M/M Al Shields (J3/12/20)

SPANGLER, Fannie - 1915 grad 8th grade Mill Twp (J6/18/15); grad, Jnsbr HS 1919 (J4/18/19)

SPANGLER, Mrs. Margaret - of North Grove; dt M/M John Hilton of Hackleman (G3/9/17); bought a new Mitchell-Six auto (J4/25/19); mother of Mrs. Lloyd Hopkins (J5/9/19)

SPANGLER, Noah W. - of Sweetser; age 82; widower; d 20 May 1919 (J5/23/19)

SPARKS, Elias - Lake Sch area boy (J6/18/15); won "dirtiest man" contest at Zeek Sch box social last Fri (G11/30/17); mbr Jnsbr Liberty Guards (G9/20/18); stationed at Camp Taylor; m since joining army (J10/24/19)

SPARKS, John - officer in GC Baptist SS (G6/24/95)

SPENCE, Samuel R. - age 79; f Jnsbr Postmaster; m 2 times; serv in CW; d 1 Mar 1916, bur GC Cem (J3/3/16)

SPENCE, Wick - the "hairless" barber of Jnsbr (G1/29/97); has joined the US Army Signal Corps (G5/6/98)

SPRINKLE, A.D. - combined his barbershop with that of Alex Howard; they are W of Centre Grocery, GC (G4/9/97)

SPRINKLE, Andra Armedia (HIATT) - b near Upland 3 Dec 1877; dt William S. and Nancy Hiatt; m 5 Dec 1893 Arthur D. Sprinkle; mbr Upland M.E. Ch.; lived in GC one yr; d 10 Mar 1898, bur Jefferson Cem (G3/18/98)

SPROWL, Otto - barber in Wilson Barber Shop, 3rd St., GC (G7/9/97; G8/6/97); took 30 frogs from river Mon night while with 3 other men (G7/30/97)

SPROWL, Will - of Marion; brother of Mrs. Anna Zent and of Mrs. Jennie Stech (G2/19/97)

SPRUNCE, R. Earl - b New Castle 4 Jul 1874; s Henry and Martha Sprunce; m 9 Mar 1900 Edna L. Ballinger of Upland; d 10 Sep 1917, bur Jefferson Cem (G9/14/17)

SPURGEON, John O. - b Adams Co., OH 20 Sep 1845; m 31 Dec 1876 Emma Riggs (dec); f Jnsbr Sch Supt.; mbr Marion Christian Ch.; d 6 Apr 1916, bur Marion IOOF Cem (J4/14/16)

SQUIRES, W.E. 'Reddy' - has been motor car (i.e. street car) pilot through GC for 2 wks; will be replaced by W.A. Lucas; will then be on Jnsbr-Marion Line (G1/1/97)

SQUIRREL - Leach and Fraze were cutting out a woods just E of GC that had a lot of squirrels; they stuffed a dead squirrel & nailed it high in a tree before inviting Mayor R.E. Brashear out for a squirrel hunt; the Mayor shot the stuffed squirrel with his gun and with their guns without effect, then said the tree was too big to climb; they said they doubted that since the boy they hired to nail up the squirrel did not have difficulty climbing the tree (G6/11/97); hunting season Jul 1-Nov 1, no bag limit (J7/9/15)

STACE, Clara - dt M/M Fred Stace; d 30 Jul 1916, bur Elizabethtown Cem 4.5 mi NE Matthews (J8/4/16)

STACE, Edna Fay (PETTY) - 1916-17 att Zeek Sch (J3/30/17)

STACE, Ollie Floyd - farmer of near Jnsbr; age 19; buys m license with Edna Petty, age 17 (J8/15/19)

STALKER, Ralph - of GC; accidentally shot in arm Sun while he was fishing (G5/28/97); m 29 Oct 1898 Maggie Price, dt M/M Robert Price of South F St., GC (G11/4/98)

STAMBAUGH, Harry - enlisted in army (G5/18/17); of North Grove area, is a returned soldier (J4/18/19)

STANDER, L.F. - moved his cigar factory from Fairmount to North B St. near 4th St., GC (G3/12/97)

STANLEY, John - age 27; s M/M Jesse Stanley; m; d; bur Jefferson Cem (J11/24/16)

STECH, A.D. - is leaving for Klondike gold fields by 1 Mar 1898 (G2/11/98)

STECH, Forest - snare drummer, GC Brass Band (G10/1/97)

STECH, Joe - plays bass trombone, GC Brass Band (G10/1/97)

STEGALL, W.D. - and Ed Magoto as Stegall & Magoto will run a grocery store on Main St., GC (G6/10/98)

STELTS, William - age 77; father of Mrs. Enoch Burgoon of GC; d 3 Sep 1915 at his home in Upland (J9/10/15)

STEPHENS, Mrs. B.H. - mbr of Jefferson WCTU (J1/7/16)

STEPHENS/STEVENS, Sallie (WINSLOW) - dt Allen and Celia Winslow, medical Dr. missionary in India for 30 yrs (J4/9/15); a good friend of Mrs. Clem Roush; her dt, Mrs. Clark Bateman of Bombay, India visited Mrs. Clem Roush recently for 2 wks (J8/1/19); f of Jnsbr; Jnsbr sch tchr before going to India, has been in India for many yrs; is retired missionary; is on way to USA; dt, Mrs. Clark Bateman, is with her (J10/15/20)

STEPHENS, Monroe - of Sweetser; age 30; killed with brother, Raymond, 27 Aug 1916 in auto wreck (J9/1/16)

STEPHENSON, Hulda Jane (GOBLE) - b Summitville 7 Apr 1889; dt John and Florence Goble; m Glenn Stephenson 2 Jun 1904 in GC; mbr Baptist Ch.; d 29 Jun 1919, bur Riverside Cem (J7/4/19)

STEPHENSON, Mrs. J.W. - lives on South B St., GC; hosted '97 Club this month (G3/25/98)

STEPHENSON, Jesse - of GC; in US Army (J6/29/17)

STEPHENSON, Verne - dt J.W. Stephenson (G7/22/98)

STEPHENSON, Walter B. - s Mrs. J.W. Stephenson; 1 Jun 1898 has 14th birthday (G6/3/98)

STEVENS, William - age 90; lived in Pleasant Twp since 1848; d 22 Mar 1919 (J3/28/19)

STEWARD, Harriet (McCAREY) - b Marion Co. 22 Aug 1836; m 1852 Samuel Steward (dec); mother of Mrs. Amanda Keenan; mbr Christian Ch. at Somerset; d 27 Jun 1915, bur Riverside Cem (J7/2/15)

STEWART, Hudson - Jnsbr's oldest and most prominant merchant (G2/12/97)

STEWART, John - of Fairmount; brother of Mrs. Joe Powell of Zeek area; d 28 Jun 1919 (J7/4/19)

STEWART, Mrs. Lizzie - of Fairmount; d 11 Jul 1919 (J7/18/19)

STEWART, Samuel - CW vet of Fairmount; tried to commit suicide recently (J4/20/17)

STEWART, Mrs. Wallace - of GC; dt Mrs. Jane Fish of GC (J10/6/16)

STEWART, W.R. - officer, GC Odd Fellows (J7/9/15)

STINE, Mary Elizabeth (HOFFERBERT) - only Charter Mbr of GC Rebekahs left 21 yrs after start of this lodge (J3/2/17)

STINSON, Loren - age ca 14; brother of Rudolph Stinson of GC (G5/18/17)

STINSON, Ray - mbr GC All-Stars 1916 football team (J10/6/16)

STITH, Mrs. Boone - lived W of Jnsbr; m; d 27 Feb 1919, bur Riverside Cem (J3/7/19)

STOCK, Bessie - mbr Jnsbr WCTU (J12/27/18)

STOCK, Mary Colene - badly burned while burning leaves Sun (J10/13/16); age 9; dt M/M Frank Stock of GC; d of burns 5 Nov 1916, bur GC Cem (J11/10/16)

STOCKDALE, Harry - bought new Overland touring car (J5/23/19)

STODDARD, Eva - mbr South Marion MM (G11/23/17)

STOKES, Iva (FEAR) - of Matthews; wife of Harry Stokes; neice of Mrs. David Ruley; will re-enter Marion Normal Coll (J1/7/16)

STONEBRAKER, Andrew - of Blountsville; m Mrs. Ida (MASON) Parks 1 Jun 1917 (G6/15/17)

STOREY, Joseph - of Peoria, IL; 3 Mar 1897 m Jennie Freeman of Jnsbr, will live in Peoria, IL (G3/5/97)

STOUT, Geraldine - age 8; dt Dr./M Trent Stout of Upland; killed 25 May 1916 by Albert Thomas (age 45) throwing bucket at her in car, he was angry at car; bur Jefferson Cem (J6/2/16)

STOUT, Nellis - age 22; m; declared insane (J12/24/15)

STRADLEY, Albert - m 13 Oct 1897 Minnie B. Bradford, dt M/M George Bradford of Jnsbr (G10/15/97)

STRADLEY, Jack - Jnsbr town Marshal (G9/22/93)

STRANAHAN, Rev. Edgar - pastor Jnsbr MM (G7/8/98)

STRANGE, __ - s M/M Benjamin Strange; b 13 May 1898 (G5/27/98)

STREET, Mrs. Jane - d Feb 1915 at age 54 (J2/6/20)

STREET, Jesse - attacked and struck James Persinger, Walter Phillips and Henry Sims who were trying to aid Olin Gordon, being assaulted on a GC street by Sam Holmes, a brewery teamster; Holmes and Street are both "wets" while the victims are all "drys" (J7/23/15)

STREET, Mrs. Jess - of GC; dt Mrs. Lucinda Myers (dec) (J1/16/20)

STUMP, Elmer - was plant foreman of Edge Tool Works for Bruce & Marks and will continue as foreman under the ownership of Coates & Lyons (G5/27/98)

SULLIVAN, __ - GC Mayor (G7/14/11)

SULLIVAN, Barney - GC tailor; boxed in match at Lovett's Opera House (G1/22/97)

SULLIVAN, Laura (McDONALD) - age 37; sister of Joe McDonald of South 1st St. & A St., GC; widow; attempted suicide by drinking carbolic acid (G5/27/98)

SULLIVAN, Mrs. Mina - of GC; dt Caleb Moon of Fairmount (J12/17/20)

SULLIVAN, S.E. 'Allie' - b Henry Co. 12 Aug 1874; s John and Nancy; m; d 11 Dec 1915, bur Park Cem (J12/17/15)

SUMAN, Rev. W.R. - pastor, Jnsbr M.E. Ch. (G1/15/97; G5/27/98))

SUTPHIN, Clara - 8th grade grad, Jnsbr Sch 1919 (J4/18/19)

SUTPHIN, Earl - mbr Jnsbr MM SS (J7/27/17)

SUTPHIN, Elsie - 8th grade grad, Jnsbr Sch 1918 (G5/10/18); mbr Jnsbr WCTU (J12/27/18)

SUTPHIN, Joe - of W. Jnsbr; recently bought a new motorcycle (J7/23/15)

SUTPHIN, Raymond - b TN 28 Sep 1895; s John and __ (RICHARDS) Sutphin; d 1 Aug 1918 of disease in US Army in France (G8/16/18)

SUTPHIN, Roy - grad, Jnsbr HS 1918 (G5/10/18)

SUTTON, __ - of Garthwait & Sutton dissolved partnership in GC real estate, insurance and rental (G6/4/97)

SUTTON, Miss Minnie - tchr at New Mulberry Sch; d last wk (J3/14/19)

SUTTON, Tom - Mill Twp farmer whose sheep have been killed by dogs this spring (G5/7/97)

SUTTON, Verne - b Loree 15 Jun 1900; accidentally shot to death 4 May 1919, bur Riverside Cem (J5/9/19)

SWALTZ, John - of Marion; age 85; CW vet; d 2 Jan 1917 (G1/5/17)

SWAN, Corwin - of Gary is s M/M W.O. Swan of GC (G11/2/17)

SWAN, George - grad, GC HS 1918 (G5/10/18)

SWAN, Juniata Augusta - lived in Harrisburg as a girl in 1874, now lives in GC; m (J4/27/17); was a student in Harrisburg Sch when Uriah S. Candy taught there (J6/1/17)

SWAN, W.O. - mbr GC Masonic Lodge (J12/24/20)

SWAN, William - in Gary enlisted in Co. F, 1st Ind. Inf.; will enter camp ca Aug 5th (G6/22/17); of GC; now in US Army (J6/29/17)

SWARTZ, Mrs. Chris - of Wilmington, OH is mother of Mrs. Pearl Tincher of W. Jnsbr (J10/6/16)

SWARTZ, Harold - Mill Twp 1920 8th grade grad (J5/21/20)

SWEETSER, James - Oct 1865 opened two kegs of beer for the RR crew laying the first rails into Marion (J8/24/17)

SWISHER, Ellen C. (CHAMBERLAIN) - b Yadkinville, NC 1868; m 1st __ Graves; m 2nd Tom W. Swisher ca 1911; lived in GC; mbr Christian Ch.; d 8 May 1919, bur Marion Cem (J5/16/19)

SWISHER, George - f clerk in Center Grocery, GC; 3 Jan 1897 fell dead in his home in Union City (G1/8/97)

SWISHER, Gideon B. - age 25; s M/M Thomas Swisher; d 27 Dec 1915, bur Marion Cem (J12/31/15)

SWISHER, Lee - of Benton Harbor, MI; s Mrs. Susan Benbow of GC; m; 50th birthday last Sun (G11/23/17)

SWISHER, Walter - barber on W. Main St., GC; m; given surprise birthday party 9 May 1897 (G5/14/97); mbr/officer GC IOOF Lodge (J7/9/15)

SWISHER, William A. - his lip cancer was removed by surgery last Thur by Dr. Horne and Dr. McKinney (G1/1/97)

SWITZER, Mrs. E.S. - 4 Apr 1898, 58th birthday (G4/8/98)

SWITZER, Lew - has hardware store, Jnsbr (J7/1/87; J7/22/87)

SYBRANT, Carrie - dt M/M L.V. Sybrant; 9 Mar 1898 given 12th birthday party (G3/11/98)

SYBRANT, Nellie - dt M/M L.V. Sybrant (G2/26/97); 24 Jun 1897, 3rd birthday; lives in Mississinewa Hotel (G6/25/97)

SYBRANT, L.V. - mgr, Mississinewa Hotel, GC (G1/1/97)

TAPPAN, David - age 60; m twice; divorced twice; dead in Marion of bullet wound, bur Apr 1 Riverside Cem (J4/2/15)

TATE, Paul - of GC; age 21; enlisted in army (J1/16/20)

TAYLOR, Allison - age 17; s William M. Taylor of GC; sues Morewood Tin Plate Factory for work injury suffered 27 Nov 1896 (G7/9/97)

TAYLOR, James P.- b Fayette Co. 1 Jul 1846; s Samuel and Lucinda Taylor; m 12 Mar 1869 Eleanor Adams (dec); att Jnsbr Friends; d 23 Feb 1920, bur Park Cem (J2/27/20)

TAYLOR, Mahlon D. - of GC; m 10 Feb 1897 Maggie E. Voris of Marion; will live in GC (G2/12/97)

TAYLOR, Oliver - f of GC; grandson William Taylor; is in army in a TX camp (G5/17/18)

TAYLOR, W.A. - mbr Jnsbr Masonic Lodge (G12/24/97)

TAYLOR, William M. - is filling his ice house with Mississinewa River ice (G1/29/97); with C.H. Clark purchased Holbrook Bakery on Railroad Ave., GC; continues baking bread (G2/5/97); sell river ice for $0.15 per 100 lbs; lost a leg in accident 2 yrs ago (G3/5/97); driving horse and buggy when Grace Harvey, riding a bicycle, ran into horse; horse and buggy passed over bicycle bruising her (G7/23/97); b Huntington Co. 6 Apr 1853; wife d 1912; cut Mississinewa River ice near old wooden bridge near present junction bridge and sold ice 1893-1908; d 1 Jul 1919, bur GC Cem (J7/4/19)

TAYLOR UNIVERSITY - planning new Swallow Dormitory (J10/1/15); student Nkomo of Rhodesia, East Africa, 20 yr-old after 3 yrs at Taylor d 11 May 1918, body shipped to his African home (5/17/18); grad 12 from coll and 21 from acad 16 Jun 1920 (J6/18/20)

TEMPLIN, Jesse - GC Car conductor; assaulted on Car by Arthur Elliott, and John and William Watters (G1/1/97); recently shaved off his mustache (G3/12/97)

TERRELL, Charles H. - elected Grant Co. Supt. of Schs (G7/14/11); of Jnsbr; is still Grant Co. Supt. of Schs (J7/9/15)

THARP, T.D. - b ca 1839; 1st Lieut, 57th Ind. Inf. 1861-62; Methodist Minister; early Grant Co. sch tchr; lived in Marion; d at Soldier's Home (J1/3/19)

THOMAS, Albert - trial for killing Geraldine Trout begins in Hartford City (J11/17/16); found guilty of manslaughter (J11/24/16)

THOMAS, Albert - of Jnsbr; m 23 Jul 1919 Gertrude Helm of GC; he returned from serv in France (J7/25/19)

THOMAS, Alonzo - age ca 55; used dull knife in suicide attempt, will recover (J11/7/19); age 57; m; hung himself in a chicken coop 28 Nov 1919 (J12/5/19)

THOMAS, Bernard - s M/M William Thomas; m 19 Apr 1919 Elva Roe; mbr Jnsbr MM (J4/25/19)

THOMAS, Edwin - local 6-yr old (J4/2/15)

THOMAS, Eli - age 93; 1829 came to Grant Co.; m Minerva M.; mbr Friends; d 15 Jan 1918, bur Marion IOOF Cem (G1/18/18)

THOMAS, Eli - s M/M A.J. Thomas; mbr Co. C, 139th Field Art.; home from France, to be mustered out (J12/27/18; J1/10/19)

THOMAS, Elizabeth Ann - dt M/M W.J. Thomas of GC; mbr GC Baptist Ch. (J10/8/15); - see F. TROMBGEN

THOMAS, Elva (ROE) - m Bernard Thomas last Sat; mbr Jnsbr MM (J4/25/19)

THOMAS, Emily (BENBOW) - b Grant Co. 9 Jan 1844; dt Aaron and Catharine (ELLIOTT) Benbow; m James Thomas 18 Jul 1867; mother of William Thomas; gr-mother of Hazel Fisher; mbr Friends; d 21 Aug 1916, bur GC Cem (J8/25/16)

THOMAS, Erie - s Mrs. Mary Thomas; brother of Walter Thomas; m; d 9 Mar 1920, bur Lancaster Cem (J3/12/20)

THOMAS, Everett - age 26; s M/M Nathan Thomas; FFA grad; lived on farm E of Fairmount; KIA in France by a large shell in his 1st battle 29 Jul 1918 (G11/22/18; J3/28/19)

THOMAS, Florence (LUDWIG) - m William Thomas; moved to Mansfield, OH (G11/5/20)

THOMAS, Fred - age 22; s Jesse Thomas of Auburn; d 30 Jan 1916, bur GC Cem (J2/4/16)

THOMAS, Hazel - mbr Jnsbr MM SS (J7/27/17)

THOMAS, Isaiah - age 75; m 9 Aug 1866 Carrie Evans; father of Charles C. Thomas; serv 3 1/2 yrs in Co. F, 31st Ind. Inf. during CW; mbr Jnsbr Friends, att Back Creek Friends; d 28 Sep 1919, funeral in Back Creek MH (J10/3/19)

THOMAS, Jesse - with his family lived in house on West 6th St., Jnsbr; home burned last Sun (G12/24/97)

THOMAS, Jesse - Mill Twp 1920 8th grade grad (J5/21/20)

THOMAS, John - s M/M W.J. Thomas of GC; mbr Jnsbr MM (J10/8/15)

THOMAS, Mary L. (RICH) - age 49; dt Erie Rich of Fairmount; d 5 Mar 1920, bur Park Cem (J3/12/20)

THOMAS, Matilda (AUSTIN) - b North Webster 29 Jun 1859; m 15 Apr 1880 Marion F. Thomas; mbr M.E. Ch.; d 14 Jul 1919, bur GC Cem (J7/18/19)

THOMAS, Mildred - mbr Jnsbr Friends SS (J7/27/17)

THOMAS, Raymond - Mill Twp 1920 8th grade grad (J5/21/20)

THOMAS, Mrs. Richard - of GC; sister of Owen Davies, f of GC; she has flu (G11/29/18)

THOMAS, Will - is in Charles Pitt's Jnsbr MM SS class (J10/6/16)

THOMAS, Winnifred - grad, GC HS 1918 (G5/10/18)

THOMPSON, Alex - of Deer Creek; s M/M Hill Thompson of West Branch (J10/12/17); wife is Vivienne (G11/16/17)

THOMPSON, America - of GC; age 68; husband d 1 mon ago at Soldier's Home; she d 19 Apr 1916, bur GC Cem (J4/21/16)

THOMPSON, David Hill - s Alexander and Vivienne Thompson of Deer Creek (G10/26/17; G11/16/17)

THOMPSON, Gertrude - of GC; dt John L. Thompson of GC (G11/23/17)

THOMPSON, Herman - mbr GC All-Stars 1916 football team (J10/6/16)

THOMPSON, Howell D. - grad, GC HS 1897 (G5/21/97)

THOMPSON, John L. - granddt, Lucille Nesbitt, lives with him (J5/21/15)

THOMPSON, Samuel R. - of Monroe Twp; b Centre Co., PA 20 Apr 1813; d last Sun, bur McKinney Cem (G12/3/97)

THOMPSON, Will - is arranging to go to Klondike gold fields (G2/4/98)

THORNBURG, __ (ARNETT) - age 36; m Clarence Thornburg; d 16 Sep 1916 (J9/22/16)

THRIFT, Minnie - age 12; dt M/M Alex Thrift of Fairmount; her cousin, Delbert Henley (age 24, of Fairmount) raped her; she is pregnant (G12/31/97)

TILSON, Mrs. __ - of Indianapolis; hired to teach in GC Sch 1895-96 (G6/24/95)

TIMMONS, F.E. - of Marion; age 43; killed on RR Mar 1918 (G3/15/18)

TINCHER, Inez (GILLESPIE) - of W. Jnsbr; visited by her mother, Mrs. Chris Swartz of Wilmington, OH (J10/6/16)

TINKLE/TRINKLE, Poe - of GC; m; s Rev./M G.H. Trinkle of Frankfort (J12/31/20)

TINKLE/TRINKLE, Mrs. Poe - of GC is mbr GC Baptist Ch. (G11/5/20)

TINER, William E. - bought marriage license with Maude E. Lewis last wk (G4/9/97)

TIPPEY, Mrs. John - m; of E of GC is mbr Jefferson WCTU (G12/7/17)

TOMLINSON, Harry - age 5; s M/M Bert Tomlinson of Fairmount; d 20 Dec 1916 (J12/22/16)

TOWNSEND, Mrs. Cora - of Kokomo is dt Mrs. Nancy Eakins of GC (G11/12/20)

TRIBBY, Miss __ - GC Sch tchr 1894-96 (G6/24/95)

TRIBBY, Blanche (MARINE) - f of Zeek Sch area; m Frank Tribby; sister of Mrs. W.E. Mason; mbr Marion Baptist Ch.; d 13 Apr 1919 in Marion, bur GC Cem (J4/18/19)

TRIBBY, Ernest B. - GC HS Football Team player; injured in game Sat with Jnsbr HS (G1/1/97); s M/M Jason Tribby; m 22 Oct 1898 Minnie Powell (G10/28/98)

TRIBBY, George C. - m 23 Oct 1897 Elsie Hoagwood in a triple wedding (G10/29/97)

TRIBBY, Robert Ewing - s M/M J.A. Tribby of S. A St., GC; 11 Jun 1898 given party for his 4th birthday (G6/17/98)

TROMBGEN/FROMBGEN, Forrest - f of Fairmount; now a Marion glassblower; 6 Oct 1915 m Elizabeth Ann Thomas, dt M/M W.J. Thomas of GC; live in GC (J10/8/15)

TROTTER, Hazel - 8th grade grad Jnsbr Sch 1919 (J4/18/19)

TROTTER, Lyle - 8th grade grad Jnsbr Sch 1919 (J4/18/19)

TROUT, __ - s M/M Theodore Trout; b 21 Feb 1897 (G2/26/97)

TROUT, Nora (JONES) - lived SE of GC; age 45; sister of Lloyd and Floyd Jones of Upland; m Theodore Trout; d 27/28 Feb 1917, bur Riverside Cem (G3/2/17; J3/2/17)

TROUT, Russell - m Amanda Ellen Beedy (dt M/M John Beedy) 24 Aug 1915, live on farm near GC (J8/27/15)

TROXELL, Charles - of Jnsbr; s M/M J.W. Troxell of GC (J10/1/15)

TROXELL, Jesse J. - b Blackford Co. 29 Nov 1895; s M/M J.W. Troxell of GC; was a cripple all his life; drank carbolic acid; d 26 Sep 1915, bur GC Cem (J10/1/15)

TROXELL, John - lived in Jnsbr; d recently; wife dec; will is probated, to build stone structure over graves of he and his wife at Walnut Creek Cem (G2/16/17; J2/16/17)

TROXEl, Lawrence - mbr GC All-Stars 1916 football team (J10/6/16)

TROYER, Joseph - f of GC; age ca 37; d 3 Sep 1916, bur Marion Cem (J9/8/16)

TRULOCK, John Francis - one of men who rescued Wood Huff and Belle Whitson from Mississinewa River when they fell in due to ice breaking under them (G1/1/97)

TUCKER, Elon W. - Frog Coll 2A tchr, 1916-20 (J9/1/16; G8/31/17; G9/6/18; J8/29/19)

TUCKER, George - b 4 Mar 1847 in Piqua Co., OH; m Mary LaMoreaux in 1888; serv Co A, 156th Regmt. Inf. in CW; d 2 Jan 1916, bur Soldiers Home Cem (J1/7/16)

TUCKER, Wayne S. - grad, Jnsbr HS 1916 (J1/5/17); Jnsbr Mason; Pvt in army (G11/29/18); s M/M Elon W. Tucker; was elected to Indiana General Assembly (J12/31/20)

TULLEY, George - f of GC; age 59; m; brother of John; d 5 Feb 1916, bur GC Cem (J2/11/16)

TULLEY, John E. - mbr/officer GC Odd Fellows (J7/9/15); brother of George (dec); their parents are bur in GC Cem (J2/11/16); b ca 1860; has lived in Harrisburg/GC since Apr 1874 (G4/20/17; J4/20/17)

TUMEY, Mae - dt M/M Morton Tumey of Jnsbr; 27 May 1898 given party for 6th birthday (G6/3/98)

TURNER, Frank - 1919 Mill Twp 8th grade grad (J4/4/19)

TURNER, M/M George - of Fairmount; gr-parents of Yevon Bliss, age 10, who was struck and injured by an auto while visiting them (J10/6/16)

TURNER, Ward - farmer of E of GC; injured when harpoon hay fork fell on him hurting his head and gashing his hand; he will recover (J7/23/15)

TURNER, Mrs. Ward - dt W.W. Worley (J4/9/15)

TUTTLE, James N. - b Union Co. 10 Nov 1844; s Isaiah and Mary Tuttle; m 18 Oct 1865 Frances M. Hutchinson; serv US Army 13 Dec 1861-5 Jun 1865; lived in GC; d 19 Jan 1920, bur Riverside Cem (J1/23/20)

TWEEDY, Marion - moved to Fairmount last Mon (J6/8/89)

TYLER, Dr. E.B. - has his dentist office upstairs in the Hussey Bldg, Jnsbr (G4/28/93)

UNION CHAPEL - pastor is Jeppe Jensen (G11/29/18)

VanARSDEL, William - age 70; of Jefferson Twp; father of Mrs. Jack Marine of Jnsbr; d 25 May 1898 (G5/27/98)

VanCANNON, Ira - lives near Fairmount; brother of Jane (VanCANNON) Larkin (J8/17/17)

VANCE, Dr. C.E. - partner of Dr. J.C. Knight, has offices on Main St. near Jnsbr Post Office and in GC in Thompson Bldg (G4/28/93); with Dr. Knight, he operated on Syms Scott of Jnsbr (G4/9/97)

VANCE, Mrs. C.E. - mbr '97 Club (G12/17/97)

VANCE, Howard - s Dr/M C.E. Vance (G8/6/97; G9/9/98))

VANCE, Walter - purchased new Inter-State auto (J10/13/16)

VanHOOK, Mary - court denied her a divorce from James T. VanHook of Jnsbr (J4/16/15); of Plymouth; dt Mrs. Eva Jones of Jnsbr (G11/23/17)

VanMETER, Ida (CARTER) - visits parents in Jnsbr (J8/10/89)

VanVACTOR, Margaret - age 92; m Joseph VanVactor; d Jun 1917, bur Marion IOOF Cem (G6/15/17)

VanVALER, Charles - of Neill & VanValer, owners of Jnsbr Flour Mill; bought out J.S. Neill, firm senior mbr (J10/22/15)

VanVALER, Mrs. Charles - of Jnsbr; dt Rev./M L.F. Walden of IL (J1/14/16; G11/26/20)

VanVALER, Mabel (RHODEHAMEL) - dt Mrs. S.A. Rhodehamel of Marion; m Charles E. VanValer; lives in GC; neice of the wife of Rev. Samuel Ballinger (G11/16/17)

VanVALER, William Russell - s M/M Charles VanValer, of Jnsbr, grad, Marion HS, ex-Ind Univ; d of disease in US Army in France 29 Sep 1918 (G11/1/18)

VanWORMER, William A. - 80th birthday was 10 Jul 1920 (J7/16/20); b PA 10 Jul 1840; m 25 May 1861 Sarah Haswell of DeKalb Co.; serv Co. K, 100th Ind. Inf. 1862 to end of CW; mbr Christian Ch.; d 15 Jul 1920, bur Marion cem (J7/23/20)

VanWYE, Enoch - b Jennings Co. 11 May 1838; m Hannah A. Green 1869; serv CW; d 1 Apr 1918 at Marion Vet Admin. Home, bur Marion Soldiers Home Cem (G4/5/18)

VATER, Rev. W.D. - Aug 1903, is GC Presbyterian Ch. pastor (J8/8/19)

VAWTERS, Howard - of Marion; age 26; m with 1 child; killed 14 Aug 1915 in motorcycle accident (J8/20/15)

VIESLET, Leopold - age 12; s M/M Leopold Vieslet, Sr.; 4 Jun 1898 drowned in Mississinewa River, bur IOOF Cem (G6/10/98)

VILLARS, George W. - with partner, John E. Ward, had a furniture store in GC ca 1895 (J3/30/17); his delivery horse d last Sat (G7/16/97)

VILLARS, Ray - 1903-04, att Washington Univ, St. Louis, MO (J8/8/19)

VINSON, Rev. J.H. - GC Christian Ch. Elder (J1/14/16); and wife moved to Fairmount; Sun is his birthday (J2/20/20)

WAGNER, __ - s M/M Robert Wagner of Jnsbr; b 11 Dec 1897 (G12/17/97)

WAGONER, Mrs. Luke - dt M/M John Deeren; Oct 1909, lives with husband in Chicago Heights (J10/10/19)

WAITE, __ (JONES) - sister of Hazel Jones; m Charles Waite of Deer Creek neighborhood (J6/1/17)

WAITE, Hazel - dt M/M Charles Waite (G5/18/17)

WALDRON, John - is given divorce from Lydia P. Waldron (G3/11/98)

WALKER, Genevieve/Geneva Mae - mbr Jnsbr Friends SS (J7/27/17)

WALLACE, George H. - f of Rochester; purchased GC store from W.H. Guthrie (G2/11/98)

WALLACE, Olive (MOSS) - f of Jnsbr; age 31; m Nick Wallace; mbr RC Ch.; d 18 Oct 1916, bur Hartford City (J9/28/16)

WALLIS, J.B. - m; new Principal of GC HS (G7/20/17)

WALLIS, Mrs. J.B. - of GC is dt Mrs. Sill of Arkansas (G10/5/17)

WALNUT CREEK LOG CHURCH - built of logs at E end of Walnut Creek Cem; preachers there ca mid-1850's include the Rev.'s Silas Parks, __ Minnick, Arthur W. Sanford, and Phineas Roberts; all of New Light/Christian faith (G6/8/17)

WALTERS, Frances - dt Mrs. H.S. Walters of GC (G6/22/17)

WALTERS, Mrs. H.S. - dt M/M M.J. Wertzberter of Decatur (G6/22/17)

WALTERS, Rev. J.W. - pastor of GC M.E. Ch. for past two yrs (J4/16/15)

WALTERS, Marjorie - dt Mrs. H.S. Walters of GC (G6/22/17)

WALTERS, William - mbr GC Christian Ch. (G2/12/97)

WALTHALL, Helen (GAMMEL) - dt M/M George Gammel; grad, Marion HS; Marion Normal grad; m Telfer Walthall 28 Dec 1918, live on farm near Jnsbr, Jnsbr Sch tchr (J1/3/19)

WALTHALL, Dr. John G. - b New Wilmington, OH 11 Aug 1854; m 1880 Lydia Bogue in Jnsbr; Ind Coll of Medicine grad; GC physician; d 27 Mar 1919 (J3/28/19)

WALTHALL, Telfer - s M/M Joseph Walthall; lives on farm near Jnsbr; m 28 Dec 1918 Helen Gammel; his grandfather, Rev. David Harris, m them (J1/3/19); neighbors belled he and his wife (J1/10/19)

WARD, __ - with __ Bond had sawmill near river bridge ca 1870; sawmill was later moved to Muncie Road near Jack Crawford residence where its boiler exploded killing Ward, Bond was not injured (J6/8/17)

WARD, Charles - plays clarinet in GC Brass Band (G10/1/97)

WARD, Clyde - s M/M J.E. Ward (G7/23/97); 26 Oct 1898 given 8th birthday party (G10/28/98); Acting GC Fire Chief in absence of Fire Chief Burr Saunders (J10/6/16)

WARD, Jay E. - of Ward & Gordon; have furniture store/ undertaking parlor at #148 Main St., GC (G6/24/95; G1/1/97); grad Champion Coll of Embalming, Indianapolis (G1/8//97); mbr GC K of P (G7/23/97); bought undertaking stock of J.E. Robbins (G10/8/97); sold out to Gordon but keeps his undertaker business (G4/29/98); passed State Undertaker License exam (G12/30/98)

WARD, John E. - with partner George Villars had furniture store in GC ca 1895 (J3/30/17); brother of Charles Ward of Frankfort (G7/9/97); mbr GC Tribe of Ben Hur (G7/30/97); is Mill Twp Assessor (G5/20/98); mbr GC Christian Ch. (J2/20/20)

WARD, Mrs. John E. - mbr GC Tribe of Ben Hur Lodge (G7/30/97); dt Mrs. Mariah Lee (G12/24/97)

WARD, May/Mae - mbr GC Baptist Ch. (G1/14/98)

WARRICK, W.O. - Supt., GC Schs 1895-96 (G6/24/95)

WASSON, Grace - age 7; dt Robert Wasson; playing on W side of Mississinewa River near covered bridge, she fell into river but was rescued (G10/29/97)

WASSON, Robert - opens saloon at river bridge (G11/19/97)

WATSON, Dorothy - new baby dt M/M Fred Watson of Kempton Heights, Jnsbr (G7/13/17)

WATSON, Esther - of Jnsbr; twin of Ethel; mbr Jnsbr M.E. Ch.; had 18th birthday 5 Oct 1915 (J10/8/15)

WATTERS, John - and William Watters assaulted GC street car conductor Jesse Templin on street car (G1/1/97)

WATTS, Ernest - local 14-yr old (JI4/2/15)

WATTS, Rev. S.D. - Aug 1903, is GC Christian Ch. pastor (J8/8/19)

WEAVER, Rev. A.L. - Jnsbr M.E. Ch. pastor (J4/16/15)

WEBER, George - age 8; s M/M John Weber of Muncie Pike S of Jnsbr; fell into Mississinewa River where men, cutting ice, rescued him (G2/5/97)

WEBSTER, Charles - lives across street from GC Lumber Co. (G1/15/97); Chief of GC Vol Fire Dept. (G9/30/98); is Chief GC Fire Dept. (J3/4/04)

WEBSTER, George - s Marion Webster; contractor who built the wooden covered bridge in 1861 over Mississinewa River between Jnsbr and what is now GC (J6/8/17)

WEDDINGTON, Manta (RULEY) - f of Jnsbr; dt D.W. Ruley, Sr. (dec); m Nathan Weddington; d 28 Nov 1915, bur GC Cem (J12/3/15)

WEESNER, Micajah - b near Jnsbr; age 79; wife dec; d 27 Apr 1917 (G5/4/17)

WEESNER, Walter - of Marion; age 17; drowned 3 Mar 1918 in Mississinewa River downstream from McFeeley Bridge (G3/8/18); body found in river 27 Mar 1918 (G4/5/18)

WEICHMAN, Rev. F.A. - pastor, GC RC Ch. (G1/15/97)

WEIMER, Arthur - tchr in singing school he started for East Bethel PM children (G6/15/17)

WEIMER, Earl - grad, Jnsbr HS 1919 (J4/18/19)

WEIMER, Kenneth A. - grad, Jnsbr HS 1918 (G5/10/18)

WEINSTEIN, J. - has a GC clothing store (G9/22/93)

WELBORNE, E.J. - of GC; age 70; sent to prison for 6 mons. for assaulting 10-yr old girl (G11/26/20)

WELBORNE, Mrs. E.J. - mother of Mrs. Jesse Bowman of GC; d, bur GC Cem (G9/6/18)

WELBOURN(E), Mrs. Daisy - now of IA, dt M/M J.H. Vinson (G12/13/18)

WELBOURN(E), Esther - granddt of Rev./Mrs. J.H. Vinson; m Arthur Graham; now lives in SD (J5/16/19)

WELLS, Bennie - age ca 30; lived with parents in GC; threatened neighbor with a revolver; last wk is sent to a Hospital for the Insane (G6/22/17)

WELLS, Earl - fined last Fri by GC Mayor Brashear for public intoxication (G1/1/97)

WELLS, Harry - of GC; has been discharged from Army after overseas duty (J4/25/19)

WELSH PERSONS (living mainly in GC) - M/M Rees Lewis; M/M W.A. Davies; Mrs. R. Price; Mrs. R. Morgan; Mrs. D. Jones; Mrs. John Jones; Mrs. T.J. Davis; Mrs. W. Davies; Mrs. D. Davies; Mrs. W.J. Davies; Mrs. J.W. John; Mrs. J. Jenkins; Mrs. J. Cole; Mrs. D.J. Lewis; Maggie Jones; Mrs. Sam Lewis of Jnsbr; W.A. Davies; S. Jenkins; Rev/M M. Hussey; S. Jane Davies; Edith Phillips; Alin Glasgodine; Annie B. Jones; Polly Phillips; Alice Roberts; R. Chappel; W.H. Davies; Maggie Morgan; Elizabeth Ann Lewis; John Roberts; Dan Morgan; T. Price; Daisy Phillips; Philip Davies; Joseph Morgan; Richard Morgan (G3/5/97); William Brennen; Anna Jones (G12/10/97); David Reese; Harry Reese; John Nichols; David Williams; Harry Jones (G1/14/98); W.J. Davis

(G4/8/98); J.D. Gape (G5/20/98); Mrs. David Davis (G5/27/98); Dai Morgan (G10/26/17)

WELSHEIMER, Lewis - of Ft. Wayne; s M/M Shafer Welsheimer of Ft. Wayne (G11/23/17)

WELSHEIMER, Mrs. Lewis - f of Jnsbr and GC; dt M/M Henderson Oliver; age 50; m Lewis Welsheimer; lived in Ft. Wayne; d last wk, bur GC cem (G11/23/17)

WERSING, Ruby - 8th grade grad, Jnsbr Sch 1918 (G5/10/18); Jnsbr HS grad 1919 (J4/18/19)

WESLEYAN METHODIST CHURCH - had Theological Seminary at Fairmount past 13 yrs; takes over Marion Normal Coll fall 1919 and closes Fairmount Seminary (J7/18/19)

WEST, C.G. - elected Warden of GC St. Paul's Episcopal Ch. at its organization last Sun (G9/22/93)

WEST, J.R. - has GC hardware store; J.R. West & Co. has hardware store in Jnsbr (G6/24/95); with s Robert left for England where Robert will be placed in sch (G6/11/97)

WEST, Mrs. J.R. - mbr GC Tribe of Ben Hur (G7/30/97); mbr '97 Club (G10/7/98)

WHEELER, Mrs. E.W.W. - dt Dr. F.S. Horner (dec); mother of Burr Wheeler; d at home in Indianapolis (J11/5/15)

WHEELER, Emma I. (CROWDER) - dt Mrs. S.M. Crowder; m 10 May 1881 Paxton E. Wheeler; lived in GC (G6/17/98)

WHEELER, Oscar - 15 Jul 1897 had 16th birthday party (G7/23/97); 18 Nov 1897 injured at work in U.S. Glass Factory (G11/19/97); of GC; now in US Army (J6/29/17)

WHITE, Rev. Charles E. - Aug 1903, is GC M.E. Ch. pastor (J8/8/19); is pastor of Jnsbr M.E. Ch. (J4/25/19)

WHITE, Mary F. (SETTLE) - dt Louis Settle of PA; m Marvin White; lives in GC (G6/22/17)

WHITSON, _ - dt Dr/M J.L. Whitson; b 8 Feb 1898 (G2/11/98)

WHITSON, _ - s M/M Elvie Whitson; b 9 May 1898 (G5/13/98)

WHITSON, Belle - dt Rufus Whitson of Jnsbr; skating with Wood Huff on Mississinewa River last Sun when ice broke under them near iron bridge W of Tinplate Works; Huff could stand on bottom with his head above water and hold Belle up so she could breath; they were soon rescued by William Wilson, Rich Price, Arthur Brushwiler, John Trulock and Joe Baker (G1/1/97)

WHITSON, Dr. E.M. - Physician/Surgeon; office in Stewart's Blk., Jnsbr (G4/28/93); officer, Jnsbr Methodist Ch. (G1/29/97); traded his Jnsbr Bank stock to Alex Myers for 70-acre farm 2 mi. SE of Jnsbr (G3/5/97)

WHITSON, Eli M. - recently divorced Almeda L. Whitson (G12/2/98)

WHITSON, Mrs. Elvie - mbr Jnsbr M.E. Ch. (J12/24/20)

WHITSON, Emma (CARL) - b Grant Co. 23 Mar 1862; dt Jacob Carl; m 25 Jan 1885 Rufus A. Whitson; mbr Jnsbr M.P. Ch.; d 5 Sep 1917, bur GC Cem (G9/7/17)

WHITSON, M/M Ervin - live SE of GC (G2/12/97)

WHITSON, Georgia - Dec 1910, att DePauw Univ (J12/24/20)

WHITSON, James L. - has harness shop on High St., Jnsbr (G7/22/87); harness shop is on 5th St. between Water St. & Main St., Jnsbr (G11/5/97)

WHITSON, Dr. J.S. - candidate for Co. Coroner (G2/11/98)

WHITSON, John - att Valparaiso Coll 1888-89 (J6/1/89)

WHITSON, M.V. - of S of Jnsbr; lost 21 out of a flock of 25 sheep to dogs recently (G7/9/97)

WHITSON, Mrs. M.V. - dt A.L. Barnard of Jnsbr (G5/7/97)

WHITSON, Mark - lives on Muncie Pike (G10/15/97)

WHITSON, M/M Mart - live S of Jnsbr (G10/22/97)

WHITSON, Martin - b 1.5 mi. S of Jnsbr 10 May 1898; s M/M Elvie Whitson; mbr Jnsbr M.E. Ch.; d 1 Jul 1919 (J7/4/19)

WHITSON, Rufus A./F. - father of Belle Whitson (G1/1/97); Supt., IOOF Cem (G9/3/97); will command vol. co. of troops (G4/29/98); of Co. A, 160th Ind. Vol., is home in Jnsbr on furlough (G10/7/98); b Jnsbr ca 1855; m 25 Jan 1885 Emma Carl (dec); Spanish-American War vet; f Jnsbr Town Marshall; brother of Rolinda Whitson; d 9 Mar 1919, bur GC Cem (J3/14/19)

WHITSON, Sarah Jane - f of Jnsbr; widow of Ira J. Whitson (serv Co. F, 34th Ind. Inf. during CW); d Aug 1917 in MO (G8/31/17)

WHYBREW, Rev. Mort - preached his farewell sermon at East Bethel PM Sun 22 Jul 1917 (G7/27/17)

WICKERSHAM, Mrs. __ - last Tue, 53rd birthday (J8/10/89)

WICKERSHAM, Oscar - of Jnsbr; age 73; serv 2 yrs during CW, mbr GAR; d 25 Jan 1919 at Marion Soldier's Home, bur GC (J1/31/19)

WICKS, Miss __ - sister of Mrs. U.S. Candy (J6/1/89)

WIECHMAN, Rev. F.C. - pastor, GC RC Ch. (G5/27/98)

WIEGEL, A.F. - b Woodfield, OH 6 Aug 1854; m; d 30 Aug 1917, bur GC Cem (G8/31/17)

WILCUTS, Anna - mbr South Marion Friends WCTU (G10/22/97)

WILDLIFE AND FISH - 26 Jul 1897 John and Holl Hoagwood, Otto Sprowl, and Ernest Bales took 30 frogs from Mississinewa River (G7/30/97); Charles Hodupp and Lorin Pemberton on 14 Nov 1898 bagged 40 quail without going 3 mi. from GC (G11/18/98)

WILEY, B.F. - has Furniture Store at corner of High & Water St., Jnsbr; Amos Cray has his Justice of Peace/insurance agency office in Wiley's store (J6/8/89)

WILEY, C.A. - mbr GC Tribe of Ben Hur (G7/30/97); works for Western Strawboard Co., GC (G5/20/98)

WILEY, Mrs. C.A. - mbr GC Tribe of Ben Hur (G7/30/97)

WILEY, Dick - s Harry Wiley of Jnsbr (J4/6/17)

WILEY, Fern - mbr Jnsbr Friends SS (J7/27/17)

WILEY, H.H. - age 85; of Fairmount; d Mon, bur Park Cem (J3/12/15)

WILEY, Harry - of Jnsbr; in 1871 had a planing mill on W riverbank just N of present Street Car Bridge (J4/6/17)

WILEY, Margaret (BROWNLEE) - of Jnsbro; dt James and __ (GOLDTHWAIT) Brownlee (G8/13/97)

WILHOIT, John - of GC has dec; his will is probated; he left his estate to his neice, Lillie Bay (J10/13/16)

WILKINS, Edith (DeWESE) - GC tchr last yr; now has m Ernest Wilkins and lives in Kokomo (G11/26/20)

WILLIAMS, Brian - mbr GC All-Stars 1916 football team (J10/6/16)

WILLIAMS, D.W. - is GC Christian Ch. Elder (J1/14/16), and now is Board President (J10/6/16)

WILLIAMS, Mrs. D.W. - mbr GC WCTU (J1/14/16)

WILLIAMS, David - GC Welshman (G1/14/98)

WILLIAMS, George - glass blower; m; drank 4 oz laudanum, d 16 Feb 1897; bur IOOF Cem (G2/19/97)

WILLIAMS, John - starts barber shop at 3rd & South D St., GC (G7/30/97)

WILLIAMS, Laura (SIMONS) - dt M/M W.J. Simons of Jnsbr; 16 Jun 1917 m Albert Williams of Marion; will live in Marion (G6/22/17)

WILLIAMS, Lillie - of GC; age 46; m J.T. Williams; d 17 Feb 1917, bur Corinth, KY (G2/23/17)

WILLIAMS, Lizzie (EVANS) - b Wales 15 Mar 1861; dt William and Lizzie Evans; m William Williams 5 Nov 1880; mbr GC Baptist Ch.; d 31 Aug 1918, bur OH (G9/6/18)

WILLIAMS, Nellie - mbr Jnsbr MM Young Friends group (J8/27/20)

WILLIAMS, Yevonne E. - grad, GC HS 1919 (J4/11/19); b GC 2 Jun 1901 (J5/16/19); dt M/M D.W. Williams of GC; att Ind Univ (G11/26/20)

WILLMAN, Henry Keller - b Hartford City 7 Oct 1841; m 29 Dec 1879 Maggie Ruley of Jnsbr; Jnsbr Postmaster for 4 yrs; mbr Jnsbr Presbyterian Ch.; d of flu 7 May 1919, bur Riverside Cem (J5/9/19)

WILLS, M/M J.L. - live on South C St., GC; celebrated 50th wedding anniv last wk (G4/1/98)

WILSON, A.E. - Major, Battalion of Liberty Guards that includes Companies in Matthews, Fowlerton, Rigdon, Swayzee, Converse and Fairmount (G7/12/18)

WILSON, Eunice - mbr BC Friends WCTU (G10/22/97); m Robert Wilson; was Ind State President of WCTU 1900-02; d at home of M/M William Kirkpatrick N of Fairmount (J8/29/19)

WILSON, Fremont - Grant Co. Surveyor 1908-12; m; killed 15 Sep 1916 when his auto hit interurban RR car (J9/22/16)

WILSON, George W. - Big Four RR agent in Jnsbr; 25 Oct 1897 given party for 28th birthday (G10/29/97); s George F./T. Wilson of Lapel (G3/25/98)

WILSON, Mrs. George W. - dt M/M __ Lockwood of Warren (G7/2/97)

WILSON, George - 1917-18 att Purdue Univ (G12/28/17)

WILSON, Harry - employee of American Strawboard Works; had right hand injured at work; may have amputation (G5/28/97)

WILSON, Homer - brother of Mrs. Ethel Davis of Deer Creek and of Ora Wilson (J8/27/17)

WILSON, Ira T. - grad, Jnsbr HS 1914 (J5/2/24); Wise Sch tchr 1914-15 (J6/18/15); Research Assist. to Prof. W.C. Allee, Head of Biology Dept., Lake Forest Univ, IL (J6/15/17); att Lake Forest Univ, IL; mbr Jnsbr Presbyterian Ch.; s M/M Eugene Wilson of Jnsbr; m 20 Jun 1918 Lillian Tufford, dt Mrs. Emma Tufford (G6/21/18)

WILSON, Isa - 8th grade grad, Mill Twp 1916 (J5/12/16); grad, Jnsbr HS 1920 (J4/16/20)

WILSON, Leonora - mbr Jnsbr Friends SS (J7/27/17)

WILSON, Mrs. Lin - mbr Back Creek WCTU (J12/10/20)

WILSON, Mack - union barber in GC (G1/1/97)

WILSON, Ora - brother of Mrs. Ethel Davis of Deer Creek and of Homer Wilson (J8/27/17)

WILSON, Porter - s Rufus Wilson of Jnsbr; injured when an old cannon exploded as he and another boy were playing with it (G4/8/98)

WILSON, Robert - helped start Hopewell Presbyterian Ch. in his home near Ink Ford on Mississinewa River 31 May 1839 (G6/7/18)

WILSON, Samuel C. - of Fairmount Twp; age 84; was in Ind. Legislature in 1890; mbr Friends; d at home of his son, Lin Wilson (J8/1/19)

WILSON, William - one of the men who rescued Wood Huff and Belle Whitson when they fell through the ice of Mississinewa River (G1/1/97)

WILSON, Wood - Marion banker; b 3 Nov 1854 Louisville, KY; d 21 Oct 1916, bur Marion IOOF Cem (J10/27/16)

WIMER, Max - Mill Twp 1920 8th grade grad (J5/21/20)

WIMMER, Edith - age 6; dt M/M Herman Wimmer; d Jun 1917, bur Park Cem (G6/8/17)

WIMPY, A.N. - 1898-99 Frog Coll Sch tchr (G9/19/98)

WIMPY, Corintha B. 'Rinta' (CLARK) - of W of Jnsbr; sister of Mrs. Leslie G. Lemon (J10/1/15); b 26 Mar 1870; dt Simon and Julia Clark; m 4 Dec 1889 Francis Wimpy (dec); d 25 Nov 1916 (J11/30/16)

WINGER, John - of Fox Station; b VA ca 1834; mbr Dunkard Church; d 1 May 1918 (G5/3/18)

WINSLOW, C.M. - last wk bought marriage license with Maud Ferguson (G6/4/97)

WINSLOW, Celia - m Allen Winslow; d several yrs ago in India while visiting her missionary dt, Mrs. Stephens, M.D.; bur in India (J4/9/15)

WINSLOW, Daniel - his team frightened by train 20 Jun 1887, ran away and damaged wagon (J6/24/87); has d; John H. Rook appointed administrator of his estate (J6/8/89)

WINSLOW, David W. - Jnsbr Methodist Ch. officer (G1/29/97); has Jnsbr livery stable; has 3 matched teams plus several other horses, fine carriages, surries, and buggies; has had telephone put in, call "No. 9" (G5/7/97); of Jnsbr; d Feb 1910 (J2/13/20)

WINSLOW, Hattie - and brother Leslie are ch Maud Winslow of Fairmount (G9/22/93)

WINSLOW, J.P. - may have helped dynamite the Fairmount saloon of Ira J. Smith 25 Jun 1887 (J7/1/87)

WINSLOW, Levi - b 3 or 20 Jul 1836; of Mill Twp (G7/27/17); of S of Jnsbr; father of Mrs. John Flanagan of Fairmount (G10/26/17)

WINSLOW, Levi - of Fairmount; brother of Obadiah (J10/6/16)

WINSLOW, Mary E. (RUSSELL) - age 76; dt John and Mary Russell; m Levi Winslow; lived 1 mi. S of Jnsbr; mbr Jnsbr Presbyterian; d 2 Oct 1918, bur Fairmount Cem (G10/4/18)

WINSLOW, Nixon - may have helped dynamite the Fairmount saloon of Ira J. Smith on 25 Jun 1887 (J7/1/87)

WINSLOW, Thomas - b ca 1850; of Fairmount; m; father of Lee Winslow (KIA in France); d last wk (J1/30/20)

WINTER, J.A. - f of Dayton, OH; hired as representative of GC Land Co. (G4/15/98)

WINTERS, Mrs. Mary J. - f of Zeek Sch area; m 27 Oct 1917 Jacob Boon Gilson, farmer near Greentown (J11/16/17)

WINTERS, Thomas - age 60; of Washington Twp; d 25 Nov 1898; bur Jnsbr IOOF Cem (G12/2/98)

WISCHMEIER, Rev. A.C. - m; is reappointed pastor for another year at GC Methodist Ch. (J4/25/19)

WISE, Catarine - dt Shingleton Wise; lived with parents and siblings in Harrisburg ca 1869 (J6/8/17)

WISE, E. Ethel - dt M/M Sol Wise; m Edward B. Drischel in Louisville, KY (J6/18/15)

WISE, Edith - local 5-yr old (J4/2/15)

WISE, Elizabeth - age 80; b Wayne Co.; m 1856 Jacob Wise (d ca 1909); d 13 Apr 1916, bur Jefferson Cem (J4/21/16)

WISE, Frank - of College Hill area is having good success fattening hogs on hominy hearts; bought new Ford (J2/11/16); has new Ford truck (J2/21/19)

WISE, Fredith - dt Mrs. Daniel Wise of College Hill area (J10/10/19)

WISE, Henry - farmer 3 mi. E of GC; 20 Jul 1897 began threshing his 70 acres of wheat (G7/23/97); b 25 Mar 1835 (G7/27/17); one of the best and most productive gas wells in the 1890's was on his farm N of GC (J6/1/17)

WISE, Lillie - 8th grade Mill Twp student who passed exam for County Diploma (G4/29/98); 8th grade grad (G5/13/98)

WISE, Shingleton - lived in Harrisburg with his family (including sons, John and Jordan, and two daughters) ca 1869 (J6/8/17)

WISE, Sol - barn is burned 10 Aug 1918; Charles William Newcomb, age 48 of Upland, arrested for sending Sol Wise "black hand" letters demanding money, when he wasn't paid, he burned the barn located E of GC (G9/6/18); C.W. Newcomb sent back to Kentucky Penitentary where he was on parole for murder (G9/27/18)

WISE, Mrs. Sol - sister of Solomon Johnson (G4/12/18)

WOLF, Daniel - age 46; not m; d Wed, bur Shilo Church Cem 3 mi. SE of Upland (J4/23/15; J4/30/15)

WOOD, Audrey Helen - b GC 7 Oct 1909; dt M/M W.C. Wood of GC; d of flu Mon, bur Star City cem (G11/29/18)

WOOD, Cleo - dt M/M Clyde Wood of Lake Galatia area (G6/22/17)

WOOD, Mrs. Della - of Upland; d 14 Sep 1920 (J9/17/20)

WOOD, Elsie - 8th grade grad, Mill Twp Sch 1916 (J5/12/16)

WOOD, Ernest - att belling of M/M Telfer Walthall with his brother, Howard, and parents, M/M Cliff Wood (J1/10/19)

WOOD, Helen Louise - b Jnsbr 27 Apr 1914; dt Joseph H. and Nellie F. Wood; d 12 Nov 1916, bur Marion (J11/17/16)

WOOD, Lottie - of Lake Galatia area; dt Mrs. Alice Fite of Jnsbr; m (J1/5/17)

WOOD, Merle - Mill Twp 1920 8th grade grad (J5/21/20)

WOOD, Nora - of GC; dt Robert T. and Sarah E. (STROUP) Wood; is Forelady, Lindley Box Factory (G11/23/17)

WOOD, Russell - s M/M Clyde Wood of Lake Galatia area (G6/22/17)

WOOD, Sarah Elizabeth (STROUP) - b near Warren 22 Sep 1842; dt Joseph and Sarah Stroup; m 18 Mar 1866 Robert T. Woods (dec); d 12 Nov 1917, bur Marion Cem (G11/23/17)

WOOD, Susie - of North Grove has att Marion Normal; will teach in Mt. Ayre (J8/24/17)

WOODRUFF, Charles - Mill Twp Sch pupil; passed exam for teaching license (G5/14/97); 8th grade grad in Mill Twp Schs Commencement held in Deer Creek Friends MH 10 Jun 1897 (G6/11/97)

WOODWORTH, Mrs. Maria - celebrated evangelist, recently bought real estate in GC (G1/1/97)

WOOLLARD, Mrs. Maggie - managed GC's Avalon Hotel before it closed recently (G12/7/17)

WOOTRING, Charles - of Jnsbr; m; mbr Presbyterian Ch.; d 27 Feb 1919, bur GC Cem (J5/7/19)

WORLEY, Bertha May - Mill Twp 8th grade grad 1917 (G5/11/17)

WORLEY, Mrs. J.L. - of GC is dt Mrs. James Huston of GC (G10/5/17)

WORLEY, William W. - has 74th birthday; has 10 children including Mrs. J.A. Ludlow and Mrs. Ward Turner (J4/9/15)

WRIGHT, Eli - Candy Sch tchr prior to CW ca 1860, dec in Army during CW (G6/1/17; J6/1/17)

WRIGHT, Miss Ethel - new clerk, Big Four Depot, Jnsbr (G6/22/17)

WRIGHT, Frank - officer in Jnsbr M.E. SS (J1/12/17)

WRIGHT, Harriett - dt Mrs. Frank Wright of Jnsbr (G7/20/17); 8th grade grad, Jnsbr Sch 1919 (J4/18/19)

WRIGHT, Jacob - of Jnsbr; age is over 60; recently rode on a train for the first time (G9/16/98)

WRIGHT, Lucille - grad, Jnsbr HS 1919 (J4/18/19)

WRIGHT, Margaret - 8th grade grad Jnsbr Sch 1919 (J4/18/19)

WRIGHT, Myrtle - 8th grade grad, Jnsbr Sch 1918 (G5/10/18)

WRIGHT, P.B. - officer, Jnsbr Methodist Ch. (G1/29/97)

WRIGHT, Ralph - has birthday party 22 Feb 1897 (G2/26/97)

WRIGHT, Thana (WINSLOW) - dt Allen and Celia Winslow; m R. Norman Wright; d 3 Apr 1915, bur GC (J4/9/15)

WYATT, Clarence W. - of Jnsbr; injured Sat night while fighting a fire in Gas City business dist. (J4/16/15)

WYATT, Miss Marie - given birthday party (J10/29/15)

WYKLE, Mary Belle - dt M/M M.E. Wykle; 16th birthday 8 Apr 1920 (J4/16/20); Mill Twp 1920 8th grade grad (J5/21/20)

WYNANT, Mrs. Sarah - age 82; lives with step-dt, Mrs. A.J. Clay in GC (G1/26/17)

YARBER/YARBROUGH, Hillary - m; trampled to death 2 Aug 1916 by team of horses, bur Park Cem (J8/4/16)

YARBROUGH, Mrs. Mary - of Lake Galatia area; mother of Hazel and Louise Yarbrough (J10/13/16; J8/3/17; J10/31/19)

YEAGER, James E. - of Marion; last Mon m Elizabeth K. Reel of GC (J4/2/15)

YOUNG, __ - infant child of M/M John L. Young; d 20 Jan 1897 (G1/22/97)

YOUNG, George - runs River Saloon, Jnsbr (G7/16/97)

YOUNG, Harry 'Brigham' - is GC Constable (J7/23/15); resigns as Constable (G1/26/17)

YOUNG, Jeanette Olive - b GC 1899; grad, GC HS 1917 (J5/18/17)

YOUNG, Joe - brother of Mrs. Mary Jane Custer (G10/22/98)

YOUNG, John - last wk bought marriage license with Minnie E. Waltz (G5/20/98)

YOUNG, John L. - drives GC bus (G3/5/97); returns to work in his Tin Shop after being ill (G7/14/11); b Darke Co., OH 16 Oct 1850; s M/M Harry Young; m Emma Oliver 27 Jul 1876 Harrisburg; d 20 Jul 1919, bur GC Cem (J7/25/19)

YOUNG, Mrs. John S. - of Jnsbr; dt M/M George W. Gibson of Muncie (J10/22/15)

YOUNG, Joseph R. - of Jnsbr; brother of Mary Jane (YOUNG) Sinkler of KS (G3/12/97); Jnsbr Marshall; has 70th birthday (J10/15/15)

YOUNG, W.C. - of Wellington, IL; is s of Joseph R. Young of Jnsbr (G1/1/97)

YOUNG, William F. - Mill Twp Trustee; has office over D.K. Ruley's Grocery (G9/22/93); receiver, Bruce & Marks Manufacturing Co. (G10/29/97); mbr Jnsbr K of P (G10/7/98)

ZEEK SCHOOL, Mill Twp Dist. No. 5 - lets out Apr 23 (J4/2/15); last day of sch 2 May 1916; Maude Smith 1915-16 tchr (J5/5/16), and 1916-17; students include Edna Petty, Laura and Jason Corn, Charles Osborn, Fred Meredith, Marion Howell, Nolia Patterson (3/30/17); sch yr closes 27 Apr 1917 (G4/27/17); box social at sch (G11/23/17); Elias Sparks won "dirtiest man" contest at box social (G11/30/17); will let out 26 Apr 1918 (GC4/19/18); Miss Ruth Jones is tchr 1919-20 (J8/29/19); box social 21 Nov 1919 (J11/21/19)

ZEEK SCHOOL NEIGHBORHOOD THRESHING RING - 18 Aug 1916 ice cream and cake social at home of M/M Chester Buffington; M/M there included James Kirkpatrick, P.B. Smith, M.E. Wykle, Mark Petty, Leroy Horner, George Ryder, Joe Powell, L.E. Patterson, A.N. Lucas, L.G. Lemons, Fred Cray; also Mrs. Elva Whitson, Thomas Cole, Emory Kirkpatrick, George Groves, Mrs. C.A.Craig, Mrs. Ashton Horner,

Mrs. Maggie Pennington, Sherman Thomas, Mrs. Thomas Buffington, Maud Smith, Maud Horner, Edna Petty, Francis Craig, Dorothy Craig, Lillian Grant, Mary Belle Wykle, Gladys Smith, Joe Smith, Georgia Carr, Woody Smith, William Graves, Omer Hort, Martin Whitson, Harold Craig, Lindley Kirkpatrick, and Elias Sparks (J8/25/16); this ring began threshing wheat 30 Jul 1917; Henry and Dee Smith are doing the threshing (J8/3/17); threshing crew started on oats Mon (J8/24/17); 1 Sep 1917 ice cream social at home of M/M Leslie Lemons, M/M att were: A.N. Lucas, Joe Powell, James Kirkpatrick, Pete Horner, Mark Petty, Tude Brown, Harold Small, Leslie Horner, Clayton Jay, Chester Buffington, Fred Cray, George Ryder, Eldo Patterson, Ora Campbell, Emory Kirkpatrick; also Thomas Cole and dt, Charles Osborn, Elsie Bowers, Edna Petty, Maude Smith, Gladys Smith, Lindley Kirkpatrick, Elias Sparks, Woody Smith, Joe Smith, Harold Craig (G9/7/17); ring of 19 families had ice cream and cake social at home of John Brown 22 Aug 1918 (G8/30/18); farmers began threshing 11 Aug 1920 (J8/13/20)

ZEEK, __ - of Zeek & Co.; grocery/restaurant, NW corner of 4th St. & Main St., Jnsbr burned last wk (G10/1/97)

ZEEK, Gage - of Jnsbr was almost struck by Big Four train while out with his horse and cutter (G2/5/97)

ZEEK, George - of Jnsbr; is a millwright; returns home from working in MI (G8/6/97)

ZEEK, William - of Jnsbr sold his feed mill to John King (G3/11/98)

ZEIS, Ed L. - Jnsbr Methodist Ch. officer (G1/29/97); is Cashier, Jnsbr Bank (G2/26/97); s of C.H. Zeis of Oxford (G5/21/97)

ZENT, Anna (SPROWL) - sister of Will Sprowl of Marion and of Mrs. Jennie Stech (G2/19/97); - see J. COOK

Other Heritage Books by Ralph D. Kirkpatrick, Ph.D.

Back Creek Friends Cemetery Burial Records
Revised Edition

Burial Records of Four Grant County, Indiana
Quaker Cemeteries

Local History and Genealogy Abstracts from
Fairmount News, *Fairmount, Indiana, 1888–1900*

Local History and Genealogy Abstracts from
Fairmount News, *Fairmount, Indiana, 1901–1905*

Local History and Genealogical Abstracts from
Jonesboro and Gas City, Indiana Newspapers, 1889–1920

Local History and Genealogy Abstracts from
Marion, Indiana Newspapers, 1865–1870

Local History and Genealogy Abstracts from
Marion, Indiana Newspapers, 1871–1875

Local History and Genealogy Abstracts from
Marion, Indiana Newspapers, 1876–1880

Local History and Genealogy Abstracts from
Marion, Indiana Newspapers, 1881–1885

Local History and Genealogical Abstracts from
Upland, Indiana Newspapers, 1891–1901